Return items to **<u>any</u>** Swindon Library by closing
time on or before the date stamped. Only books
and Audio Books can be renewed - phone your
library or visit our website,

www.swindon.gov.uk/libraries

CENTRAL LIBRARY
SWINDON
TEL: 463238

Copying recordings is illegal. All recorded items
are hired entirely at hirer's own risk

DODO PRESS

THE

SPIRIT OF THE AGE:

OR

CONTEMPORARY PORTRAITS.

"To know another well were to know one's self. "

CONTENTS.

JEREMY BENTHAM.

Mr. Bentham is one of those persons who verify the old adage, that "A prophet has no honour, except out of his own country. " His reputation lies at the circumference; and the lights of his understanding are reflected, with increasing lustre, on the other side of the globe. His name is little known in England, better in Europe, best of all in the plains of Chili and the mines of Mexico. He has offered constitutions for the New World, and legislated for future times. The people of Westminster, where he lives, hardly know of such a person; but the Siberian savage has received cold comfort from his lunar aspect, and may say to him with Caliban—"I know thee, and thy dog and thy bush! " The tawny Indian may hold out the hand of fellowship to him across the GREAT PACIFIC. We believe that the Empress Catherine corresponded with him; and we know that the Emperor Alexander called upon him, and presented him with his miniature in a gold snuff-box, which the philosopher, to his eternal honour, returned. Mr. Hobhouse is a greater man at the hustings, Lord Rolle at Plymouth Dock; but Mr. Bentham would carry it hollow, on the score of popularity, at Paris or Pegu. The reason is, that our author's influence is purely intellectual. He has devoted his life to the pursuit of abstract and general truths, and to those studies—

"That waft a *thought* from Indus to the Pole" —

and has never mixed himself up with personal intrigues or party politics. He once, indeed, stuck up a hand-bill to say that he (Jeremy Bentham) being of sound mind, was of opinion that Sir Samuel Romilly was the most proper person to represent Westminster; but this was the whim of the moment. Otherwise, his reasonings, if true at all, are true everywhere alike: his speculations concern humanity at large, and are not confined to the hundred or the bills of mortality. It is in moral as in physical magnitude. The little is seen best near: the great appears in its proper dimensions, only from a more commanding point of view, and gains strength with time, and elevation from distance!

Mr. Bentham is very much among philosophers what La Fontaine was among poets: —in general habits and in all but his professional pursuits, he is a mere child. He has lived for the last forty years in a house in Westminster, overlooking the Park, like an anchoret in his cell, reducing law to a system, and the mind of man to a machine. He scarcely ever goes out, and sees very little company. The favoured few, who have the privilege of the *entrée*, are always admitted one by one. He does not like to have witnesses to his conversation. He talks a great deal, and listens to nothing but facts. When any one calls upon him, he invites them to take a turn round his garden with him (Mr. Bentham is an economist of his time, and sets apart this portion of it to air and exercise)—and there you may see the lively old man, his mind still buoyant with thought and with the prospect of futurity, in eager conversation with some Opposition Member, some expatriated Patriot, or Transatlantic Adventurer, urging the extinction of Close Boroughs, or planning a code of laws for some "lone island in the watery waste, " his walk almost amounting to a run, his tongue keeping pace with it in shrill, cluttering accents, negligent of his person, his dress, and his manner, intent only on his grand theme of UTILITY—or pausing, perhaps, for want of breath and with lack-lustre eye to point out to the stranger a stone in the wall at the end of his garden (overarched by two beautiful cotton-trees) *Inscribed to the Prince of Poets*, which marks the house where Milton formerly lived. To shew how little the refinements of taste or fancy enter into our author's system, he proposed at one time to cut down these beautiful trees, to convert the garden where he had breathed the air of Truth and Heaven for near half a century into a paltry *Chreistomathic School*, and to make Milton's house (the cradle of Paradise Lost) a thoroughfare, like a three-stalled stable, for the idle rabble of Westminster to pass backwards and forwards to it with their cloven hoofs. Let us not, however, be getting on too fast— Milton himself taught school! There is something not altogether dissimilar between Mr. Bentham's appearance, and the portraits of Milton, the same silvery tone, a few dishevelled hairs, a peevish, yet puritanical expression, an irritable temperament corrected by habit and discipline. Or in modern times, he is something between Franklin and Charles Fox, with the comfortable double-chin and sleek thriving look of the one, and the quivering lip, the restless eye, and animated acuteness of the other. His eye is quick and lively; but it glances not from object to object, but from thought to thought. He is evidently a man occupied with some train of fine and inward association. He regards the people about him no more than the flies of a summer. He meditates the coming age. He hears and sees only what suits his purpose, or some "foregone conclusion; " and looks out for facts and passing occurrences in order to put them into his logical machinery and grind them into the dust and powder of some subtle theory, as the miller looks out for grist to his mill! Add to this physiognomical sketch the minor points of costume, the open shirt-collar, the single-breasted coat, the old-fashioned half-boots and ribbed stockings; and you will find in Mr. Bentham's general appearance a singular mixture of boyish simplicity and of the venerableness of age. In a word, our celebrated jurist presents a striking illustration of the difference between the *philosophical* and the *regal* look; that is, between the merely abstracted and the merely personal. There is a lackadaisical *bonhommie* about his whole aspect, none of the fierceness of pride or power; an unconscious neglect of his own person, instead of a stately assumption of superiority; a good-humoured, placid intelligence, instead of a lynx-eyed watchfulness, as if it wished to make others its prey, or was afraid they might turn and rend him; he is a beneficent spirit, prying into the universe, not lording it over it; a thoughtful spectator of the scenes of life, or ruminator on the fate of mankind, not a painted pageant, a stupid idol set up on its pedestal of pride for men to fall down and worship with idiot fear and wonder at the thing themselves have made, and which, without that fear and wonder, would in itself be nothing!

Mr. Bentham, perhaps, over-rates the importance of his own theories. He has been heard to say (without any appearance of pride or affectation) that "he should like to live the remaining years of his life, a year at a time at the end of the next six or eight centuries, to see the effect which his writings would by that time have had upon the world. " Alas! his name will hardly live so long! Nor do we think, in point of fact, that Mr. Bentham has given any new or decided impulse to the human mind. He cannot be looked upon in the light of a discoverer in legislation or morals. He has not struck out any great leading principle or parent-truth, from which a number of others might be deduced; nor has he enriched the common and established stock of intelligence with original observations, like pearls thrown into wine. One truth discovered is immortal, and entitles its author to be so: for, like a new substance in nature, it cannot be destroyed. But Mr. Bentham's *forte* is arrangement; and the form of truth, though not its essence, varies with time and circumstance. He has methodised, collated, and condensed all the materials prepared to his hand on the subjects of which he treats, in a masterly and scientific manner; but we should find a difficulty in adducing from his different works (however elaborate or closely reasoned) any new element of thought, or even a new fact or illustration. His writings are, therefore, chiefly valuable as *books of reference*, as bringing down the account of intellectual inquiry to the present period, and disposing the results in a compendious, connected, and tangible shape; but books of reference are chiefly serviceable for facilitating the acquisition of knowledge, and are constantly liable to be superseded and to grow out of fashion with its progress, as the scaffolding is thrown down as soon as the building is completed. Mr. Bentham is not the first writer (by a great many) who has assumed the principle of UTILITY as the foundation of just laws, and of all moral and political reasoning: —his merit is, that he has applied this principle more closely and literally; that he has brought all the objections and arguments, more distinctly labelled and ticketted, under this one head, and made a more constant and explicit reference to it at every step of his progress, than any other writer. Perhaps the weak side of his conclusions also is, that he has carried this single view of his subject too far, and not made sufficient allowance for the varieties of human nature, and the caprices and irregularities of the human will. "He has not allowed for the *wind.* " It is not that you can be said to see his favourite doctrine of Utility glittering everywhere through his system, like a vein of rich, shining ore (that is not the nature of the material)—but it might be plausibly objected that he had struck the whole mass of fancy, prejudice, passion, sense, whim, with his petrific, leaden mace, that he had "bound volatile Hermes, " and reduced the theory and practice of human life to a *caput mortuum* of reason, and dull, plodding, technical calculation. The gentleman is himself a capital logician; and he has been led by this circumstance to consider man as a logical animal. We fear this view of the matter will hardly hold water. If we attend to the *moral* man, the constitution of his mind will scarcely be found to be built up of pure reason and a regard to consequences: if we consider the *criminal* man (with whom the legislator has chiefly to do) it will be found to be still less so.

Every pleasure, says Mr. Bentham, is equally a good, and is to be taken into the account as such in a moral estimate, whether it be the pleasure of sense or of conscience, whether it arise from the exercise of virtue or the perpetration of crime. We are afraid the human mind does not readily come into this doctrine, this *ultima ratio philosophorum*, interpreted according to the letter. Our moral sentiments are made up of sympathies and antipathies, of sense and imagination, of understanding and prejudice. The soul, by reason of its weakness, is an aggregating and an exclusive principle; it clings obstinately to some things, and violently rejects others. And it must do so, in a great measure, or it would act contrary to its own nature. It needs helps and stages in its progress, and "all appliances and means to boot, " which can raise it to a partial conformity to truth and good (the utmost it is capable of) and bring it into a tolerable harmony with the universe. By aiming at too much, by dismissing collateral aids, by extending itself to the farthest verge of the conceivable and possible, it loses its elasticity and vigour, its impulse and its direction. The moralist can no more do without the intermediate use of rules and principles, without the 'vantage ground of habit, without the levers of the understanding, than the mechanist can discard the use of wheels and pulleys, and perform every thing by simple motion. If the mind of man were competent to comprehend the whole of truth and good, and act upon it at once, and independently of all other considerations, Mr. Bentham's plan would be a feasible one, and *the truth, the whole truth, and nothing but the truth* would be the best possible ground to place morality upon. But it is not so. In ascertaining the rules of moral conduct, we must have regard not merely to the nature of the object, but to the capacity of the agent, and to his fitness for apprehending or attaining it. Pleasure is that which is so in itself: good is that which approves itself as such on reflection, or the idea of which is a source of satisfaction. All pleasure is not, therefore (morally speaking) equally a good; for all pleasure does not equally bear reflecting on. There are some tastes that are sweet in the mouth and bitter in the belly; and there is a similar contradiction and anomaly in the mind and heart of man. Again, what would become of the *Posthaec meminisse juvabit* of the poet, if a principle of fluctuation and reaction is not inherent in the very constitution of our nature, or if all moral truth is a mere literal truism? We are not, then, so much to inquire what certain things are abstractedly or in themselves, as how they affect the mind, and to approve or condemn them accordingly. The same object seen near strikes us more powerfully than at a distance: things thrown into masses give a greater blow to the imagination than when scattered and divided into their component parts. A number of mole-hills do not make a mountain, though a mountain is actually made up of atoms: so moral truth must present itself under a certain aspect and from a certain point of view, in order to produce its full and proper effect upon the mind. The laws of the affections are as necessary as those of optics. A calculation of consequences is no more equivalent to a sentiment, than a *seriatim* enumeration of square yards or feet touches the fancy like the sight of the Alps or Andes!

To give an instance or two of what we mean. Those who on pure cosmopolite principles, or on the ground of abstract humanity affect an extraordinary regard for the Turks and Tartars, have been accused of neglecting their duties to their friends and next-door neighbours. Well, then, what is the state of the question here? One human being is, no doubt, as much worth in himself, independently of the circumstances of time or place, as another; but he is not of so much value to us and our affections. Could our imagination take wing (with our speculative faculties) to the other side of the globe or to the ends of the universe, could our eyes behold whatever our reason teaches us to be possible, could our hands reach as far as our thoughts or wishes, we might then busy ourselves to advantage with the Hottentots, or hold intimate converse with the inhabitants of the Moon; but being as we are, our feelings evaporate in so large a space—we must draw the circle of our affections and duties somewhat closer—the heart hovers and fixes nearer home. It is true, the bands of private, or of local and natural affection are often, nay in general, too tightly strained, so as frequently to do harm instead of good: but the present question is whether we can, with safety and effect, be wholly emancipated from them? Whether we should shake them off at pleasure and without mercy, as the only bar to the triumph of truth and justice? Or whether benevolence, constructed upon a logical scale, would not be merely *nominal*, whether duty, raised to too lofty a pitch of refinement, might not sink into callous indifference or hollow selfishness? Again, is it not to exact too high a strain from humanity, to ask us to qualify the degree of abhorrence we feel against a murderer by taking into our cool consideration the pleasure he may have in committing the deed, and in the prospect of gratifying his avarice or his revenge? We are hardly so formed as to sympathise at the same moment with the assassin and his victim. The degree of pleasure the former may feel, instead of extenuating, aggravates his guilt, and shews the depth of his malignity. Now the mind revolts against this by mere natural antipathy, if it is itself well-disposed; or the slow process of reason would afford but a feeble resistance to violence and wrong. The will, which is necessary to give consistency and promptness to our good intentions, cannot extend so much candour and courtesy to the antagonist principle of evil: virtue, to be sincere and practical, cannot be divested entirely of the blindness and impetuosity of passion! It has been made a plea (half jest, half earnest) for the horrors of war, that they promote trade and manufactures. It has been said, as a set-off for the atrocities practised upon the negro slaves in the West Indies, that without their blood and sweat, so many millions of people could not have sugar to sweeten their tea. Fires and murders have been argued to be beneficial, as they serve to fill the newspapers, and for a subject to talk of— this is a sort of sophistry that it might be difficult to disprove on the bare scheme of contingent utility; but on the ground that we have stated, it must pass for a mere irony. What the proportion between the good and the evil will really be found in any of the supposed cases, may be a question to the understanding; but to the imagination and the heart, that is, to the natural feelings of mankind, it admits of none!

Mr. Bentham, in adjusting the provisions of a penal code, lays too little stress on the cooperation of the natural prejudices of mankind, and the habitual feelings of that class of persons for whom they are more particularly designed. Legislators (we mean writers on legislation) are philosophers, and governed by their reason: criminals, for whose controul laws are made, are a set of desperadoes, governed only by their passions. What wonder that so little progress has been made towards a mutual understanding between the two parties! They are quite a different species, and speak a different language, and are sadly at a loss for a common interpreter between them. Perhaps the Ordinary of Newgate bids as fair for this office as any one. What should Mr. Bentham, sitting at ease in his arm-chair, composing his mind before he begins to write by a prelude on the organ, and looking out at a beautiful prospect when he is at a loss for an idea, know of the principles of action of rogues, outlaws, and vagabonds? No more than Montaigne of the motions of his cat! If sanguine and tender-hearted philanthropists have set on foot an inquiry into the barbarity and the defects of penal laws, the practical improvements have been mostly suggested by reformed cut-throats, turnkeys, and thief-takers. What even can the Honourable House, who when the Speaker has pronounced the well-known, wished-for sounds "That this house do now adjourn, " retire, after voting a royal crusade or a loan of millions, to lie on down, and feed on plate in spacious palaces, know of what passes in the hearts of wretches in garrets and night-cellars, petty pilferers and marauders, who cut throats and pick pockets with their own hands? The thing is impossible. The laws of the country are, therefore, ineffectual and abortive, because they are made by the rich for the poor, by the wise for the ignorant, by the respectable and exalted in station for the very scum and refuse of the community. If Newgate would resolve itself into a committee of the whole Press-yard, with Jack Ketch at its head, aided by confidential persons from the county prisons or the Hulks, and would make a clear breast, some *data* might be found out to proceed upon; but as it is, the *criminal mind* of the country is a book sealed, no one has been able to penetrate to the inside! Mr. Bentham, in his attempts to revise and amend our criminal jurisprudence, proceeds entirely on his favourite principle of Utility. Convince highwaymen and house-breakers that it will be for their interest to reform, and they will reform and lead honest lives; according to Mr. Bentham. He says, "All men act from calculation, even madmen reason. " And, in our opinion, he might as well carry this maxim to Bedlam or St. Luke's, and apply it to the inhabitants, as think to coerce or overawe the inmates of a gaol, or those whose practices make them candidates for that distinction, by the mere dry, detailed convictions of the understanding. Criminals are not to be influenced by reason; for it is of the very essence of crime to disregard consequences both to ourselves and others. You may as well preach philosophy to a drunken man, or to the dead, as to those who are under the instigation of any mischievous passion. A man is a drunkard, and you tell him he ought to be sober; he is debauched, and you ask him to reform; he is idle, and you recommend industry to him as his wisest course; he gambles, and you remind him that he may be ruined by this foible; he has lost his character, and you advise him to get into some reputable service or lucrative situation; vice becomes a habit with him, and you request him to rouse himself and shake it off; he is starving, and you warn him that if he breaks the law, he will be hanged. None of this reasoning reaches the mark it aims at. The culprit, who violates and suffers the vengeance of the laws, is not the dupe of ignorance, but the slave of passion, the victim of habit or necessity. To argue with strong passion, with inveterate habit, with desperate circumstances, is to talk to the winds. Clownish ignorance may indeed be dispelled, and taught better; but it is seldom that a criminal is not aware of the consequences of his act, or has not made up his mind to the alternative. They are, in general, *too knowing by half*. You tell a person of this stamp what is his interest; he says he does not care about his interest, or the world and he differ on that particular. But there is one point on which he must agree with them, namely, what *they* think of his conduct, and that is the only hold you have of him. A man may be callous and indifferent to what happens to himself; but he is never indifferent to public opinion, or proof against open scorn and infamy. Shame, then, not fear, is the sheet-anchor of the law. He who is not afraid of being pointed at as a *thief*, will not mind a month's hard labour. He who is prepared to take the life of another, is already reckless of his own. But every one makes a sorry figure in the pillory; and the being launched from the New Drop lowers a man in his own opinion. The lawless and violent spirit, who is hurried by headstrong self-will to break the laws, does not like to have the ground of pride and obstinacy struck from under his feet. This is what gives the *swells* of the metropolis such a dread of the *tread-mill*—it makes them ridiculous. It must be confessed, that this very circumstance renders the reform of criminals nearly hopeless. It is the apprehension of being stigmatized by public opinion, the fear of what will be thought and said of them, that deters men from the violation of the laws, while their character remains unimpeached; but honour once lost, all is lost. The man can never be himself again! A citizen is like a soldier, a part of a machine, who submits to certain hardships, privations, and dangers, not for his own ease, pleasure, profit, or even conscience, but—*for shame*. What is it that keeps the machine together in either case? Not punishment or discipline, but sympathy. The soldier mounts the breach or stands in the trenches, the peasant hedges and ditches, or the mechanic plies his ceaseless task, because the one will not be called a *coward*, the other a *rogue*: but let the one turn deserter and the other vagabond, and there is an end of him. The grinding law of necessity, which is no other than a name, a breath, loses its force; he is no longer sustained by the good opinion of others, and he drops out of his place in society, a useless clog! Mr. Bentham takes a culprit, and puts him into what he calls a *Panopticon*, that is, a sort of circular prison, with open cells, like a glass bee-hive. He sits in the middle, and sees all the other does. He gives him work to do, and lectures him if he does not do it. He takes liquor from him, and society, and liberty; but he feeds and clothes him, and keeps him out of mischief; and when he has convinced him, by force and reason together, that this life is for his good, he turns him out upon the world a reformed man, and as confident of the success of his handy-work, as the shoemaker of that which he has just taken off the last, or the Parisian barber in Sterne, of the buckle of his wig. "Dip it in the ocean, " said the perruquier, "and it will stand! " But we doubt the durability of our projector's patchwork. Will our convert to the great principle of Utility work when he is from under Mr. Bentham's eye, because he was forced to work when under it? Will he keep sober, because he has been kept from liquor so long? Will he not return to loose company, because he has had the pleasure of sitting vis-a-vis with a philosopher of late? Will he not steal, now that his hands are untied? Will he not take the road, now that it is free to him? Will he not call his benefactor all the names he can set his tongue to, the moment his back is turned? All this is more than to be feared. The charm of criminal life, like that of savage life, consists in liberty, in hardship, in danger, and in the contempt of death, in one word, in extraordinary excitement; and he who has tasted of it, will no more return to regular habits of life, than a man will take to water after drinking brandy, or than a wild beast will give over hunting its prey. Miracles never cease, to be sure; but they are not to be had wholesale, or *to order*. Mr. Owen, who is another of these proprietors and patentees of reform, has lately got an American savage with him, whom he carries about in great triumph and complacency, as an antithesis to his *New View of Society*, and as winding up his reasoning to what it mainly wanted, an epigrammatic point. Does the benevolent visionary of the Lanark cotton-mills really think this *natural man* will act as a foil to his *artificial man*? Does he for a moment imagine that his *Address to the higher and middle classes*, with all its advantages of fiction, makes any thing like so interesting a romance as *Hunter's Captivity among the North American Indians?* Has he any thing to shew, in all the apparatus of New Lanark and its desolate monotony, to excite the thrill of imagination like the blankets made of wreaths of snow under which the wild wood-rovers bury themselves for weeks in winter? Or the skin of a leopard, which our hardy adventurer slew, and which served him for great coat and bedding? Or the rattle-snake that he found by his side as a bedfellow? Or his rolling himself into a ball to escape from him? Or his suddenly placing himself against a tree to avoid being trampled to death by the herd of wild buffaloes, that came rushing on like the sound of thunder? Or his account of the huge spiders that prey on bluebottles and gilded flies in green pathless forests; or of the great Pacific Ocean, that the natives look upon as the gulf that parts time from eternity, and that is to waft them to the spirits of their fathers? After all this, Mr. Hunter must find Mr. Owen and his parallellograms trite and flat, and will, we suspect, take an opportunity to escape from them!

Mr. Bentham's method of reasoning, though comprehensive and exact, labours under the defect of most systems—it is too *topical*. It includes every thing; but it includes every thing alike. It is rather like an inventory, than a valuation of different arguments. Every possible suggestion finds a place, so that the mind is distracted as much as enlightened by this perplexing accuracy. The exceptions seem as important as the rule. By attending to the minute, we overlook the great; and in summing up an account, it will not do merely to insist on the number of items without considering their amount. Our author's page presents a very nicely dove-tailed mosaic pavement of legal common-places. We slip and slide over its even surface without being arrested any where. Or his view of the human mind resembles a map, rather than a picture: the outline, the disposition is correct, but it wants colouring and relief. There is a technicality of manner, which renders his writings of more value to the professional inquirer than to the general reader. Again, his style is unpopular, not to say unintelligible. He writes a language of his own, that *darkens knowledge*. His works have been translated into French—they ought to be translated into English. People wonder that Mr. Bentham has not been prosecuted for the boldness and severity of some of his invectives. He might wrap up high treason in one of his inextricable periods, and it would never find its way into Westminster-Hall. He is a kind of Manuscript author—he writes a cypher-hand, which the vulgar have no key to. The construction of his sentences is a curious framework with pegs and hooks to hang his thoughts upon, for his own use and guidance, but almost out of the reach of every body else. It is a barbarous philosophical jargon, with all the repetitions, parentheses, formalities, uncouth nomenclature and verbiage of law-Latin; and what makes it worse, it is not mere verbiage, but has a great deal of acuteness and meaning in it, which you would be glad to pick out if you could. In short, Mr. Bentham writes as if he was allowed but a single sentence to express his whole view of a subject in, and as if, should he omit a single circumstance or step of the argument, it would be lost to the world for ever, like an estate by a flaw in the title-deeds. This is over-rating the importance of our own discoveries, and mistaking the nature and object of language altogether. Mr. Bentham has *acquired* this disability—it is not natural to him. His admirable little work *On Usury*, published forty years ago, is clear, easy, and vigorous. But Mr. Bentham has shut himself up since then "in nook monastic, " conversing only with followers of his own, or with "men of Ind, " and has endeavoured to overlay his natural humour, sense, spirit, and style with the dust and cobwebs of an obscure solitude. The best of it is, he thinks his present mode of expressing himself perfect, and that whatever may be objected to his law or logic, no one can find the least fault with the purity, simplicity, and perspicuity of his style.

Mr. Bentham, in private life, is an amiable and exemplary character. He is a little romantic, or so; and has dissipated part of a handsome fortune in practical speculations. He lends an ear to plausible projectors, and, if he cannot prove them to be wrong in their premises or their conclusions, thinks himself bound *in reason* to stake his money on the venture. Strict logicians are licensed visionaries. Mr. Bentham is half-brother to the late Mr. Speaker Abbott[A]—*Proh pudor*! He was educated at Eton, and still takes our novices to task about a passage in Homer, or a metre in Virgil. He was afterwards at the University, and he has described the scruples of an ingenuous youthful mind about subscribing the articles, in a passage in his *Church-of-Englandism*, which smacks of truth and honour both, and does one good to read it in an age, when "to be honest" (or not to laugh at the very idea of honesty) "is to be one man picked out of ten thousand! " Mr. Bentham relieves his mind sometimes, after the fatigue of study, by playing on a fine old organ, and has a relish for Hogarth's prints. He turns wooden utensils in a lathe for exercise, and fancies he can turn men in the same manner. He has no great fondness for poetry, and can hardly extract a moral out of Shakespear. His house is warmed and lighted by steam. He is one of those who prefer the artificial to the natural in most things, and think the mind of man omnipotent. He has a great contempt for out-of-door prospects, for green fields and trees, and is for referring every thing to Utility. There is a little narrowness in this; for if all the sources of satisfaction are taken away, what is to become of utility itself? It is, indeed, the great fault of this able and extraordinary man, that he has concentrated his faculties and feelings too entirely on one subject and pursuit, and has not "looked enough abroad into universality. "[B]

[Footnote A: Now Lord Colchester.]

[Footnote B: Lord Bacon's Advancement of Learning.]

* * * * *

WILLIAM GODWIN

The Spirit of the Age was never more fully-shewn than in its treatment of this writer—its love of paradox and change, its dastard submission to prejudice and to the fashion of the day. Five-and-twenty years ago he was in the very zenith of a sultry and unwholesome popularity; he blazed as a sun in the firmament of reputation; no one was more talked of, more looked up to, more sought after, and wherever liberty, truth, justice was the theme, his name was not far off: —now he has sunk below the horizon, and enjoys the serene twilight of a doubtful immortality. Mr. Godwin, during his lifetime, has secured to himself the triumphs and the mortifications of an extreme notoriety and of a sort of posthumous fame.

His bark, after being tossed in the revolutionary tempest, now raised to heaven by all the fury of popular breath, now almost dashed in pieces, and buried in the quicksands of ignorance, or scorched with the lightning of momentary indignation, at length floats on the calm wave that is to bear it down the stream of time. Mr. Godwin's person is not known, he is not pointed out in the street, his conversation is not courted, his opinions are not asked, he is at the head of no cabal, he belongs to no party in the State, he has no train of admirers, no one thinks it worth his while even to traduce and vilify him, he has scarcely friend or foe, the world make a point (as Goldsmith used to say) of taking no more notice of him than if such an individual had never existed; he is to all ordinary intents and purposes dead and buried; but the author of *Political Justice* and of *Caleb Williams* can never die, his name is an abstraction in letters, his works are standard in the history of intellect. He is thought of now like any eminent writer a hundred-and-fifty years ago, or just as he will be a hundred-and-fifty years hence. He knows this, and smiles in silent mockery of himself, reposing on the monument of his fame—

"Sedet, in eternumque sedebit infelix Theseus. "

No work in our time gave such a blow to the philosophical mind of the country as the celebrated *Enquiry concerning Political Justice*. Tom Paine was considered for the time as a Tom Fool to him; Paley an old woman; Edmund Burke a flashy sophist. Truth, moral truth, it was supposed, had here taken up its abode; and these were the oracles of thought. "Throw aside your books of chemistry, " said Wordsworth

to a young man, a student in the Temple, "and read Godwin on
Necessity. " Sad necessity! Fatal reverse! Is truth then so variable? Is
it one thing at twenty, and another at forty? Is it at a burning heat in
1793, and below *zero* in 1814? Not so, in the name of manhood and of
common sense! Let us pause here a little. —Mr. Godwin indulged in
extreme opinions, and carried with him all the most sanguine and
fearless understandings of the time. What then? Because those
opinions were overcharged, were they therefore altogether
groundless? Is the very God of our idolatry all of a sudden to
become an abomination and an anathema? Could so many young
men of talent, of education, and of principle have been hurried away
by what had neither truth, nor nature, not one particle of honest
feeling nor the least shew of reason in it? Is the *Modern Philosophy* (as
it has been called) at one moment a youthful bride, and the next a
withered beldame, like the false Duessa in Spenser? Or is the
vaunted edifice of Reason, like his House of Pride, gorgeous in front,
and dazzling to approach, while "its hinder parts are ruinous,
decayed, and old? " Has the main prop, which supported the mighty
fabric, been shaken and given way under the strong grasp of some
Samson; or has it not rather been undermined by rats and vermin?
At one time, it almost seemed, that "if this failed,

> "The pillar'd firmament was rottenness,
> And earth's base built of stubble: "

now scarce a shadow of it remains, it is crumbled to dust, nor is it
even talked of! "What then, went ye forth for to see, a reed shaken
with the wind? " Was it for this that our young gownsmen of the
greatest expectation and promise, versed in classic lore, steeped in
dialectics, armed at all points for the foe, well read, well nurtured,
well provided for, left the University and the prospect of lawn
sleeves, tearing asunder the shackles of the free born spirit, and the
cobwebs of school-divinity, to throw themselves at the feet of the
new Gamaliel, and learn wisdom from him? Was it for this, that
students at the bar, acute, inquisitive, sceptical (here only wild
enthusiasts) neglected for a while the paths of preferment and the
law as too narrow, tortuous, and unseemly to bear the pure and
broad light of reason? Was it for this, that students in medicine
missed their way to Lecturerships and the top of their profession,
deeming lightly of the health of the body, and dreaming only of the
renovation of society and the march of mind? Was it to this that Mr.
Southey's *Inscriptions* pointed? to this that Mr. Coleridge's *Religious
Musings* tended? Was it for this, that Mr. Godwin himself sat with

arms folded, and, "like Cato, gave his little senate laws? " Or rather, like another Prospero, uttered syllables that with their enchanted breath were to change the world, and might almost stop the stars in their courses? Oh! and is all forgot? Is this sun of intellect blotted from the sky? Or has it suffered total eclipse? Or is it we who make the fancied gloom, by looking at it through the paltry, broken, stained fragments of our own interests and prejudices? Were we fools then, or are we dishonest now? Or was the impulse of the mind less likely to be true and sound when it arose from high thought and warm feeling, than afterwards, when it was warped and debased by the example, the vices, and follies of the world?

The fault, then, of Mr. Godwin's philosophy, in one word, was too much ambition—"by that sin fell the angels! " He conceived too nobly of his fellows (the most unpardonable crime against them, for there is nothing that annoys our self-love so much as being complimented on imaginary achievements, to which we are wholly unequal)—he raised the standard of morality above the reach of humanity, and by directing virtue to the most airy and romantic heights, made her path dangerous, solitary, and impracticable. The author of the *Political Justice* took abstract reason for the rule of conduct, and abstract good for its end. He places the human mind on an elevation, from which it commands a view of the whole line of moral consequences; and requires it to conform its acts to the larger and more enlightened conscience which it has thus acquired. He absolves man from the gross and narrow ties of sense, custom, authority, private and local attachment, in order that he may devote himself to the boundless pursuit of universal benevolence. Mr. Godwin gives no quarter to the amiable weaknesses of our nature, nor does he stoop to avail himself of the supplementary aids of an imperfect virtue. Gratitude, promises, friendship, family affection give way, not that they may be merged in the opposite vices or in want of principle; but that the void may be filled up by the disinterested love of good, and the dictates of inflexible justice, which is "the law of laws, and sovereign of sovereigns. " All minor considerations yield, in his system, to the stern sense of duty, as they do, in the ordinary and established ones, to the voice of necessity. Mr. Godwin's theory and that of more approved reasoners differ only in this, that what are with them the exceptions, the extreme cases, he makes the every-day rule. No one denies that on great occasions, in moments of fearful excitement, or when a mighty object is at stake, the lesser and merely instrumental points of duty are to be sacrificed without remorse at the shrine of patriotism, of honour, and of conscience. But the disciple of the *New School* (no wonder it found so many impugners, even in its own bosom!) is to be always the hero of duty; the law to which he has bound himself never swerves nor relaxes; his feeling of what is right is to be at all times wrought up to a pitch of enthusiastic self-devotion; he must become the unshrinking martyr and confessor of the public good. If it be said that this scheme is chimerical and impracticable on ordinary occasions, and to the generality of mankind, well and good; but those who accuse the author of having trampled on the common feelings and prejudices of mankind in wantonness or insult, or without wishing to substitute something better (and only unattainable, because it is better) in their stead, accuse him wrongfully. We may not be able to launch the bark of our affections on the ocean-tide of humanity, we may be forced to paddle along its shores, or shelter in its creeks and rivulets: but we have no right to reproach the bold and adventurous pilot, who dared us to tempt the uncertain abyss, with our own want of courage or of skill, or with the jealousies and impatience, which deter us from undertaking, or might prevent us from accomplishing the voyage!

The *Enquiry concerning Political Justice* (it was urged by its favourers and defenders at the time, and may still be so, without either profaneness or levity) is a metaphysical and logical commentary on some of the most beautiful and striking texts of Scripture. Mr. Godwin is a mixture of the Stoic and of the Christian philosopher. To break the force of the vulgar objections and outcry that have been raised against the Modern Philosophy, as if it were a new and monstrous birth in morals, it may be worth noticing, that volumes of sermons have been written to excuse the founder of Christianity for not including friendship and private affection among its golden rules, but rather excluding them. [A] Moreover, the answer to the question, "Who is thy neighbour? " added to the divine precept, "Thou shalt love thy neighbour as thyself, " is the same as in the exploded pages of our author, —"He to whom we can do most good. " In determining this point, we were not to be influenced by any extrinsic or collateral considerations, by our own predilections, or the expectations of others, by our obligations to them or any services they might be able to render us, by the climate they were born in, by the house they lived in, by rank or religion, or party, or personal ties, but by the abstract merits, the pure and unbiassed justice of the case. The artificial helps and checks to moral conduct were set aside as spurious and unnecessary, and we came at once to the grand and simple question—"In what manner we could best contribute to the greatest possible good? " This was the paramount obligation in all cases whatever, from which we had no right to free ourselves upon any idle or formal pretext, and of which each person was to judge for himself, under the infallible authority of his own opinion and the inviolable sanction of his self-approbation. "There was the rub that made *philosophy* of so short life! " Mr. Godwin's definition of morals was the same as the admired one of law, *reason without passion*; but with the unlimited scope of private opinion, and in a boundless field of speculation (for nothing less would satisfy the pretensions of the New School), there was danger that the unseasoned novice might substitute some pragmatical conceit of his own for the rule of right reason, and mistake a heartless indifference for a superiority to more natural and generous feelings. Our ardent and dauntless reformer followed out the moral of the parable of the Good Samaritan into its most rigid and repulsive consequences with a pen of steel, and let fall his "trenchant blade" on every vulnerable point of human infirmity; but there is a want in his system of the mild and persuasive tone of the Gospel, where "all is conscience and tender heart. " Man was indeed screwed up, by mood and figure, into a logical machine, that was to forward the public good with the utmost punctuality and effect, and it might go very well on smooth ground and under favourable circumstances; but would it work up-hill or *against the grain*? It was to be feared that the proud Temple of Reason, which at a distance and in stately supposition shone like the palaces of the New Jerusalem, might (when placed on actual ground) be broken up into the sordid styes of sensuality, and the petty huckster's shops of self-interest! Every man (it was proposed—"so ran the tenour of the bond") was to be a Regulus, a Codrus, a Cato, or a Brutus—every woman a Mother of the Gracchi.

> " — — — — — —It was well said,
> And 'tis a kind of good deed to say well. "

But heroes on paper might degenerate into vagabonds in practice, Corinnas into courtezans. Thus a refined and permanent individual attachment is intended to supply the place and avoid the inconveniences of marriage; but vows of eternal constancy, without church security, are found to be fragile. A member of the *ideal* and perfect commonwealth of letters lends another a hundred pounds for immediate and pressing use; and when he applies for it again, the borrower has still more need of it than he, and retains it for his own especial, which is tantamount to the public good. The Exchequer of pure reason, like that of the State, never refunds. The political as well as the religious fanatic appeals from the over-weening opinion and claims of others to the highest and most impartial tribunal, namely, his own breast. Two persons agree to live together in Chambers on principles of pure equality and mutual assistance—but when it comes to the push, one of them finds that the other always insists on his fetching water from the pump in Hare-court, and cleaning his shoes for him. A modest assurance was not the least indispensable virtue in the new perfectibility code; and it was hence discovered to be a scheme, like other schemes where there are all prizes and no blanks, for the accommodation of the enterprizing and cunning, at the expence of the credulous and honest. This broke up the system, and left no good odour behind it! Reason has become a sort of bye-word, and philosophy has "fallen first into a fasting, then into a sadness, then into a decline, and last, into the dissolution of which we all complain! " This is a worse error than the former: we may be said to have "lost the immortal part of ourselves, and what remains is beastly! " The point of view from which this matter may be fairly considered, is two-fold, and may be stated thus: —In the first place, it by no means follows, because reason is found not to be the only infallible or safe rule of conduct, that it is no rule at all; or that we are to discard it altogether with derision and ignominy. On the contrary, if not the sole, it is the principal ground of action; it is "the guide, the stay and anchor of our purest thoughts, and soul of all our moral being. " In proportion as we strengthen and expand this principle, and bring our affections and subordinate, but perhaps more powerful motives of action into harmony with it, it will not admit of a doubt that we advance to the goal of perfection, and answer the ends of our creation, those ends which not only morality enjoins, but which religion sanctions. If with the utmost stretch of reason, man cannot (as some seemed inclined to suppose) soar up to the God, and quit the ground of human frailty, yet, stripped wholly of it, he sinks at once into the brute. If it cannot stand alone, in its naked simplicity, but requires other props to buttress it up, or ornaments to set it off; yet without it the moral structure would fall flat and dishonoured to the ground. Private reason is that which raises the individual above his mere animal instincts, appetites and passions: public reason in its gradual progress separates the savage from the civilized state. Without the one, men would resemble wild beasts in their dens; without the other, they would be speedily converted into hordes of barbarians or banditti. Sir Walter Scott, in his zeal to restore the spirit of loyalty, of passive obedience and non-resistance as an acknowledgment for his having been created a Baronet by a Prince of the House of Brunswick, may think it a fine thing to return in imagination to the good old times, "when in Auvergne alone, there were three hundred nobles whose most ordinary actions were robbery, rape, and murder, " when the castle of each Norman baron was a strong hold from which the lordly proprietor issued to oppress and plunder the neighbouring districts, and when the Saxon peasantry were treated by their gay and gallant tyrants as a herd of loathsome swine—but for our own parts we beg to be excused; we had rather live in the same age with the author of Waverley and Blackwood's Magazine. Reason is the meter and alnager in civil intercourse, by which each person's upstart and contradictory pretensions are weighed and approved or found wanting, and without which it could not subsist, any more than traffic or the exchange of commodities could be carried on without weights and measures. It is the medium of knowledge, and the polisher of manners, by creating common interests and ideas. Or in the words of a contemporary writer, "Reason is the queen of the moral world, the soul of the universe, the lamp of human life, the pillar of society, the foundation of law, the beacon of nations, the golden chain let down from heaven, which links all accountable and all intelligent natures in one common system—and in the vain strife between fanatic innovation and fanatic prejudice, we are exhorted to dethrone this queen of the world, to blot out this light of the mind, to deface this fair column, to break in pieces this golden chain! We are to discard and throw from us with loud taunts and bitter execrations that reason, which has been the lofty theme of the philosopher, the poet, the moralist, and the divine, whose name was not first named to be abused by the enthusiasts of the French Revolution, or to be blasphemed by the madder enthusiasts, the advocates of Divine Right, but which is coeval with, and inseparable from the nature and faculties of man—is the image of his Maker stamped upon him at his birth, the understanding breathed into him with the breath of life, and in the participation and improvement of which alone he is raised above the brute creation and his own physical nature! "—The overstrained and ridiculous pretensions of monks and ascetics were never thought to justify a return to unbridled licence of manners, or the throwing aside of all decency. The hypocrisy, cruelty, and fanaticism, often attendant on peculiar professions of sanctity, have not banished the name of religion from the world. Neither can "the unreasonableness of the reason" of some modern sciolists "so unreason our reason, " as to debar us of the benefit of this principle in future, or to disfranchise us of the highest privilege of our nature. In the second place, if it is admitted that Reason alone is not the sole and self-sufficient ground of morals, it is to Mr. Godwin that we are indebted for having settled the point. No one denied or distrusted this principle (before his time) as the absolute judge and interpreter in all questions of difficulty; and if this is no longer the case, it is because he has taken this principle, and followed it into its remotest consequences with more keenness of eye and steadiness of hand than any other expounder of ethics. His grand work is (at least) an *experimentum crucis* to shew the weak sides and imperfections of human reason as the sole law of human action. By overshooting the mark, or by "flying an eagle flight, forth and right on, " he has pointed out the limit or line of separation, between what is practicable and what is barely conceivable—by imposing impossible tasks on the naked strength of the will, he has discovered how far it is or is not in our power to dispense with the illusions of sense, to resist the calls of affection, to emancipate ourselves from the force of habit; and thus, though he has not said it himself, has enabled others to say to the towering aspirations after good, and to the over-bearing pride of human intellect—"Thus far shalt thou come, and no farther! " Captain Parry would be thought to have rendered a service to navigation and his country, no less by proving that there is no North-West Passage, than if he had ascertained that there is one: so Mr. Godwin has rendered an essential service to moral science, by attempting (in vain) to pass the Arctic Circle and Frozen Regions, where the understanding is no longer warmed by the affections, nor fanned by the breeze of fancy! This is the effect of all bold, original, and powerful thinking, that it either discovers the truth, or detects where error lies; and the only crime with which Mr. Godwin can be charged as a political and moral reasoner is, that he has displayed a more ardent spirit, and a more independent activity of thought than others, in establishing the fallacy (if fallacy it be) of an old popular prejudice that *the Just and True were one*, by "championing it to the Outrance, " and in the final result placing the Gothic structure of human virtue on an humbler, but a wider and safer foundation than it had hitherto occupied in the volumes and systems of the learned. Mr. Godwin is an inventor in the regions of romance, as well as a skilful and hardy explorer of those of moral truth. *Caleb Williams* and *St. Leon* are two of the most splendid and impressive works of the imagination that have appeared in our times. It is not merely that these novels are very well for a philosopher to have produced—they are admirable and complete in themselves, and would not lead you to suppose that the author, who is so entirely at home in human character and dramatic situation, had ever dabbled in logic or metaphysics. The first of these, particularly, is a master-piece, both as to invention and execution. The romantic and chivalrous principle of the love of personal fame is embodied in the finest possible manner in the character of Falkland; [B] as in Caleb Williams (who is not the first, but the second character in the piece) we see the very demon of curiosity personified. Perhaps the art with which these two characters are contrived to relieve and set off each other, has never been surpassed in any work of fiction, with the exception of the immortal satire of Cervantes. The restless and inquisitive spirit of Caleb Williams, in search and in possession of his patron's fatal secret, haunts the latter like a second conscience, plants stings in his tortured mind, fans the flame of his jealous ambition, struggling with agonized remorse; and the hapless but noble-minded Falkland at length falls a martyr to the persecution of that morbid and overpowering interest, of which his mingled virtues and vices have rendered him the object. We conceive no one ever began Caleb Williams that did not read it through: no one that ever read it could possibly forget it, or speak of it after any length of time, but with an impression as if the events and feelings had been personal to himself. This is the case also with the story of St. Leon, which, with less dramatic interest and intensity of purpose, is set off by a more gorgeous and flowing eloquence, and by a crown of preternatural imagery, that waves over it like a palm-tree! It is the beauty and the charm of Mr. Godwin's descriptions that the reader identifies himself with the author; and the secret of this is, that the author has identified himself with his personages. Indeed, he has created them. They are the proper issue of his brain, lawfully begot, not foundlings, nor the "bastards of his art. " He is not an indifferent, callous spectator of the scenes which he himself pourtrays, but without seeming to feel them. There is no look of patch-work and plagiarism, the beggarly copiousness of borrowed wealth; no tracery-work from worm-eaten manuscripts, from forgotten chronicles, nor piecing out of vague traditions with fragments and snatches of old ballads, so that the result resembles a gaudy, staring transparency, in which you cannot distinguish the daubing of the painter from the light that shines through the flimsy colours and gives them brilliancy. Here all is clearly made out with strokes of the pencil, by fair, not by factitious means. Our author takes a given subject from nature or from books, and then fills it up with the ardent workings of his own mind, with the teeming and audible pulses of his own heart. The effect is entire and satisfactory in proportion. The work (so to speak) and the author are one. We are not puzzled to decide upon their respective pretensions. In reading Mr. Godwin's novels, we know what share of merit the author has in them. In reading the *Scotch Novels*, we are perpetually embarrassed in asking ourselves this question; and perhaps it is not altogether a false modesty that prevents the editor from putting his name in the title-page—he is (for any thing we know to the contrary) only a more voluminous sort of Allen-a-Dale. At least, we may claim this advantage for the English author, that the chains with which he rivets our attention are forged out of his own thoughts, link by link, blow for blow, with glowing enthusiasm: we see the genuine ore melted in the furnace of fervid feeling, and moulded into stately and *ideal* forms; and this is so far better than peeping into an old iron shop, or pilfering from a dealer in marine stores! There is one drawback, however, attending this mode of proceeding, which attaches generally, indeed, to all originality of composition; namely, that it has a tendency to a certain degree of monotony. He who draws upon his own resources, easily comes to an end of his wealth. Mr. Godwin, in all his writings, dwells upon one idea or exclusive view of a subject, aggrandises a sentiment, exaggerates a character, or pushes an argument to extremes, and makes up by the force of style and continuity of feeling for what he wants in variety of incident or ease of manner. This necessary defect is observable in his best works, and is still more so in Fleetwood and Mandeville; the one of which, compared with his more admired performances, is mawkish, and the other morbid. Mr. Godwin is also an essayist, an historian—in short, what is he not, that belongs to the character of an indefatigable and accomplished author? His *Life of Chaucer* would have given celebrity to any man of letters possessed of three thousand a year, with leisure to write quartos: as the legal acuteness displayed in his *Remarks on Judge Eyre's Charge to the Jury* would have raised any briefless barrister to the height of his profession. This temporary effusion did more—it gave a turn to the trials for high treason in the year 1794, and possibly saved the lives of twelve innocent individuals, marked out as political victims to the Moloch of Legitimacy, which then skulked behind a British throne, and had not yet dared to stalk forth (as it has done since) from its lurking-place, in the face of day, to brave the opinion of the world. If it had then glutted its maw with its intended prey (the sharpness of Mr. Godwin's pen cut the legal cords with which it was attempted to bind them), it might have done so sooner, and with more lasting effect. The world do not know (and we are not sure but the intelligence may startle Mr. Godwin himself), that he is the author of a volume of Sermons, and of a Life of Chatham. [C]

Mr. Fawcett (an old friend and fellow-student of our author, and who always spoke of his writings with admiration, tinctured with wonder) used to mention a circumstance with respect to the last-mentioned work, which may throw some light on the history and progress of Mr. Godwin's mind. He was anxious to make his biographical account as complete as he could, and applied for this purpose to many of his acquaintance to furnish him with anecdotes or to suggest criticisms. Amongst others Mr. Fawcett repeated to him what he thought a striking passage in a speech on *General Warrants* delivered by Lord Chatham, at which he (Mr. Fawcett) had been present. "Every man's house" (said this emphatic thinker and speaker) "has been called his castle. And why is it called his castle? Is it because it is defended by a wall, because it is surrounded with a moat? No, it may be nothing more than a straw-built shed. It may be open to all the elements: the wind may enter in, the rain may enter in—but the king *cannot* enter in! " His friend thought that the point was here palpable enough: but when he came to read the printed volume, he found it thus *transposed*: "Every man's house is his castle. And why is it called so? Is it because it is defended by a wall, because it is surrounded with a moat? No, it may be nothing more than a straw-built shed. It may be exposed to all the elements: the rain may enter into it, *all the winds of Heaven may whistle round it*, but the king cannot, &c. " This was what Fawcett called a defect of *natural imagination*. He at the same time admitted that Mr. Godwin had improved his native sterility in this respect; or atoned for it by incessant activity of mind and by accumulated stores of thought and powers of language. In fact, his *forte* is not the spontaneous, but the voluntary exercise of talent. He fixes his ambition on a high point of excellence, and spares no pains or time in attaining it. He has less of the appearance of a man of genius, than any one who has given such decided and ample proofs of it. He is ready only on reflection: dangerous only at the rebound. He gathers himself up, and strains every nerve and faculty with deliberate aim to some heroic and dazzling atchievement of intellect: but he must make a career before he flings himself, armed, upon the enemy, or he is sure to be unhorsed. Or he resembles an eight-day clock that must be wound up long before it can strike. Therefore, his powers of conversation are but limited. He has neither acuteness of remark, nor a flow of language, both which might be expected from his writings, as these are no less distinguished by a sustained and impassioned tone of declamation than by novelty of opinion or brilliant tracks of invention. In company, Horne Tooke used to make a mere child of him—or of any man! Mr. Godwin liked this treatment[D], and indeed it is his foible to fawn on those who use him *cavalierly*, and to be cavalier to those who express an undue or unqualified admiration of him. He looks up with unfeigned respect to acknowledged reputation (but then it must be very well ascertained before he admits it)—and has a favourite hypothesis that Understanding and Virtue are the same thing. Mr. Godwin possesses a high degree of philosophical candour, and studiously paid the homage of his pen and person to Mr. Malthus, Sir James Macintosh, and Dr. Parr, for their unsparing attacks on him; but woe to any poor devil who had the hardihood to defend him against them! In private, the author of *Political Justice* at one time reminded those who knew him of the metaphysician engrafted on the Dissenting Minister. There was a dictatorial, captious, quibbling pettiness of manner. He lost this with the first blush and awkwardness of popularity, which surprised him in the retirement of his study; and he has since, with the wear and tear of society, from being too pragmatical, become somewhat too careless. He is, at present, as easy as an old glove. Perhaps there is a little attention to effect in this, and he wishes to appear a foil to himself. His best moments are with an intimate acquaintance or two, when he gossips in a fine vein about old authors, Clarendon's *History of the Rebellion*, or Burnet's *History of his own Times*; and you perceive by your host's talk, as by the taste of seasoned wine, that he has a *cellarage* in his understanding! Mr. Godwin also has a correct *acquired* taste in poetry and the drama. He relishes Donne and Ben Jonson, and recites a passage from either with an agreeable mixture of pedantry and *bonhommie*. He is not one of those who do not grow wiser with opportunity and reflection: he changes his opinions, and changes them for the better. The alteration of his taste in poetry, from an exclusive admiration of the age of Queen Anne to an almost equally exclusive one of that of Elizabeth, is, we suspect, owing to Mr. Coleridge, who some twenty years ago, threw a great stone into the standing pool of criticism, which splashed some persons with the mud, but which gave a motion to the surface and a reverberation to the neighbouring echoes, which has not since subsided. In common company, Mr. Godwin either goes to sleep himself, or sets others to sleep. He is at present engaged in a History of the Commonwealth of England. —*Esto perpetua!* In size Mr. Godwin is below the common stature, nor is his deportment graceful or animated. His face is, however, fine, with an expression of placid temper and recondite thought. He is not unlike the common portraits of Locke. There is a very admirable likeness of him by Mr. Northcote, which with a more heroic and dignified air, only does justice to the profound sagacity and benevolent aspirations of our author's mind. Mr. Godwin has kept the best company of his time, but he has survived most of the celebrated persons with whom he lived in habits of intimacy. He speaks of them with enthusiasm and with discrimination; and sometimes dwells with peculiar delight on a day passed at John Kemble's in company with Mr. Sheridan, Mr. Curran, Mrs. Wolstonecraft and Mrs. Inchbald, when the conversation took a most animated turn and the subject was of Love. Of all these our author is the only one remaining. Frail tenure, on which human life and genius are lent us for a while to improve or to enjoy!

[Footnote A: Shaftesbury made this an objection to Christianity, which was answered by Foster, Leland, and other eminent divines, on the ground that Christianity had a higher object in view, namely, general philanthropy.]

[Footnote B: Mr. Fuseli used to object to this striking delineation a want of historical correctness, inasmuch as the animating principle of the true chivalrous character was the sense of honour, not the mere regard to, or saving of, appearances. This, we think, must be an hypercriticism, from all we remember of books of chivalry and heroes of romance.]

[Footnote C: We had forgotten the tragedies of Antonio and Ferdinand. Peace be with their *manes*!]

[Footnote D: To be sure, it was redeemed by a high respect, and by some magnificent compliments. Once in particular, at his own table, after a good deal of *badinage* and cross-questioning about his being the author of the Reply to Judge Eyre's Charge, on Mr. Godwin's acknowledging that he was, Mr. Tooke said, "Come here then, " — and when his guest went round to his chair, he took his hand, and pressed it to his lips, saying—"I can do no less for the hand that saved my life! "]

* * * * *

MR. COLERIDGE.

The present is an age of talkers, and not of doers; and the reason is, that the world is growing old. We are so far advanced in the Arts and Sciences, that we live in retrospect, and doat on past atchievements. The accumulation of knowledge has been so great, that we are lost in wonder at the height it has reached, instead of attempting to climb or add to it; while the variety of objects distracts and dazzles the looker-on. What *niche* remains unoccupied? What path untried? What is the use of doing anything, unless we could do better than all those who have gone before us? What hope is there of this? We are like those who have been to see some noble monument of art, who are content to admire without thinking of rivalling it; or like guests after a feast, who praise the hospitality of the donor "and thank the bounteous Pan"—perhaps carrying away some trifling fragments; or like the spectators of a mighty battle, who still hear its sound afar off, and the clashing of armour and the neighing of the war-horse and the shout of victory is in their ears, like the rushing of innumerable waters!

Mr. Coleridge has "a mind reflecting ages past: " his voice is like the echo of the congregated roar of the "dark rearward and abyss" of thought. He who has seen a mouldering tower by the side of a chrystal lake, hid by the mist, but glittering in the wave below, may conceive the dim, gleaming, uncertain intelligence of his eye: he who has marked the evening clouds uprolled (a world of vapours), has seen the picture of his mind, unearthly, unsubstantial, with gorgeous tints and ever-varying forms—

> "That which was now a horse, even with a thought
> The rack dislimns, and makes it indistinct
> As water is in water. "

Our author's mind is (as he himself might express it) *tangential.* There is no subject on which he has not touched, none on which he has rested. With an understanding fertile, subtle, expansive, "quick, forgetive, apprehensive, " beyond all living precedent, few traces of it will perhaps remain. He lends himself to all impressions alike; he gives up his mind and liberty of thought to none. He is a general lover of art and science, and wedded to no one in particular. He pursues knowledge as a mistress, with outstretched hands and winged speed; but as he is about to embrace her, his Daphne turns—

alas! not to a laurel! Hardly a speculation has been left on record from the earliest time, but it is loosely folded up in Mr. Coleridge's memory, like a rich, but somewhat tattered piece of tapestry; we might add (with more seeming than real extravagance), that scarce a thought can pass through the mind of man, but its sound has at some time or other passed over his head with rustling pinions. On whatever question or author you speak, he is prepared to take up the theme with advantage—from Peter Abelard down to Thomas Moore, from the subtlest metaphysics to the politics of the *Courier*. There is no man of genius, in whose praise he descants, but the critic seems to stand above the author, and "what in him is weak, to strengthen, what is low, to raise and support: " nor is there any work of genius that does not come out of his hands like an Illuminated Missal, sparkling even in its defects. If Mr. Coleridge had not been the most impressive talker of his age, he would probably have been the finest writer; but he lays down his pen to make sure of an auditor, and mortgages the admiration of posterity for the stare of an idler. If he had not been a poet, he would have been a powerful logician; if he had not dipped his wing in the Unitarian controversy, he might have soared to the very summit of fancy. But in writing verse, he is trying to subject the Muse to *transcendental* theories: in his abstract reasoning, he misses his way by strewing it with flowers. All that he has done of moment, he had done twenty years ago: since then, he may be said to have lived on the sound of his own voice. Mr. Coleridge is too rich in intellectual wealth, to need to task himself to any drudgery: he has only to draw the sliders of his imagination, and a thousand subjects expand before him, startling him with their brilliancy, or losing themselves in endless obscurity—

> "And by the force of blear illusion,
> They draw him on to his confusion. "

What is the little he could add to the stock, compared with the countless stores that lie about him, that he should stoop to pick up a name, or to polish an idle fancy? He walks abroad in the majesty of an universal understanding, eyeing the "rich strond, " or golden sky above him, and "goes sounding on his way, " in eloquent accents, uncompelled and free!

Persons of the greatest capacity are often those, who for this reason do the least; for surveying themselves from the highest point of view, amidst the infinite variety of the universe, their own share in it seems trifling, and scarce worth a thought, and they prefer the contemplation of all that is, or has been, or can be, to the making a coil about doing what, when done, is no better than vanity. It is hard to concentrate all our attention and efforts on one pursuit, except from ignorance of others; and without this concentration of our faculties, no great progress can be made in any one thing. It is not merely that the mind is not capable of the effort; it does not think the effort worth making. Action is one; but thought is manifold. He whose restless eye glances through the wide compass of nature and art, will not consent to have "his own nothings monstered: " but he must do this, before he can give his whole soul to them. The mind, after "letting contemplation have its fill, " or

"Sailing with supreme dominion
Through the azure deep of air, "

sinks down on the ground, breathless, exhausted, powerless, inactive; or if it must have some vent to its feelings, seeks the most easy and obvious; is soothed by friendly flattery, lulled by the murmur of immediate applause, thinks as it were aloud, and babbles in its dreams! A scholar (so to speak) is a more disinterested and abstracted character than a mere author. The first looks at the numberless volumes of a library, and says, "All these are mine: " the other points to a single volume (perhaps it may be an immortal one) and says, "My name is written on the back of it. " This is a puny and groveling ambition, beneath the lofty amplitude of Mr. Coleridge's mind. No, he revolves in his wayward soul, or utters to the passing wind, or discourses to his own shadow, things mightier and more various! —Let us draw the curtain, and unlock the shrine. Learning rocked him in his cradle, and, while yet a child,

"He lisped in numbers, for the numbers came. "

At sixteen he wrote his *Ode on Chatterton*, and he still reverts to that period with delight, not so much as it relates to himself (for that string of his own early promise of fame rather jars than otherwise) but as exemplifying the youth of a poet. Mr. Coleridge talks of himself, without being an egotist, for in him the individual is always merged in the abstract and general. He distinguished himself at school and at the University by his knowledge of the classics, and gained several prizes for Greek epigrams. How many men are there (great scholars, celebrated names in literature) who having done the same thing in their youth, have no other idea all the rest of their lives but of this achievement, of a fellowship and dinner, and who, installed in academic honours, would look down on our author as a mere strolling bard! At Christ's Hospital, where he was brought up, he was the idol of those among his schoolfellows, who mingled with their bookish studies the music of thought and of humanity; and he was usually attended round the cloisters by a group of these (inspiring and inspired) whose hearts, even then, burnt within them as he talked, and where the sounds yet linger to mock ELIA on his way, still turning pensive to the past! One of the finest and rarest parts of Mr. Coleridge's conversation, is when he expatiates on the Greek tragedians (not that he is not well acquainted, when he pleases, with the epic poets, or the philosophers, or orators, or historians of antiquity)—on the subtle reasonings and melting pathos of Euripides, on the harmonious gracefulness of Sophocles, tuning his love-laboured song, like sweetest warblings from a sacred grove; on the high-wrought trumpet-tongued eloquence of Aeschylus, whose Prometheus, above all, is like an Ode to Fate, and a pleading with Providence, his thoughts being let loose as his body is chained on his solitary rock, and his afflicted will (the emblem of mortality)

"Struggling in vain with ruthless destiny. "

As the impassioned critic speaks and rises in his theme, you would think you heard the voice of the Man hated by the Gods, contending with the wild winds as they roar, and his eye glitters with the spirit of Antiquity!

Next, he was engaged with Hartley's tribes of mind, "etherial braid, thought-woven, "—and he busied himself for a year or two with vibrations and vibratiuncles and the great law of association that binds all things in its mystic chain, and the doctrine of Necessity (the mild teacher of Charity) and the Millennium, anticipative of a life to come—and he plunged deep into the controversy on Matter and Spirit, and, as an escape from Dr. Priestley's Materialism, where he felt himself imprisoned by the logician's spell, like Ariel in the cloven pine-tree, he became suddenly enamoured of Bishop Berkeley's fairy-world, [A] and used in all companies to build the universe, like a brave poetical fiction, of fine words—and he was deep-read in Malebranche, and in Cudworth's Intellectual System (a huge pile of learning, unwieldy, enormous) and in Lord Brook's hieroglyphic theories, and in Bishop Butler's Sermons, and in the Duchess of Newcastle's fantastic folios, and in Clarke and South and Tillotson, and all the fine thinkers and masculine reasoners of that age—and

Leibnitz's *Pre-established Harmony* reared its arch above his head, like the rainbow in the cloud, covenanting with the hopes of man—and then he fell plump, ten thousand fathoms down (but his wings saved him harmless) into the *hortus siccus* of Dissent, where he pared religion down to the standard of reason and stripped faith of mystery, and preached Christ crucified and the Unity of the Godhead, and so dwelt for a while in the spirit with John Huss and Jerome of Prague and Socinus and old John Zisca, and ran through Neal's History of the Puritans, and Calamy's Non-Conformists' Memorial, having like thoughts and passions with them—but then Spinoza became his God, and he took up the vast chain of being in his hand, and the round world became the centre and the soul of all things in some shadowy sense, forlorn of meaning, and around him he beheld the living traces and the sky-pointing proportions of the mighty Pan—but poetry redeemed him from this spectral philosophy, and he bathed his heart in beauty, and gazed at the golden light of heaven, and drank of the spirit of the universe, and wandered at eve by fairy-stream or fountain,

> "———When he saw nought but beauty,
> When he heard the voice of that Almighty One
> In every breeze that blew, or wave that murmured"—

and wedded with truth in Plato's shade, and in the writings of Proclus and Plotinus saw the ideas of things in the eternal mind, and unfolded all mysteries with the Schoolmen and fathomed the depths of Duns Scotus and Thomas Aquinas, and entered the third heaven with Jacob Behmen, and walked hand in hand with Swedenborg through the pavilions of the New Jerusalem, and sung his faith in the promise and in the word in his *Religious Musings*—and lowering himself from that dizzy height, poised himself on Milton's wings, and spread out his thoughts in charity with the glad prose of Jeremy Taylor, and wept over Bowles's Sonnets, and studied Cowper's blankverse, and betook himself to Thomson's Castle of Indolence, and sported with the wits of Charles the Second's days and of Queen Anne, and relished Swift's style and that of the John Bull (Arbuthnot's we mean, not Mr. Croker's) and dallied with the British Essayists and Novelists, and knew all qualities of more modern writers with a learned spirit, Johnson, and Goldsmith, and Junius, and Burke, and Godwin, and the Sorrows of Werter, and Jean Jacques Rousseau, and Voltaire, and Marivaux, and Crebillon, and thousands more—now "laughed with Rabelais in his easy chair" or pointed to Hogarth, or afterwards dwelt on Claude's classic scenes or spoke with rapture of Raphael, and compared the women at Rome to figures that had walked out of his pictures, or visited the Oratory of Pisa, and described the works of Giotto and Ghirlandaio and Massaccio, and gave the moral of the picture of the Triumph of Death, where the beggars and the wretched invoke his dreadful dart, but the rich and mighty of the earth quail and shrink before it; and in that land of siren sights and sounds, saw a dance of peasant girls, and was charmed with lutes and gondolas, —or wandered into Germany and lost himself in the labyrinths of the Hartz Forest and of the Kantean philosophy, and amongst the cabalistic names of Fichtè and Schelling and Lessing, and God knows who—this was long after, but all the former while, he had nerved his heart and filled his eyes with tears, as he hailed the rising orb of liberty, since quenched in darkness and in blood, and had kindled his affections at the blaze of the French Revolution, and sang for joy when the towers of the Bastile and the proud places of the insolent and the oppressor fell, and would have floated his bark, freighted with fondest fancies, across the Atlantic wave with Southey and others to seek for peace and freedom—

"In Philarmonia's undivided dale! "

Alas! "Frailty, thy name is *Genius*! " —What is become of all this mighty heap of hope, of thought, of learning, and humanity? It has ended in swallowing doses of oblivion and in writing paragraphs in the *Courier*. —Such, and so little is the mind of man!

It was not to be supposed that Mr. Coleridge could keep on at the rate he set off; he could not realize all he knew or thought, and less could not fix his desultory ambition; other stimulants supplied the place, and kept up the intoxicating dream, the fever and the madness of his early impressions. Liberty (the philosopher's and the poet's bride) had fallen a victim, meanwhile, to the murderous practices of the hag, Legitimacy. Proscribed by court-hirelings, too romantic for the herd of vulgar politicians, our enthusiast stood at bay, and at last turned on the pivot of a subtle casuistry to the *unclean side:* but his discursive reason would not let him trammel himself into a poet-laureate or stamp-distributor, and he stopped, ere he had quite passed that well-known "bourne from whence no traveller returns" —and so has sunk into torpid, uneasy repose, tantalized by useless resources, haunted by vain imaginings, his lips idly moving, but his heart forever still, or, as the shattered chords vibrate of themselves, making melancholy music to the ear of memory! Such is the fate of genius in an age, when in the unequal contest with sovereign wrong, every man is ground to powder who is not either a born slave, or who does not willingly and at once offer up the yearnings of humanity and the dictates of reason as a welcome sacrifice to besotted prejudice and loathsome power.

Of all Mr. Coleridge's productions, the *Ancient Mariner* is the only one that we could with confidence put into any person's hands, on whom we wished to impress a favourable idea of his extraordinary powers. Let whatever other objections be made to it, it is unquestionably a work of genius—of wild, irregular, overwhelming imagination, and has that rich, varied movement in the verse, which gives a distant idea of the lofty or changeful tones of Mr. Coleridge's voice. In the *Christobel*, there is one splendid passage on divided friendship. The *Translation of Schiller's Wallenstein* is also a masterly production in its kind, faithful and spirited. Among his smaller pieces there are occasional bursts of pathos and fancy, equal to what we might expect from him; but these form the exception, and not the rule. Such, for instance, is his affecting Sonnet to the author of the Robbers.

> Schiller! that hour I would have wish'd to die,
> If through the shudd'ring midnight I had sent
> From the dark dungeon of the tower time-rent,
> That fearful voice, a famish'd father's cry—
>
> That in no after-moment aught less vast
> Might stamp me mortal! A triumphant shout
> Black horror scream'd, and all her goblin rout
> From the more with'ring scene diminish'd pass'd.
>
> Ah! Bard tremendous in sublimity!
> Could I behold thee in thy loftier mood,
> Wand'ring at eve, with finely frenzied eye,
> Beneath some vast old tempest-swinging wood!
> Awhile, with mute awe gazing, I would brood,
> Then weep aloud in a wild ecstasy.

His Tragedy, entitled *Remorse*, is full of beautiful and striking passages, but it does not place the author in the first rank of dramatic writers. But if Mr. Coleridge's works do not place him in that rank, they injure instead of conveying a just idea of the man, for he himself is certainly in the first class of general intellect.

If our author's poetry is inferior to his conversation, his prose is utterly abortive. Hardly a gleam is to be found in it of the brilliancy and richness of those stores of thought and language that he pours out incessantly, when they are lost like drops of water in the ground. The principal work, in which he has attempted to embody his general views of things, is the FRIEND, of which, though it contains some noble passages and fine trains of thought, prolixity and obscurity are the most frequent characteristics.

No two persons can be conceived more opposite in character or genius than the subject of the present and of the preceding sketch. Mr. Godwin, with less natural capacity, and with fewer acquired advantages, by concentrating his mind on some given object, and doing what he had to do with all his might, has accomplished much, and will leave more than one monument of a powerful intellect behind him; Mr. Coleridge, by dissipating his, and dallying with every subject by turns, has done little or nothing to justify to the world or to posterity, the high opinion which all who have ever heard him converse, or known him intimately, with one accord entertain of him. Mr. Godwin's faculties have kept house, and plied their task in the work-shop of the brain, diligently and effectually: Mr. Coleridge's have gossipped away their time, and gadded about from house to house, as if life's business were to melt the hours in listless talk. Mr. Godwin is intent on a subject, only as it concerns himself and his reputation; he works it out as a matter of duty, and discards from his mind whatever does not forward his main object as impertinent and vain. Mr. Coleridge, on the other hand, delights in nothing but episodes and digressions, neglects whatever he undertakes to perform, and can act only on spontaneous impulses, without object or method. "He cannot be constrained by mastery. " While he should be occupied with a given pursuit, he is thinking of a thousand other things; a thousand tastes, a thousand objects tempt him, and distract his mind, which keeps open house, and entertains all comers; and after being fatigued and amused with morning calls from idle visitors, finds the day consumed and its business unconcluded. Mr. Godwin, on the contrary, is somewhat exclusive and unsocial in his habits of mind, entertains no company but what he gives his whole time and attention to, and wisely writes over the doors of his understanding, his fancy, and his senses—"No admittance except on business. " He has none of that fastidious refinement and false delicacy, which might lead him to balance between the endless variety of modern attainments. He does not throw away his life (nor a single half-hour of it) in adjusting the claims of different accomplishments, and in choosing between them or making himself master of them all. He sets about his task, (whatever it may be) and goes through it with spirit and fortitude. He has the happiness to think an author the greatest character in the world, and himself the greatest author in it. Mr. Coleridge, in writing an harmonious stanza, would stop to consider whether there was not more grace and beauty in a *Pas de trois*, and would not proceed till he had resolved this question by a chain of metaphysical reasoning without end. Not so Mr. Godwin. That is best to him, which he can do best. He does not waste himself in vain aspirations and effeminate sympathies. He is blind, deaf, insensible to all but the trump of Fame. Plays, operas, painting, music, ball-rooms, wealth, fashion, titles, lords, ladies, touch him not—all these are no more to him than to the magician in his cell, and he writes on to the end of the chapter, through good report and evil report. *Pingo in eternitatem*—is his motto. He neither envies nor admires what others are, but is contented to be what he is, and strives to do the utmost he can. Mr. Coleridge has flirted with the Muses as with a set of mistresses: Mr. Godwin has been married twice, to Reason and to Fancy, and has to boast no short-lived progeny by each. So to speak, he has *valves* belonging to his mind, to regulate the quantity of gas admitted into it, so that like the bare, unsightly, but well-compacted steam-vessel, it cuts its liquid way, and arrives at its promised end: while Mr. Coleridge's bark, "taught with the little nautilus to sail, " the sport of every breath, dancing to every wave,

"Youth at its prow, and Pleasure at its helm, "

flutters its gaudy pennons in the air, glitters in the sun, but we wait in vain to hear of its arrival in the destined harbour. Mr. Godwin, with less variety and vividness, with less subtlety and susceptibility both of thought and feeling, has had firmer nerves, a more determined purpose, a more comprehensive grasp of his subject, and the results are as we find them. Each has met with his reward: for justice has, after all, been done to the pretensions of each; and we must, in all cases, use means to ends!

[Footnote A: Mr. Coleridge named his eldest son (the writer of some beautiful Sonnets) after Hartley, and the second after Berkeley. The third was called Derwent, after the river of that name. Nothing can be more characteristic of his mind than this circumstance. All his ideas indeed are like a river, flowing on for ever, and still murmuring as it flows, discharging its waters and still replenished—

The Spirit of the Age

"And so by many winding nooks it strays,
With willing sport to the wild ocean! "]

* * * * *

REV. MR. IRVING.

This gentleman has gained an almost unprecedented, and not an altogether unmerited popularity as a preacher. As he is, perhaps, though a burning and a shining light, not "one of the fixed, " we shall take this opportunity of discussing his merits, while he is at his meridian height; and in doing so, shall "nothing extenuate, nor set down aught in malice. "

Few circumstances shew the prevailing and preposterous rage for novelty in a more striking point of view, than the success of Mr. Irving's oratory. People go to hear him in crowds, and come away with a mixture of delight and astonishment—they go again to see if the effect will continue, and send others to try to find out the mystery—and in the noisy conflict between extravagant encomiums and splenetic objections, the true secret escapes observation, which is, that the whole thing is, nearly from beginning to end, a *transposition of ideas*. If the subject of these remarks had come out as a player, with all his advantages of figure, voice, and action, we think he would have failed: if, as a preacher, he had kept within the strict bounds of pulpit-oratory, he would scarcely have been much distinguished among his Calvinistic brethren: as a mere author, he would have excited attention rather by his quaintness and affectation of an obsolete style and mode of thinking, than by any thing else. But he has contrived to jumble these several characters together in an unheard-of and unwarranted manner, and the fascination is altogether irresistible. Our Caledonian divine is equally an anomaly in religion, in literature, in personal appearance, and in public speaking. To hear a person spout Shakspeare on the stage is nothing—the charm is nearly worn out—but to hear any one spout Shakspeare (and that not in a sneaking under-tone, but at the top of his voice, and with the full breadth of his chest) from a Calvinistic pulpit, is new and wonderful. The *Fancy* have lately lost something of their gloss in public estimation, and after the last fight, few would go far to see a Neat or a Spring set-to; —but to see a man who is able to enter the ring with either of them, or brandish a quarter-staff with Friar Tuck, or a broad-sword with Shaw the Lifeguards' man, stand up in a strait-laced old-fashioned pulpit, and bandy dialectics with modern philosophers or give a *cross-buttock* to a cabinet minister, there is something in a sight like this also, that is a cure for sore eyes. It is as if Crib or Molyneux had turned Methodist parson, or as if a Patagonian savage were to come forward as the patron-saint of

Evangelical religion. Again, the doctrine of eternal punishment was one of the staple arguments with which, everlastingly drawled out, the old school of Presbyterian divines used to keep their audiences awake, or lull them to sleep; but to which people of taste and fashion paid little attention, as inelegant and barbarous, till Mr. Irving, with his cast-iron features and sledge-hammer blows, puffing like a grim Vulcan, set to work to forge more classic thunderbolts, and kindle the expiring flames anew with the very sweepings of sceptical and infidel libraries, so as to excite a pleasing horror in the female part of his congregation. In short, our popular declaimer has, contrary to the Scripture-caution, put new wine into old bottles, or new cloth on old garments. He has, with an unlimited and daring licence, mixed the sacred and the profane together, the carnal and the spiritual man, the petulance of the bar with the dogmatism of the pulpit, the theatrical and theological, the modern and the obsolete; —what wonder that this splendid piece of patchwork, splendid by contradiction and contrast, has delighted some and confounded others? The more serious part of his congregation indeed complain, though not bitterly, that their pastor has converted their meeting-house into a play-house: but when a lady of quality, introducing herself and her three daughters to the preacher, assures him that they have been to all the most fashionable places of resort, the opera, the theatre, assemblies, Miss Macauley's readings, and Exeter-Change, and have been equally entertained no where else, we apprehend that no remonstrances of a committee of ruling-elders will be able to bring him to his senses again, or make him forego such sweet, but ill-assorted praise. What we mean to insist upon is, that Mr. Irving owes his triumphant success, not to any one quality for which he has been extolled, but to a combination of qualities, the more striking in their immediate effect, in proportion as they are unlooked-for and heterogeneous, like the violent opposition of light and shade in a picture. We shall endeavour to explain this view of the subject more at large.

Mr. Irving, then, is no common or mean man. He has four or five qualities, possessed in a moderate or in a paramount degree, which, added or multiplied together, fill up the important space he occupies in the public eye. Mr. Irving's intellect itself is of a superior order; he has undoubtedly both talents and acquirements beyond the ordinary run of every-day preachers. These alone, however, we hold, would not account for a twentieth part of the effect he has produced: they would have lifted him perhaps out of the mire and slough of sordid obscurity, but would never have launched him into the ocean-stream of popularity, in which he "lies floating many a rood; "—but to these he adds uncommon height, a graceful figure and action, a clear and powerful voice, a striking, if not a fine face, a bold and fiery spirit, and a most portentous obliquity of vision, which throw him to an immeasurable distance beyond all competition, and effectually relieve whatever there might be of common-place or bombast in his style of composition. Put the case that Mr. Irving had been five feet high—Would he ever have been heard of, or, as he does now, have "bestrode the world like a Colossus? " No, the thing speaks for itself. He would in vain have lifted his Lilliputian arm to Heaven, people would have laughed at his monkey-tricks. Again, had he been as tall as he is, but had wanted other recommendations, he would have been nothing.

> "The player's province they but vainly try,
> Who want these powers, deportment, voice, and eye. "

Conceive a rough, ugly, shock-headed Scotchman, standing up in the Caledonian chapel, and dealing "damnation round the land" in a broad northern dialect, and with a harsh, screaking voice, what ear polite, what smile serene would have hailed the barbarous prodigy, or not consigned him to utter neglect and derision? But the Rev. Edward Irving, with all his native wildness, "hath a smooth aspect framed to make women" saints; his very unusual size and height are carried off and moulded into elegance by the most admirable symmetry of form and ease of gesture; his sable locks, his clear iron-grey complexion, and firm-set features, turn the raw, uncouth Scotchman into the likeness of a noble Italian picture; and even his distortion of sight only redeems the otherwise "faultless monster" within the bounds of humanity, and, when admiration is exhausted and curiosity ceases, excites a new interest by leading to the idle question whether it is an advantage to the preacher or not. Farther, give him all his actual and remarkable advantages of body and mind, let him be as tall, as strait, as dark and clear of skin, as much at his ease, as silver-tongued, as eloquent and as argumentative as he is, yet with all these, and without a little charlatanery to set them off, he had been nothing. He might, keeping within the rigid line of his duty and professed calling, have preached on for ever; he might have divided the old-fashioned doctrines of election, grace, reprobation, predestination, into his sixteenth, seventeenth, and eighteenth heads, and his *lastly* have been looked for as a "consummation devoutly to be wished; " he might have defied the devil and all his works, and by the help of a loud voice and strong-set person—

"A lusty man to ben an Abbot able; "—

have increased his own congregation, and been quoted among the godly as a powerful preacher of the word; but in addition to this, he went out of his way to attack Jeremy Bentham, and the town was up in arms. The thing was new. He thus wiped the stain of musty ignorance and formal bigotry out of his style. Mr. Irving must have something superior in him, to look over the shining close-packed heads of his congregation to have a hit at the *Great Jurisconsult* in his study. He next, ere the report of the former blow had subsided, made a lunge at Mr. Brougham, and glanced an eye at Mr. Canning; *mystified* Mr. Coleridge, and *stultified* Lord Liverpool in his place—in the Gallery. It was rare sport to see him, "like an eagle in a dovecote, flutter the Volscians in Corioli. " He has found out the secret of attracting by repelling. Those whom he is likely to attack are curious to hear what he says of them: they go again, to show that they do not mind it. It is no less interesting to the by-standers, who like to witness this sort of *onslaught*—like a charge of cavalry, the shock, and the resistance. Mr. Irving has, in fact, without leave asked or a licence granted, converted the Caledonian Chapel into a Westminster Forum or Debating Society, with the sanctity of religion added to it. Our spirited polemic is not contented to defend the citadel of orthodoxy against all impugners, and shut himself up in texts of Scripture and huge volumes of the Commentators as an impregnable fortress; —he merely makes use of the stronghold of religion as a resting-place, from which he sallies forth, armed with modern topics and with penal fire, like Achilles of old rushing from the Grecian tents, against the adversaries of God and man. Peter Aretine is said to have laid the Princes of Europe under contribution by penning satires against them: so Mr. Irving keeps the public in awe by insulting all their favourite idols. He does not spare their politicians, their rulers, their moralists, their poets, their players, their critics, their reviewers, their magazine-writers; he levels their resorts of business, their places of amusement, at a blow—their cities, churches, palaces, ranks and professions, refinements, and elegances—and leaves nothing standing but himself, a mighty landmark in a degenerate age, overlooking the wide havoc he has made! He makes war upon all arts and sciences, upon the faculties and nature of man, on his vices and his virtues, on all existing institutions, and all possible improvements, that nothing may be left but the Kirk of Scotland, and that he may be the head of it. He literally sends a challenge to all London in the name of the KING of HEAVEN, to evacuate its streets, to disperse its population, to lay aside its employments, to burn its wealth, to renounce its vanities and pomp; and for what? —that he may enter in as the *King of Glory*; or after enforcing his threat with the battering-ram of logic, the grape-shot of rhetoric, and the crossfire of his double vision, reduce the British metropolis to a Scottish heath, with a few miserable hovels upon it, where they may worship God according to *the root of the matter*, and an old man with a blue bonnet, a fair-haired girl, and a little child would form the flower of his flock! Such is the pretension and the boast of this new Peter the Hermit, who would get rid of all we have done in the way of improvement on a state of barbarous ignorance, or still more barbarous prejudice, in order to begin again on a *tabula rasa* of Calvinism, and have a world of his own making. It is not very surprising that when nearly the whole mass and texture of civil society is indicted as a nuisance, and threatened to be pulled down as a rotten building ready to fall on the heads of the inhabitants, that all classes of people run to hear the crash, and to see the engines and levers at work which are to effect this laudable purpose. What else can be the meaning of our preacher's taking upon himself to denounce the sentiments of the most serious professors in great cities, as vitiated and stark-naught, of relegating religion to his native glens, and pretending that the hymn of praise or the sigh of contrition cannot ascend acceptably to the throne of grace from the crowded street as well as from the barren rock or silent valley? Why put this affront upon his hearers? Why belie his own aspirations?

"God made the country, and man made the town. "

So says the poet; does Mr. Irving say so? If he does, and finds the air of the city death to his piety, why does he not return home again? But if he can breathe it with impunity, and still retain the fervour of his early enthusiasm, and the simplicity and purity of the faith that was once delivered to the saints, why not extend the benefit of his own experience to others, instead of taunting them with a vapid pastoral theory? Or, if our popular and eloquent divine finds a change in himself, that flattery prevents the growth of grace, that he is becoming the God of his own idolatry by being that of others, that the glittering of coronet-coaches rolling down Holborn-Hill to Hatton Garden, that titled beauty, that the parliamentary complexion of his audience, the compliments of poets, and the stare of peers discompose his wandering thoughts a little; and yet that he cannot give up these strong temptations tugging at his heart; why not extend more charity to others, and shew more candour in speaking of himself? There is either a good deal of bigoted intolerance with a deplorable want of self-knowledge in all this; or at least an equal degree of cant and quackery.

To whichever cause we are to attribute this hyperbolical tone, we hold it certain he could not have adopted it, if he had been *a little man*. But his imposing figure and dignified manner enable him to hazard sentiments or assertions that would be fatal to others. His controversial daring is *backed* by his bodily prowess; and by bringing his intellectual pretensions boldly into a line with his physical accomplishments, he, indeed, presents a very formidable front to the sceptic or the scoffer. Take a cubit from his stature, and his whole manner resolves itself into an impertinence. But with that addition, he *overcrows* the town, browbeats their prejudices, and bullies them out of their senses, and is not afraid of being contradicted by any one *less than himself.* It may be said, that individuals with great personal defects have made a considerable figure as public speakers; and Mr. Wilberforce, among others, may be held out as an instance. Nothing can be more insignificant as to mere outward appearance, and yet he is listened to in the House of Commons. But he does not wield it, he does not insult or bully it. He leads by following opinion, he trims, he shifts, he glides on the silvery sounds of his undulating, flexible, cautiously modulated voice, winding his way betwixt heaven and earth, now courting popularity, now calling servility to his aid, and with a large estate, the "saints, " and the population of Yorkshire to swell his influence, never venturing on the forlorn hope, or doing any thing more than "hitting the house between wind and water. " Yet he is probably a cleverer man than Mr. Irving.

There is a Mr. Fox, a Dissenting Minister, as fluent a speaker, with a sweeter voice and a more animated and beneficent countenance than Mr. Irving, who expresses himself with manly spirit at a public meeting, takes a hand at whist, and is the darling of his congregation; but he is no more, because he is diminutive in person. His head is not seen above the crowd the length of a street off. He is the Duke of Sussex in miniature, but the Duke of Sussex does not go to hear him preach, as he attends Mr. Irving, who rises up against him like a martello tower, and is nothing loth to confront the spirit of a man of genius with the blood-royal. We allow there are, or may be, talents sufficient to produce this equality without a single personal advantage; but we deny that this would be the effect of any that our great preacher possesses. We conceive it not improbable that the consciousness of muscular power, that the admiration of his person by strangers might first have inspired Mr. Irving with an ambition to be something, intellectually speaking, and have given him confidence to attempt the greatest things. He has not failed for want of courage. The public, as well as the fair, are won by a show of gallantry. Mr. Irving has shrunk from no opinion, however paradoxical. He has scrupled to avow no sentiment, however obnoxious. He has revived exploded prejudices, he has scouted prevailing fashions. He has opposed the spirit of the age, and not consulted the *esprit de corps*. He has brought back the doctrines of Calvinism in all their inveteracy, and relaxed the inveteracy of his northern accents. He has turned religion and the Caledonian Chapel topsy-turvy. He has held a play-book in one hand, and a Bible in the other, and quoted Shakspeare and Melancthon in the same breath. The tree of the knowledge of good and evil is no longer, with his grafting, a dry withered stump; it shoots its branches to the skies, and hangs out its blossoms to the gale —

"Miraturque novos fructus, et non sua poma. "

He has taken the thorns and briars of scholastic divinity, and garlanded them with the flowers of modern literature. He has done all this, relying on the strength of a remarkably fine person and manner, and through that he has succeeded — otherwise he would have perished miserably.

Dr. Chalmers is not by any means so good a looking man, nor so accomplished a speaker as Mr. Irving; yet he at one time almost equalled his oratorical celebrity, and certainly paved the way for him. He has therefore more merit than his admired pupil, as he has done as much with fewer means. He has more scope of intellect and more intensity of purpose. Both his matter and his manner, setting aside his face and figure, are more impressive. Take the volume of "Sermons on Astronomy, " by Dr. Chalmers, and the "Four Orations for the Oracles of God" which Mr. Irving lately published, and we apprehend there can be no comparison as to their success. The first ran like wild-fire through the country, were the darlings of watering-places, were laid in the windows of inns, [A] and were to be met with in all places of public resort; while the "Orations" get on but slowly, on Milton's stilts, and are pompously announced as in a Third Edition. We believe the fairest and fondest of his admirers

42

would rather see and hear Mr. Irving than read him. The reason is, that the groundwork of his compositions is trashy and hackneyed, though set off by extravagant metaphors and an affected phraseology; that without the turn of his head and wave of his hand, his periods have nothing in them; and that he himself is the only *idea* with which he has yet enriched the public mind! He must play off his person, as Orator Henley used to dazzle his hearers with his diamond-ring. The small frontispiece prefixed to the "Orations" does not serve to convey an adequate idea of the magnitude of the man, nor of the ease and freedom of his motions in the pulpit. How different is Dr. Chalmers! He is like "a monkey-preacher" to the other. He cannot boast of personal appearance to set him off. But then he is like the very genius or demon of theological controversy personified. He has neither airs nor graces at command; he thinks nothing of himself; he has nothing theatrical about him (which cannot be said of his successor and rival); but you see a man in mortal throes and agony with doubts and difficulties, seizing stubborn knotty points with his teeth, tearing them with his hands, and straining his eyeballs till they almost start out of their sockets, in pursuit of a train of visionary reasoning, like a Highland-seer with his second sight. The description of Balfour of Burley in his cave, with his Bible in one hand and his sword in the other, contending with the imaginary enemy of mankind, gasping for breath, and with the cold moisture running down his face, gives a lively idea of Dr. Chalmers's prophetic fury in the pulpit. If we could have looked in to have seen Burley hard-beset "by the coinage of his heat-oppressed brain, " who would have asked whether he was a handsome man or not? It would be enough to see a man haunted by a spirit, under the strong and entire dominion of a wilful hallucination. So the integrity and vehemence of Dr. Chalmers's manner, the determined way in which he gives himself up to his subject, or lays about him and buffets sceptics and gainsayers, arrests attention in spite of every other circumstance, and fixes it on that, and that alone, which excites such interest and such eagerness in his own breast! Besides, he is a logician, has a theory in support of whatever he chooses to advance, and weaves the tissue of his sophistry so close and intricate, that it is difficult not to be entangled in it, or to escape from it. "There's magic in the web. " Whatever appeals to the pride of the human understanding, has a subtle charm in it. The mind is naturally pugnacious, cannot refuse a challenge of strength or skill, sturdily enters the lists and resolves to conquer, or to yield itself vanquished in the forms. This is the chief hold Dr. Chalmers had upon his hearers, and upon the readers of his "Astronomical Discourses. " No one was satisfied with his arguments, no one could answer them, but every one wanted to try what he could make of them, as we try to find out a riddle. "By his so potent art, " the art of laying down problematical premises, and drawing from them still more doubtful, but not impossible, conclusions, "he could bedim the noonday sun, betwixt the green sea and the azure vault set roaring war, " and almost compel the stars in their courses to testify to his opinions. The mode in which he undertook to make the circuit of the universe, and demand categorical information "now of the planetary and now of the fixed, " might put one in mind of Hecate's mode of ascending in a machine from the stage, "midst troops of spirits, " in which you now admire the skill of the artist, and next tremble for the fate of the performer, fearing that the audacity of the attempt will turn his head or break his neck. The style of these "Discourses" also, though not elegant or poetical, was, like the subject, intricate and endless. It was that of a man pushing his way through a labyrinth of difficulties, and determined not to flinch. The impression on the reader was proportionate; for, whatever were the merits of the style or matter, both were new and striking; and the train of thought that was unfolded at such length and with such strenuousness, was bold, well-sustained, and consistent with itself.

Mr. Irving wants the continuity of thought and manner which distinguishes his rival—and shines by patches and in bursts. He does not warm or acquire increasing force or rapidity with his progress. He is never hurried away by a deep or lofty enthusiasm, nor touches the highest point of genius or fanaticism, but "in the very storm and whirlwind of his passion, he acquires and begets a temperance that may give it smoothness. " He has the self-possession and masterly execution of an experienced player or fencer, and does not seem to express his natural convictions, or to be engaged in a mortal struggle. This greater ease and indifference is the result of vast superiority of personal appearance, which "to be admired needs but to be seen, " and does not require the possessor to work himself up into a passion, or to use any violent contortions to gain attention or to keep it. These two celebrated preachers are in almost all respects an antithesis to each other. If Mr. Irving is an example of what can be done by the help of external advantages, Dr. Chalmers is a proof of what can be done without them. The one is most indebted to his mind, the other to his body. If Mr. Irving inclines one to suspect fashionable or popular religion of a little *anthropomorphitism*, Dr. Chalmers effectually redeems it from that scandal.

[Footnote A: We remember finding the volume in the orchard at Burford-bridge near Boxhill, and passing a whole and very delightful morning in reading it, without quitting the shade of an apple-tree. We have not been able to pay Mr. Irving's back the same compliment of reading it at a sitting.]

* * * * *

THE LATE MR. HORNE TOOKE.

Mr. Horne Tooke was one of those who may be considered as connecting links between a former period and the existing generation. His education and accomplishments, nay, his political opinions, were of the last age; his mind, and the tone of his feelings were *modern*. There was a hard, dry materialism in the very texture of his understanding, varnished over by the external refinements of the old school. Mr. Tooke had great scope of attainment, and great versatility of pursuit; but the same shrewdness, quickness, cool self-possession, the same *literalness* of perception, and absence of passion and enthusiasm, characterised nearly all he did, said, or wrote. He was without a rival (almost) in private conversation, an expert public speaker, a keen politician, a first-rate grammarian, and the finest gentleman (to say the least) of his own party. He had no imagination (or he would not have scorned it!)—no delicacy of taste, no rooted prejudices or strong attachments: his intellect was like a bow of polished steel, from which he shot sharp-pointed poisoned arrows at his friends in private, at his enemies in public. His mind (so to speak) had no *religion* in it, and very little even of the moral qualities of genius; but he was a man of the world, a scholar bred, and a most acute and powerful logician. He was also a wit, and a formidable one: yet it may be questioned whether his wit was any thing more than an excess of his logical faculty: it did not consist in the play of fancy, but in close and cutting combinations of the understanding. "The law is open to every one: *so,* " said Mr. Tooke, "*is the London Tavern!* " It is the previous deduction formed in the mind, and the splenetic contempt felt for a practical sophism, that *beats about the bush for*, and at last finds the apt illustration; not the casual, glancing coincidence of two objects, that points out an absurdity to the understanding. So, on another occasion, when Sir Allan Gardiner (who was a candidate for Westminster) had objected to Mr. Fox, that "he was always against the minister, *whether right or wrong,* " and Mr. Fox, in his reply, had overlooked this slip of the tongue, Mr. Tooke immediately seized on it, and said, "he thought it at least an equal objection to Sir Allan, that he was always *with* the minister, whether right or wrong. " This retort had all the effect, and produced the same surprise as the most brilliant display of wit or fancy: yet it was only the detecting a flaw in an argument, like a flaw in an indictment, by a kind of legal pertinacity, or rather by a rigid and constant habit of attending to the exact import of every word and clause in a sentence. Mr. Tooke had the mind of a lawyer; but it was applied to a vast variety of topics and general trains of speculation.

Mr. Horne Tooke was in private company, and among his friends, the finished gentleman of the last age. His manners were as fascinating as his conversation was spirited and delightful. He put one in mind of the burden of the song of *"The King's Old Courtier, and an Old Courtier of the King's. "* He was, however, of the opposite party. It was curious to hear our modern sciolist advancing opinions of the most radical kind without any mixture of radical heat or violence, in a tone of fashionable *nonchalance,* with elegance of gesture and attitude, and with the most perfect good-humour. In the spirit of opposition, or in the pride of logical superiority, he too often shocked the prejudices or wounded the self-love of those about him, while he himself displayed the same unmoved indifference or equanimity. He said the most provoking things with a laughing gaiety, and a polite attention, that there was no withstanding. He threw others off their guard by thwarting their favourite theories, and then availed himself of the temperance of his own pulse to chafe them into madness. He had not one particle of deference for the opinion of others, nor of sympathy with their feelings; nor had he any obstinate convictions of his own to defend—

"Lord of himself, uncumbered with a *creed*! "

He took up any topic by chance, and played with it at will, like a juggler with his cups and balls. He generally ranged himself on the losing side; and had rather an ill-natured delight in contradiction, and in perplexing the understandings of others, without leaving them any clue to guide them out of the labyrinth into which he had led them. He understood, in its perfection, the great art of throwing the *onus probandi* on his adversary; and so could maintain almost any opinion, however absurd or fantastical, with fearless impunity. I have heard a sensible and well-informed man say, that he never was in company with Mr. Tooke without being delighted and surprised, or without feeling the conversation of every other person to be flat in the comparison; but that he did not recollect having ever heard him make a remark that struck him as a sound and true one, or that he himself appeared to think so. He used to plague Fuseli by asking him after the origin of the Teutonic dialects, and Dr. Parr, by wishing to know the meaning of the common copulative, *Is*. Once at G——'s, he defended Pitt from a charge of verbiage, and endeavoured to prove him superior to Fox. Some one imitated Pitt's manner, to show that it was monotonous, and he imitated him also, to show that it was not. He maintained (what would he not maintain?) that young Betty's acting was finer than John Kemble's, and recited a passage from Douglas in the manner of each, to justify the preference he gave to the former. The mentioning this will please the living; it cannot hurt the dead. He argued on the same occasion and in the same breath, that Addison's style was without modulation, and that it was physically impossible for any one to write well, who was habitually silent in company. He sat like a king at his own table, and gave law to his guests—and to the world! No man knew better how to manage his immediate circle, to foil or bring them out. A professed orator, beginning to address some observations to Mr. Tooke with a voluminous apology for his youth and inexperience, he said, "Speak up, young man! "—and by taking him at his word, cut short the flower of orations. Porson was the only person of whom he stood in some degree of awe, on account of his prodigious memory and knowledge of his favourite subject, Languages. Sheridan, it has been remarked, said more good things, but had not an equal flow of pleasantry. As an instance of Mr. Horne Tooke's extreme coolness and command of nerve, it has been mentioned that once at a public dinner when he had got on the table to return thanks for his health being drank with a glass of wine in his hand, and when there was a great clamour and opposition for some time, after it had subsided, he pointed to the glass to shew that it was still full. Mr. Holcroft (the author of the *Road to Ruin*) was one of the most violent and fiery-spirited of all that motley crew of persons, who attended the Sunday meetings at Wimbledon. One day he was so enraged by some paradox or raillery of his host, that he indignantly rose from his chair, and said, "Mr. Tooke, you are a scoundrel! " His opponent without manifesting the least emotion, replied, "Mr. Holcroft, when is it that I am to dine with you? shall it be next Thursday? "—"If you please, Mr. Tooke! " answered the angry philosopher, and sat down again. —It was delightful to see him sometimes turn from these waspish or ludicrous altercations with over-weening antagonists to some old friend and veteran politician seated at his elbow; to hear him recal the time of Wilkes and Liberty, the conversation mellowing like the wine with the smack of age; assenting to all the old man said, bringing out his pleasant *traits*, and pampering him into childish self-importance, and sending him away thirty years younger than he came!

As a public or at least as a parliamentary speaker, Mr. Tooke did not answer the expectations that had been conceived of him, or probably that he had conceived of himself. It is natural for men who have felt a superiority over all those whom they happen to have encountered, to fancy that this superiority will continue, and that it will extend from individuals to public bodies. There is no rule in the case; or rather, the probability lies the contrary way. That which constitutes the excellence of conversation is of little use in addressing large assemblies of people; while other qualities are required that are hardly to be looked for in one and the same capacity. The way to move great masses of men is to shew that you yourself are moved. In a private circle, a ready repartee, a shrewd cross-question, ridicule and banter, a caustic remark or an amusing anecdote, whatever sets off the individual to advantage, or gratifies the curiosity or piques the self-love of the hearers, keeps attention alive, and secures the triumph of the speaker—it is a personal contest, and depends on personal and momentary advantages. But in appealing to the public, no one triumphs but in the triumph of some public cause, or by shewing a sympathy with the general and predominant feelings of mankind. In a private room, a satirist, a sophist may provoke admiration by expressing his contempt for each of his adversaries in turn, and by setting their opinion at defiance—but when men are congregated together on a great public question and for a weighty object, they must be treated with more respect; they are touched with what affects themselves or the general weal, not with what flatters the vanity of the speaker; they must be moved altogether, if they are moved at all; they are impressed with gratitude for a luminous exposition of their claims or for zeal in their cause; and the lightning of generous indignation at bad men and bad measures is followed by thunders of applause—even in the House of Commons. But a man may sneer and cavil and puzzle and fly-blow every question that comes before him—be despised and feared by others, and admired by no one but himself. He who thinks first of himself, either in the world or in a popular assembly, will be sure to turn attention away from his claims, instead of fixing it there. He must make common cause with his hearers. To lead, he must follow the general bias. Mr. Tooke did not therefore succeed as a speaker in parliament. He stood aloof, he played antics, he exhibited his peculiar talent—while he was on his legs, the question before the House stood still; the only point at issue respected Mr. Tooke himself, his personal address and adroitness of intellect.

Were there to be no more places and pensions, because Mr. Tooke's style was terse and epigrammatic? Were the Opposition benches to be inflamed to an unusual pitch of "sacred vehemence, " because he gave them plainly to understand there was not a pin to choose between Ministers and Opposition? Would the House let him remain among them, because, if they turned him out on account of his *black coat*, Lord Camelford had threatened to send his *black servant* in his place? This was a good joke, but not a practical one. Would he gain the affections of the people out of doors, by scouting the question of reform? Would the King ever relish the old associate of Wilkes? What interest, then, what party did he represent? He represented nobody but himself. He was an example of an ingenious man, a clever talker, but he was out of his place in the House of Commons; where people did not come (as in his own house) to admire or break a lance with him, but to get through the business of the day, and so adjourn! He wanted effect and *momentum*. Each of his sentences told very well in itself, but they did not all together make a speech. He left off where he began. His eloquence was a succession of drops, not a stream. His arguments, though subtle and new, did not affect the main body of the question. The coldness and pettiness of his manner did not warm the hearts or expand the understandings of his hearers. Instead of encouraging, he checked the ardour of his friends; and teazed, instead of overpowering his antagonists. The only palpable hit he ever made, while he remained there, was the comparing his own situation in being rejected by the House, on account of the supposed purity of his clerical character, to the story of the girl at the Magdalen, who was told "she must turn out and qualify. "[A] This met with laughter and loud applause. It was a *home* thrust, and the House (to do them justice) are obliged to any one who, by a smart blow, relieves them of the load of grave responsibility, which sits heavy on their shoulders. —At the hustings, or as an election-candidate, Mr. Tooke did better. There was no great question to move or carry—it was an affair of political *sparring* between himself and the other candidates. He took it in a very cool and leisurely manner—watched his competitors with a wary, sarcastic eye; picked up the mistakes or absurdities that fell from them, and retorted them on their heads; told a story to the mob; and smiled and took snuff with a gentlemanly and becoming air, as if he was already seated in the House. But a Court of Law was the place where Mr. Tooke made the best figure in public. He might assuredly be said to be "native and endued unto that element. " He had here to stand merely on the defensive—not to advance himself, but to block up the way—not to impress others, but to be himself impenetrable. All he wanted was *negative success*; and to this no one was better qualified to aspire. Cross purposes, *moot-points*, pleas, demurrers, flaws in the indictment, double meanings, cases, inconsequentialities, these were the play-things, the darlings of Mr. Tooke's mind; and with these he baffled the Judge, dumb-founded the Counsel, and outwitted the Jury. The report of his trial before Lord Kenyon is a master-piece of acuteness, dexterity, modest assurance, and legal effect. It is much like his examination before the Commissioners of the Income-Tax—nothing could be got out of him in either case! Mr. Tooke, as a political leader, belonged to the class of *trimmers*; or at most, it was his delight to make mischief and spoil sport. He would rather be *against* himself than *for* any body else. He was neither a bold nor a safe leader. He enticed others into scrapes, and kept out of them himself. Provided he could say a clever or a spiteful thing, he did not care whether it served or injured the cause. Spleen or the exercise of intellectual power was the motive of his patriotism, rather than principle. He would talk treason with a saving clause; and instil sedition into the public mind, through the medium of a third (who was to be the responsible) party. He made Sir Francis Burdett his spokesman in the House and to the country, often venting his chagrin or singularity of sentiment at the expense of his friend; but what in the first was trick or reckless vanity, was in the last plain downright English honesty and singleness of heart. In the case of the State Trials, in 1794, Mr. Tooke rather compromised his friends to screen himself. He kept repeating that "others might have gone on to Windsor, but he had stopped at Hounslow, " as if to go farther might have been dangerous and unwarrantable. It was not the question how far he or others had actually gone, but how far they had a right to go, according to the law. His conduct was not the limit of the law, nor did treasonable excess begin where prudence or principle taught him to stop short, though this was the oblique inference liable to be drawn from his line of defence. Mr. Tooke was uneasy and apprehensive for the issue of the Government-prosecution while in confinement, and said, in speaking of it to a friend, with a morbid feeling and an emphasis quite unusual with him—"They want our blood—blood—blood! " It was somewhat ridiculous to implicate Mr. Tooke in a charge of High Treason (and indeed the whole charge was built on the mistaken purport of an intercepted letter relating to an engagement for a private dinnerparty)—his politics were not at all revolutionary. In this respect he was a mere pettifogger, full of chicane, and captious objections, and unmeaning discontent; but he had none of the grand whirling movements of the French Revolution, nor of the tumultuous glow of rebellion in his head or in his heart. His politics were cast in a different mould, or confined to the party distinctions and court- intrigues and pittances of popular right, that made a noise in the time of Junius and Wilkes—and even if his understanding had gone along with more modern and unqualified principles, his cautious temper would have prevented his risking them in practice. Horne Tooke (though not of the same side in politics) had much of the tone of mind and more of the spirit of moral feeling of the celebrated philosopher of Malmesbury. The narrow scale and fine-drawn distinctions of his political creed made his conversation on such subjects infinitely amusing, particularly when contrasted with that of persons who dealt in the sounding *common-places* and sweeping clauses of abstract politics. He knew all the cabals and jealousies and heart-burnings in the beginning of the late reign, the changes of administration and the springs of secret influence, the characters of the leading men, Wilkes, Barrè, Dunning, Chatham, Burke, the Marquis of Rockingham, North, Shelburne, Fox, Pitt, and all the vacillating events of the American war: —these formed a curious back-ground to the more prominent figures that occupied the present time, and Mr. Tooke worked out the minute details and touched in the evanescent *traits* with the pencil of a master. His conversation resembled a political *camera obscura*—as quaint as it was magical. To some pompous pretenders he might seem to narrate *fabellas aniles* (old wives' fables)—but not to those who study human nature, and wish to know the materials of which it is composed. Mr. Tooke's faculties might appear to have ripened and acquired a finer flavour with age. In a former period of his life he was hardly the man he was latterly; or else he had greater abilities to contend against. He no where makes so poor a figure as in his controversy with Junius. He has evidently the best of the argument, yet he makes nothing out of it. He tells a long story about himself, without wit or point in it; and whines and whimpers like a school-boy under the rod of his master. Junius, after bringing a hasty charge against him, has not a single fact to adduce in support of it; but keeps his ground and fairly beats his adversary out of the field by the mere force of style. One would think that "Parson Horne" knew who Junius was, and was afraid of him. "Under him his genius is" quite "rebuked. " With the best cause to defend, he comes off more shabbily from the contest than any other person in the LETTERS, except Sir William Draper, who is the very hero of defeat.

The great thing which Mr. Horne Tooke has done, and which he has left behind him to posterity, is his work on Grammar, oddly enough entitled THE DIVERSIONS OF PURLEY. Many people have taken it up as a description of a game—others supposing it to be a novel. It is, in truth, one of the few philosophical works on Grammar that were ever written. The essence of it (and, indeed, almost all that is really valuable in it) is contained in his *Letter to Dunning*, published about the year 1775. Mr. Tooke's work is truly elementary. Dr. Lowth described Mr. Harris's *Hermes* as "the finest specimen of analysis since the days of Aristotle"—a work in which there is no analysis at all, for analysis consists in reducing things to their principles, and not in endless details and subdivisions. Mr. Harris multiplies distinctions, and confounds his readers. Mr. Tooke clears away the rubbish of school-boy technicalities, and strikes at the root of his subject. In accomplishing his arduous task, he was, perhaps, aided not more by the strength and resources of his mind than by its limits and defects. There is a web of old associations wound round language, that is a kind of veil over its natural features; and custom puts on the mask of ignorance. But this veil, this mask the author of *The Diversions of Purley* threw aside and penetrated to the naked truth of things, by the literal, matter-of-fact, unimaginative nature of his understanding, and because he was not subject to prejudices or illusions of any kind. Words may be said to "bear a charmed life, that must not yield to one of woman born"—with womanish weaknesses and confused apprehensions. But this charm was broken in the case of Mr. Tooke, whose mind was the reverse of effeminate—hard, unbending, concrete, physical, half-savage—and who saw language stripped of the clothing of habit or sentiment, or the disguises of doting pedantry, naked in its cradle, and in its primitive state. Our author tells us that he found his discovery on Grammar among a number of papers on other subjects, which he had thrown aside and forgotten. Is this an idle boast? Or had he made other discoveries of equal importance, which he did not think it worth his while to communicate to the world, but chose to die the churl of knowledge? The whole of his reasoning turns upon shewing that the Conjunction *That* is the pronoun *That*, which is itself the participle of a verb, and in like manner that all the other mystical and hitherto unintelligible parts of speech are derived from the only two intelligible ones, the Verb and Noun. "I affirm *that* gold is yellow, " that is, "I affirm *that* fact, or that proposition, viz. gold is yellow. " The secret of the Conjunction on which so many fine heads had split, on which so many learned definitions were thrown away, as if it was its peculiar province and inborn virtue to announce oracles and formal propositions, and nothing else, like a Doctor of Laws, is here at once accounted for, inasmuch as it is clearly nothing but another part of speech, the pronoun, *that*, with a third part of speech, the noun, *thing*, understood. This is getting at a solution of words into their component parts, not glossing over one difficulty by bringing another to parallel it, nor like saying with Mr. Harris, when it is asked, "what a Conjunction is? " that there are conjunctions copulative, conjunctions disjunctive, and as many other frivolous varieties of the species as any one chooses to hunt out "with laborious foolery. " Our author hit upon his parent-discovery in the course of a law-suit, while he was examining, with jealous watchfulness, the meaning of words to prevent being entrapped by them; or rather, this circumstance might itself be traced to the habit of satisfying his own mind as to the precise sense in which he himself made use of words. Mr. Tooke, though he had no objection to puzzle others, was mightily averse to being puzzled or *mystified* himself. All was, to his determined mind, either complete light or complete darkness. There was no hazy, doubtful *chiaro-scuro* in his understanding. He wanted something "palpable to feeling as to sight. " "What, " he would say to himself, "do I mean when I use the conjunction *that?* Is it an anomaly, a class by itself, a word sealed against all inquisitive attempts? Is it enough to call it a *copula*, a bridge, a link, a word connecting sentences? That is undoubtedly its use, but what is its origin? " Mr. Tooke thought he had answered this question satisfactorily, and loosened the Gordian knot of grammarians, "familiar as his garter, " when he said, "It is the common pronoun, adjective, or participle, *that*, with the noun, *thing or proposition*, implied, and the particular example following it. " So he thought, and so every reader has thought since, with the exception of teachers and writers upon grammar. Mr. Windham, indeed, who was a sophist, but not a logician, charged him with having found "a mare's-nest; " but it is not to be doubted that Mr. Tooke's etymologies will stand the test, and last longer than Mr. Windham's ingenious derivation of the practice of bull-baiting from the principles of humanity!

Having thus laid the corner-stone, he proceeded to apply the same method of reasoning to other undecyphered and impracticable terms. Thus the word, *And*, he explained clearly enough to be the verb *add*, or a corruption of the old Saxon, *anandad*. "Two *and* two make four, " that is, "two *add* two make four. " Mr. Tooke, in fact, treated words as the chemists do substances; he separated those which are compounded of others from those which are not decompoundable. He did not explain the obscure by the more obscure, but the difficult by the plain, the complex by the simple. This alone is proceeding upon the true principles of science: the rest is pedantry and *petit-maitreship*. Our philosophical writer distinguished all words into *names of things*, and directions added for joining them together, or originally into *nouns* and *verbs*. It is a pity that he has left this matter short, by omitting to define the Verb. After enumerating sixteen different definitions (all of which he dismisses with scorn and contumely) at the end of two quarto volumes, he refers the reader for the true solution to a third volume, which he did not live to finish. This extraordinary man was in the habit of tantalizing his guests on a Sunday afternoon with sundry abstruse speculations, and putting them off to the following week for a satisfaction of their doubts; but why should he treat posterity in the same scurvy manner, or leave the world without quitting scores with it? I question whether Mr. Tooke was himself in possession of his pretended *nostrum*, and whether, after trying hard at a definition of the verb as a distinct part of speech, as a terrier-dog mumbles a hedge-hog, he did not find it too much for him, and leave it to its fate. It is also a pity that Mr. Tooke spun out his great work with prolix and dogmatical dissertations on irrelevant matters; and after denying the old metaphysical theories of language, should attempt to found a metaphysical theory of his own on the nature and mechanism of language. The nature of words, he contended (it was the basis of his whole system) had no connection with the nature of things or the objects of thought; yet he afterwards strove to limit the nature of things and of the human mind by the technical structure of language. Thus he endeavours to shew that there are no abstract ideas, by enumerating two thousand instances of words, expressing abstract ideas, that are the past participles of certain verbs. It is difficult to know what he means by this. On the other hand, he maintains that "a complex idea is as great an absurdity as a complex star, " and that words only are complex. He also makes out a triumphant list of metaphysical and moral non-entities, proved to be so on the pure principle that the names of these non-entities are participles, not nouns, or names of things. That is strange in so close a reasoner and in one who maintained that all language was a masquerade of words, and that the class to which they grammatically belonged had nothing to do with the class of ideas they represented.

It is now above twenty years since the two quarto volumes of the *Diversions of Purley* were published, and fifty since the same theory was promulgated in the celebrated *Letter to Dunning*. Yet it is a curious example of the *Spirit of the Age* that Mr. Lindley Murray's Grammar (a work out of which Mr. C— — helps himself to English, and Mr. M— — to style[B]) has proceeded to the thirtieth edition in complete defiance of all the facts and arguments there laid down. He defines a noun to be the name of a thing. Is quackery a thing, *i. e.* a substance? He defines a verb to be a word signifying *to be, to do, or to suffer.* Are being, action, suffering verbs? He defines an adjective to be the name of a quality. Are not *wooden, golden, substantial* adjectives? He maintains that there are six cases in English nouns [C], that is, six various terminations without any change of termination at all, and that English verbs have all the moods, tenses, and persons that the Latin ones have. This is an extraordinary stretch of blindness and obstinacy. He very formally translates the Latin Grammar into English (as so many had done before him) and fancies he has written an English Grammar; and divines applaud, and schoolmasters usher him into the polite world, and English scholars carry on the jest, while Horne Tooke's genuine anatomy of our native tongue is laid on the shelf. Can it be that our politicians smell a rat in the Member for Old Sarum? That our clergy do not relish Parson Horne? That the world at large are alarmed at acuteness and originality greater than their own? What has all this to do with the formation of the English language or with the first conditions and necessary foundation of speech itself? Is there nothing beyond the reach of prejudice and party-spirit? It seems in this, as in so many other instances, as if there was a patent for absurdity in the natural bias of the human mind, and that folly should be *stereotyped*!

[Footnote A: "They receive him like a virgin at the Magdalen—*Go thou and do likewise. "* —JUNIUS.]

[Footnote B: This work is not without merit in the details and examples of English construction. But its fault even in that part is that he confounds the genius of the English language, making it periphrastic and literal, instead of elliptical and idiomatic. According to Mr. Murray, hardly any of our best writers ever wrote a word of English.]

[Footnote C: At least, with only one change in the genitive case,]

* * * * *

SIR WALTER SCOTT

Sir Walter Scott is undoubtedly the most popular writer of the age—the "lord of the ascendant" for the time being. He is just half what the human intellect is capable of being: if you take the universe, and divide it into two parts, he knows all that it *has been*; all that it *is to be* is nothing to him. His is a mind brooding over antiquity—scorning "the present ignorant time. " He is "laudator temporis acti"—a "*prophesier* of things past. " The old world is to him a crowded map; the new one a dull, hateful blank. He dotes on all well- authenticated superstitions; he shudders at the shadow of innovation. His retentiveness of memory, his accumulated weight of interested prejudice or romantic association have overlaid his other faculties. The cells of his memory are vast, various, full even to bursting with life and motion; his speculative understanding is empty, flaccid, poor, and dead. His mind receives and treasures up every thing brought to it by tradition or custom—it does not project itself beyond this into the world unknown, but mechanically shrinks back as from the edge of a prejudice. The land of pure reason is to his apprehension like *Van Dieman's Land*; —barren, miserable, distant, a place of exile, the dreary abode of savages, convicts, and adventurers. Sir Walter would make a bad hand of a description of the *Millennium*, unless he could lay the scene in Scotland five hundred years ago, and then he would want facts and worm-eaten parchments to support his drooping style. Our historical novelist firmly thinks that nothing *is* but what *has been*—that the moral world stands still, as the material one was supposed to do of old—and that we can never get beyond the point where we actually are without utter destruction, though every thing changes and will change from what it was three hundred years ago to what it is now, —from what it is now to all that the bigoted admirer of the good old times most dreads and hates!

It is long since we read, and long since we thought of our author's poetry. It would probably have gone out of date with the immediate occasion, even if he himself had not contrived to banish it from our recollection. It is not to be denied that it had great merit, both of an obvious and intrinsic kind. It abounded in vivid descriptions, in spirited action, in smooth and flowing versification. But it wanted *character*. It was poetry "of no mark or likelihood. " It slid out of the mind as soon as read, like a river; and would have been forgotten, but that the public curiosity was fed with ever-new supplies from the same teeming liquid source. It is not every man that can write six quarto volumes in verse, that are caught up with avidity, even by fastidious judges. But what a difference between *their* popularity and that of the Scotch Novels! It is true, the public read and admired the *Lay of the Last Minstrel, Marmion,* and so on, and each individual was contented to read and admire because the public did so: but with regard to the prose-works of the same (supposed) author, it is quite *another-guess* sort of thing. Here every one stands forward to applaud on his own ground, would be thought to go before the public opinion, is eager to extol his favourite characters louder, to understand them better than every body else, and has his own scale of comparative excellence for each work, supported by nothing but his own enthusiastic and fearless convictions. It must be amusing to the *Author of Waverley* to hear his readers and admirers (and are not these the same thing? [A]) quarrelling which of his novels is the best, opposing character to character, quoting passage against passage, striving to surpass each other in the extravagance of their encomiums, and yet unable to settle the precedence, or to do the author's writings justice—so various, so equal, so transcendant are their merits! His volumes of poetry were received as fashionable and well-dressed acquaintances: we are ready to tear the others in pieces as old friends. There was something meretricious in Sir Walter's ballad-rhymes; and like those who keep opera *figurantes*, we were willing to have our admiration shared, and our taste confirmed by the town: but the Novels are like the betrothed of our hearts, bone of our bone, and flesh of our flesh, and we are jealous that any one should be as much delighted or as thoroughly acquainted with their beauties as ourselves. For which of his poetical heroines would the reader break a lance so soon as for Jeanie Deans? What *Lady of the Lake* can compare with the beautiful Rebecca? We believe the late Mr. John Scott went to his death-bed (though a painful and premature one) with some degree of satisfaction, inasmuch as he had penned the most elaborate panegyric on the *Scotch Novels* that had as yet appeared! —The *Epics* are not poems, so much as metrical romances. There is a glittering veil of verse thrown over the features of nature and of old romance. The deep incisions into character are "skinned and filmed over"—the details are lost or shaped into flimsy and insipid decorum; and the truth of feeling and of circumstance is translated into a tinkling sound, a tinsel *common-place*. It must be owned, there is a power in true poetry that lifts the mind from the ground of reality to a higher sphere, that penetrates the inert, scattered, incoherent materials presented to it, and by a force and inspiration of its own, melts and moulds them into sublimity and beauty. But Sir Walter (we contend, under correction) has not this creative impulse, this plastic power, this capacity of reacting on his first impressions. He is a learned, a literal, a *matter-of-fact* expounder of truth or fable: [B] he does not soar above and look down upon his subject, imparting his own lofty views and feelings to his descriptions of nature—he relies upon it, is raised by it, is one with it, or he is nothing. A poet is essentially a *maker*; that is, he must atone for what he loses in individuality and local resemblance by the energies and resources of his own mind. The writer of whom we speak is deficient in these last. He has either not the faculty or not the will to impregnate his subject by an effort of pure invention. The execution also is much upon a par with the more ephemeral effusions of the press. It is light, agreeable, effeminate, diffuse. Sir Walter's Muse is a *Modern Antique*. The smooth, glossy texture of his verse contrasts happily with the quaint, uncouth, rugged materials of which it is composed; and takes away any appearance of heaviness or harshness from the body of local traditions and obsolete costume. We see grim knights and iron armour; but then they are woven in silk with a careless, delicate hand, and have the softness of flowers. The poet's figures might be compared to old [C] tapestries copied on the finest velvet: —they are not like Raphael's *Cartoons*, but they are very like Mr. Westall's drawings, which accompany, and are intended to illustrate them. This facility and grace of execution is the more remarkable, as a story goes that not long before the appearance of the *Lay of the Last Minstrel* Sir Walter (then Mr.) Scott, having, in the company of a friend, to cross the Frith of Forth in a ferry-boat, they proposed to beguile the time by writing a number of verses on a given subject, and that at the end of an hour's hard study, they found they had produced only six lines between them. "It is plain, " said the unconscious author to his fellow-labourer, "that you and I need never think of getting our living by writing poetry! " In a year or so after this, he set to work, and poured out quarto upon quarto, as if they had been drops of water. As to the rest, and compared with true and great poets, our Scottish Minstrel is but "a metre ballad-monger. " We would rather have written one song of Burns, or a single passage in Lord Byron's *Heaven and Earth*, or one of Wordsworth's "fancies and good-nights, " than all his epics. What is he to Spenser, over whose immortal, ever-amiable verse beauty hovers and trembles, and who has shed the purple light of Fancy, from his ambrosial wings, over all nature? What is there of the might of Milton, whose head is canopied in the blue serene, and who takes us to sit with him there? What is there (in his ambling rhymes) of the deep pathos of Chaucer? Or of the o'er-informing power of

Shakespear, whose eye, watching alike the minutest traces of characters and the strongest movements of passion, "glances from heaven to earth, from earth to heaven, " and with the lambent flame of genius, playing round each object, lights up the universe in a robe of its own radiance? Sir Walter has no voluntary power of combination: all his associations (as we said before) are those of habit or of tradition. He is a mere narrative and descriptive poet, garrulous of the old time. The definition of his poetry is a pleasing superficiality.

Not so of his NOVELS AND ROMANCES. There we turn over a new leaf—another and the same—the same in matter, but in form, in power how different! The author of Waverley has got rid of the tagging of rhymes, the eking out of syllables, the supplying of epithets, the colours of style, the grouping of his characters, and the regular march of events, and comes to the point at once, and strikes at the heart of his subject, without dismay and without disguise. His poetry was a lady's waiting-maid, dressed out in cast-off finery: his prose is a beautiful, rustic nymph, that, like Dorothea in Don Quixote, when she is surprised with dishevelled tresses bathing her naked feet in the brook, looks round her, abashed at the admiration her charms have excited! The grand secret of the author's success in these latter productions is that he has completely got rid of the trammels of authorship; and torn off at one rent (as Lord Peter got rid of so many yards of lace in the *Tale of a Tub*) all the ornaments of fine writing and worn-out sentimentality. All is fresh, as from the hand of nature: by going a century or two back and laying the scene in a remote and uncultivated district, all becomes new and startling in the present advanced period. —Highland manners, characters, scenery, superstitions, Northern dialect and costume, the wars, the religion, and politics of the sixteenth and seventeenth centuries, give a charming and wholesome relief to the fastidious refinement and "over-laboured lassitude" of modern readers, like the effect of plunging a nervous valetudinarian into a cold-bath. The *Scotch Novels*, for this reason, are not so much admired in Scotland as in England. The contrast, the transition is less striking. From the top of the Calton-Hill, the inhabitants of "Auld Reekie" can descry, or fancy they descry the peaks of Ben Lomond and the waving outline of Rob Roy's country: we who live at the southern extremity of the island can only catch a glimpse of the billowy scene in the descriptions of the Author of Waverley. The mountain air is most bracing to our languid nerves, and it is brought us in ship-loads from the neighbourhood of Abbot's-Ford. There is another circumstance to be taken into the account. In Edinburgh there is a little opposition and something of the spirit of cabal between the partisans of works proceeding from Mr. Constable's and Mr. Blackwood's shops. Mr. Constable gives the highest prices; but being the Whig bookseller, it is grudged that he should do so. An attempt is therefore made to transfer a certain share of popularity to the second-rate Scotch novels, "the embryo fry, the little airy of *rickety* children, " issuing through Mr. Blackwood's shop-door. This operates a diversion, which does not affect us here. The Author of Waverley wears the palm of legendary lore alone. Sir Walter may, indeed, surfeit us: his imitators make us sick! It may be asked, it has been asked, "Have we no materials for romance in England? Must we look to Scotland for a supply of whatever is original and striking in this kind? " And we answer—"Yes! " Every foot of soil is with us worked up: nearly every movement of the social machine is calculable. We have no room left for violent catastrophes; for grotesque quaintnesses; for wizard spells. The last skirts of ignorance and barbarism are seen hovering (in Sir Walter's pages) over the Border. We have, it is true, gipsies in this country as well as at the Cairn of Derncleugh: but they live under clipped hedges, and repose in camp-beds, and do not perch on crags, like eagles, or take shelter, like sea-mews, in basaltic subterranean caverns. We have heaths with rude heaps of stones upon them: but no existing superstition converts them into the Geese of Micklestane-Moor, or sees a Black Dwarf groping among them. We have sects in religion: but the only thing sublime or ridiculous in that way is Mr. Irving, the Caledonian preacher, who "comes like a satyr staring from the woods, and yet speaks like an orator! " We had a Parson Adams not quite a hundred years ago—a Sir Roger de Coverley rather more than a hundred! Even Sir Walter is ordinarily obliged to pitch his angle (strong as the hook is) a hundred miles to the North of the "Modern Athens" or a century back. His last work, [A] indeed, is mystical, is romantic in nothing but the title-page. Instead of "a holy-water sprinkle dipped in dew, " he has given us a fashionable watering-place—and we see what he has made of it. He must not come down from his fastnesses in traditional barbarism and native rusticity: the level, the littleness, the frippery of modern civilization will undo him as it has undone us!

Sir Walter has found out (oh, rare discovery) that facts are better than fiction; that there is no romance like the romance of real life; and that if we can but arrive at what men feel, do, and say in striking and singular situations, the result will be "more lively, audible, and full of vent, " than the fine-spun cobwebs of the brain. With reverence be it spoken, he is like the man who having to imitate the squeaking of a pig upon the stage, brought the animal under his coat with him. Our author has conjured up the actual people he has to deal with, or as much as he could get of them, in "their habits as they lived. " He has ransacked old chronicles, and poured the contents upon his page; he has squeezed out musty records; he has consulted wayfaring pilgrims, bed-rid sibyls; he has invoked the spirits of the air; he has conversed with the living and the dead, and let them tell their story their own way; and by borrowing of others, has enriched his own genius with everlasting variety, truth, and freedom. He has taken his materials from the original, authentic sources, in large concrete masses, and not tampered with or too much frittered them away. He is only the amanuensis of truth and history. It is impossible to say how fine his writings in consequence are, unless we could describe how fine nature is. All that portion of the history of his country that he has touched upon (wide as the scope is) the manners, the personages, the events, the scenery, lives over again in his volumes. Nothing is wanting—the illusion is complete. There is a hurtling in the air, a trampling of feet upon the ground, as these perfect representations of human character or fanciful belief come thronging back upon our imaginations. We will merely recall a few of the subjects of his pencil to the reader's recollection; for nothing we could add, by way of note or commendation, could make the impression more vivid.

There is (first and foremost, because the earliest of our acquaintance) the Baron of Bradwardine, stately, kind-hearted, whimsical, pedantic; and Flora MacIvor (whom even *we* forgive for her Jacobitism), the fierce Vich Ian Vohr, and Evan Dhu, constant in death, and Davie Gellatly roasting his eggs or turning his rhymes with restless volubility, and the two stag-hounds that met Waverley, as fine as ever Titian painted, or Paul Veronese: —then there is old Balfour of Burley, brandishing his sword and his Bible with fire-eyed fury, trying a fall with the insolent, gigantic Bothwell at the 'Change-house, and vanquishing him at the noble battle of Loudonhill; there is Bothwell himself, drawn to the life, proud, cruel, selfish, profligate, but with the love-letters of the gentle Alice (written thirty years before), and his verses to her memory, found in his pocket after his death: in the same volume of *Old Mortality* is that lone figure, like a figure in Scripture, of the woman sitting on the stone at the turning to the mountain, to warn Burley that there is a lion in his path; and the fawning Claverhouse, beautiful as a panther, smooth-looking, blood-spotted; and the fanatics, Macbriar and Mucklewrath, crazed with zeal and sufferings; and the inflexible Morton, and the faithful Edith, who refused to "give her hand to another while her heart was with her lover in the deep and dead sea. " And in *The Heart of Mid-Lothian* we have Effie Deans (that sweet, faded flower) and Jeanie, her more than sister, and old David Deans, the patriarch of St. Leonard's Crags, and Butler, and Dumbiedikes, eloquent in his silence, and Mr. Bartoline Saddle-tree and his prudent helpmate, and Porteous swinging in the wind, and Madge Wildfire, full of finery and madness, and her ghastly mother. —Again, there is Meg Merrilies, standing on her rock, stretched on her bier with "her head to the east, " and Dirk Hatterick (equal to Shakespear's Master Barnardine), and Glossin, the soul of an attorney, and Dandy Dinmont, with his terrier-pack and his pony Dumple, and the fiery Colonel Mannering, and the modish old counsellor Pleydell, and Dominie Sampson, [D] and Rob Roy (like the eagle in his eyry), and Baillie Nicol Jarvie, and the inimitable Major Galbraith, and Rashleigh Osbaldistone, and Die Vernon, the best of secret-keepers; and in the *Antiquary*, the ingenious and abstruse Mr. Jonathan Oldbuck, and the old beadsman Edie Ochiltree, and that preternatural figure of old Edith Elspeith, a living shadow, in whom the lamp of life had been long extinguished, had it not been fed by remorse and "thick-coming" recollections; and that striking picture of the effects of feudal tyranny and fiendish pride, the unhappy Earl of Glenallan; and the Black Dwarf, and his friend Habbie of the Heughfoot (the cheerful hunter), and his cousin Grace Armstrong, fresh and laughing like the morning; and the *Children of the Mint*, and the baying of the blood-hound that tracks their steps at a distance (the hollow echoes are in our ears now), and Amy and her hapless love, and the villain Varney, and the deep voice of George of Douglas—and the immoveable Balafre, and Master Oliver the Barber in Quentin Durward—and the quaint humour of the Fortunes of Nigel, and the comic spirit of Peveril of the Peak—and the fine old English romance of Ivanhoe. What a list of names! What a host of associations! What a thing is human life! What a power is that of genius! What a world of thought and feeling is thus rescued from oblivion! How many hours of heartfelt satisfaction has our author given to the gay and thoughtless! How many sad hearts has he soothed in pain and solitude! It is no wonder that the public repay with lengthened applause and gratitude the pleasure they receive. He writes as fast as they can read, and he does not write himself down. He is always in the public eye, and we do not tire of him. His worst is better than any other person's best. His *backgrounds* (and his later works are little else but back-grounds capitally made out) are more attractive than the principal figures and most complicated actions of other writers. His works (taken together) are almost like a new edition of human nature. This is indeed to be an author!

The political bearing of the *Scotch Novels* has been a considerable recommendation to them. They are a relief to the mind, rarefied as it has been with modern philosophy, and heated with ultra-radicalism. At a time also, when we bid fair to revive the principles of the Stuarts, it is interesting to bring us acquainted with their persons and misfortunes. The candour of Sir Walter's historic pen levels our bristling prejudices on this score, and sees fair play between Roundheads and Cavaliers, between Protestant and Papist. He is a writer reconciling all the diversities of human nature to the reader. He does not enter into the distinctions of hostile sects or parties, but treats of the strength or the infirmity of the human mind, of the virtues or vices of the human breast, as they are to be found blended in the whole race of mankind. Nothing can shew more handsomely or be more gallantly executed. There was a talk at one time that our author was about to take Guy Faux for the subject of one of his novels, in order to put a more liberal and humane construction on the Gunpowder Plot than our "No Popery" prejudices have hitherto permitted. Sir Walter is a professed *clarifier* of the age from the vulgar and still lurking old-English antipathy to Popery and Slavery. Through some odd process of *servile* logic, it should seem, that in restoring the claims of the Stuarts by the courtesy of romance, the House of Brunswick are more firmly seated in point of fact, and the Bourbons, by collateral reasoning, become legitimate! In any other point of view, we cannot possibly conceive how Sir Walter imagines "he has done something to revive the declining spirit of loyalty" by these novels. His loyalty is founded on *would-be* treason: he props the actual throne by the shadow of rebellion. Does he really think of making us enamoured of the "good old times" by the faithful and harrowing portraits he has drawn of them? Would he carry us back to the early stages of barbarism, of clanship, of the feudal system as "a consummation devoutly to be wished? " Is he infatuated enough, or does he so dote and drivel over his own slothful and self-willed prejudices, as to believe that he will make a single convert to the beauty of Legitimacy, that is, of lawless power and savage bigotry, when he himself is obliged to apologise for the horrors he describes, and even render his descriptions credible to the modern reader by referring to the authentic history of these delectable times? [E] He is indeed so besotted as to the moral of his own story, that he has even the blindness to go out of his way to have a fling at *flints* and *dungs* (the contemptible ingredients, as he would have us believe, of a modern rabble) at the very time when he is describing a mob of the twelfth century—a mob (one should think) after the writer's own heart, without one particle of modern philosophy or revolutionary politics in their composition, who were to a man, to a hair, just what priests, and kings, and nobles *let* them be, and who were collected to witness (a spectacle proper to the times) the burning of the lovely Rebecca at a stake for a sorceress, because she was a Jewess, beautiful and innocent, and the consequent victim of insane bigotry and unbridled profligacy. And it is at this moment (when the heart is kindled and bursting with indignation at the revolting abuses of self-constituted power) that Sir Walter *stops the press* to have a sneer at the people, and to put a spoke (as he thinks) in the wheel of upstart innovation! This is what he "calls backing his friends"—it is thus he administers charms and philtres to our love of Legitimacy, makes us conceive a horror of all reform, civil, political, or religious, and would fain put down the *Spirit of the Age*. The author of Waverley might just as well get up and make a speech at a dinner at Edinburgh, abusing Mr. Mac-Adam for his improvements in the roads, on the ground that they were nearly *impassable* in many places "sixty years since;" or object to Mr. Peel's *Police-Bill*, by insisting that Hounslow-Heath was formerly a scene of greater interest and terror to highwaymen and travellers, and cut a greater figure in the Newgate-Calendar than it does at present. —Oh! Wickliff, Luther, Hampden, Sidney, Somers, mistaken Whigs, and thoughtless Reformers in religion and politics, and all ye, whether poets or philosophers, heroes or sages, inventors of arts or sciences, patriots, benefactors of the human race, enlighteners and civilisers of the world, who have (so far) reduced opinion to reason, and power to law, who are the cause that we no longer burn witches and heretics at slow fires, that the thumb-screws are no longer applied by ghastly, smiling judges, to extort confession of imputed crimes from sufferers for conscience sake; that men are no longer strung up like acorns on trees without judge or jury, or hunted like wild beasts through thickets and glens, who have abated the cruelty of priests, the pride of nobles, the divinity of kings in former times; to whom we owe it, that we no longer wear round our necks the collar of Gurth the swineherd, and of Wamba the jester; that the castles of great lords are no longer the dens of banditti, from whence they issue with fire and sword, to lay waste the land; that we no longer expire in loathsome dungeons without knowing the cause, or have our right hands struck off for raising them in self-defence against wanton insult; that we can sleep without fear of being burnt in our beds, or travel without making our wills; that no Amy Robsarts are thrown down trap-doors by Richard Varneys with impunity; that no Red Reiver of Westburn-Flat sets fire to peaceful cottages; that no Claverhouse signs cold-blooded death-warrants in sport; that we have no Tristan the Hermit, or Petit- Andrè, crawling near us, like spiders, and making our flesh creep, and our hearts sicken within us at every moment of our lives—ye who have produced this change in the face of nature and society, return to earth once more, and beg pardon of Sir Walter and his patrons, who sigh at not being able to undo all that you have done! Leaving this question, there are two other remarks which we wished to make on the Novels. The one was, to express our admiration at the good-nature of the mottos, in which the author has taken occasion to remember and quote almost every living author (whether illustrious or obscure) but himself—an indirect argument in favour of the general opinion as to the source from which they spring—and the other was, to hint our astonishment at the innumerable and incessant in-stances of bad and slovenly English in them, more, we believe, than in any other works now printed. We should think the writer could not possibly read the manuscript after he has once written it, or overlook the press.

If there were a writer, who "born for the universe"—

> "— — — — —-Narrow'd his mind,
> And to party gave up what was meant for mankind—"

who, from the height of his genius looking abroad into nature, and scanning the recesses of the human heart, "winked and shut his apprehension up" to every thought or purpose that tended to the future good of mankind—who, raised by affluence, the reward of successful industry, and by the voice of fame above the want of any but the most honourable patronage, stooped to the unworthy arts of adulation, and abetted the views of the great with the pettifogging feelings of the meanest dependant on office—who, having secured the admiration of the public (with the probable reversion of immortality), shewed no respect for himself, for that genius that had raised him to distinction, for that nature which he trampled under foot—who, amiable, frank, friendly, manly in private life, was seized with the dotage of age and the fury of a woman, the instant politics were concerned—who reserved all his candour and comprehensiveness of view for history, and vented his littleness, pique, resentment, bigotry, and intolerance on his contemporaries— who took the wrong side, and defended it by unfair means—who, the moment his own interest or the prejudices of others interfered, seemed to forget all that was due to the pride of intellect, to the sense of manhood—who, praised, admired by men of all parties alike, repaid the public liberality by striking a secret and envenomed blow at the reputation of every one who was not the ready tool of power— who strewed the slime of rankling malice and mercenary scorn over the bud and promise of genius, because it was not fostered in the hot-bed of corruption, or warped by the trammels of servility—who supported the worst abuses of authority in the worst spirit—who joined a gang of desperadoes to spread calumny, contempt, infamy, wherever they were merited by honesty or talent on a different side—who officiously undertook to decide public questions by private insinuations, to prop the throne by nicknames, and the altar by lies—who being (by common consent) the finest, the most humane and accomplished writer of his age, associated himself with and encouraged the lowest panders of a venal press; deluging, nauseating the public mind with the offal and garbage of Billingsgate abuse and vulgar *slang*; shewing no remorse, no relenting or compassion towards the victims of this nefarious and organized system of party-proscription, carried on under the mask of literary criticism and fair discussion, insulting the misfortunes of some, and trampling on the early grave of others—

> "Who would not grieve if such a man there be?
> Who would not weep if Atticus were he? "

But we believe there is no other age or country of the world (but ours), in which such genius could have been so degraded!

[Footnote A: No! For we met with a young lady who kept a circulating library and a milliner's-shop, in a watering-place in the country, who, when we inquired for the *Scotch Novels*, spoke indifferently about them, said they were "so dry she could hardly get through them, " and recommended us to read *Agnes*. We never thought of it before; but we would venture to lay a wager that there are many other young ladies in the same situation, and who think "Old Mortality" "dry. "]

[Footnote B: Just as Cobbett is a *matter-of-fact reasoner*.]

[Footnote C: St. Ronan's Well.]

[Footnote D: Perhaps the finest scene in all these novels, is that where the Dominie meets his pupil, Miss Lucy, the morning after her brother's arrival.]

[Footnote E: "And here we cannot but think it necessary to offer some better proof than the incidents of an idle tale, to vindicate the melancholy representation of manners which has been just laid before the reader. It is grievous to think that those valiant Barons, to whose stand against the crown the liberties of England were indebted for their existence, should themselves have been such dreadful oppressors, and capable of excesses, contrary not only to the laws of England, but to those of nature and humanity. But alas! we have only to extract from the industrious Henry one of those numerous passages which he has collected from contemporary historians, to prove that fiction itself can hardly reach the dark reality of the horrors of the period.

"The description given by the author of the Saxon Chronicle of the cruelties exercised in the reign of King Stephen by the great barons and lords of castles, who were all Normans, affords a strong proof of the excesses of which they were capable when their passions were inflamed. 'They grievously oppressed the poor people by building castles; and when they were built, they filled them with wicked men or rather devils, who seized both men and women who they imagined had any money, threw them into prison, and put them to more cruel tortures than the martyrs ever endured. They suffocated some in mud, and suspended others by the feet, or the head, or the thumbs, kindling fires below them. They squeezed the heads of some with knotted cords till they pierced their brains, while they threw others into dungeons swarming with serpents, snakes, and toads. ' But it would be cruel to put the reader to the pain of perusing the remainder of the description. " —*Henry's Hist*. edit. 1805, vol. vii. p. 346.]

* * * * *

LORD BYRON.

Lord Byron and Sir Walter Scott are among writers now living[A] the two, who would carry away a majority of suffrages as the greatest geniuses of the age. The former would, perhaps, obtain the preference with the fine gentlemen and ladies (squeamishness apart)—the latter with the critics and the vulgar. We shall treat of them in the same connection, partly on account of their distinguished pre-eminence, and partly because they afford a complete contrast to each other. In their poetry, in their prose, in their politics, and in their tempers no two men can be more unlike. If Sir Walter Scott may be thought by some to have been

"Born universal heir to all humanity, "

it is plain Lord Byron can set up no such pretension. He is, in a striking degree, the creature of his own will. He holds no communion with his kind; but stands alone, without mate or fellow—

"As if a man were author of himself,
And owned no other kin. "

He is like a solitary peak, all access to which is cut off not more by elevation than distance. He is seated on a lofty eminence, "cloud-capt, " or reflecting the last rays of setting suns; and in his poetical moods, reminds us of the fabled Titans, retired to a ridgy steep, playing on their Pan's-pipes, and taking up ordinary men and things in their hands with haughty indifference. He raises his subject to himself, or tramples on it: he neither stoops to, nor loses himself in it. He exists not by sympathy, but by antipathy. He scorns all things, even himself. Nature must come to him to sit for her picture—he does not go to her. She must consult his time, his convenience, and his humour; and wear a *sombre* or a fantastic garb, or his Lordship turns his back upon her. There is no ease, no unaffected simplicity of manner, no "golden mean. " All is strained, or petulant in the extreme. His thoughts are sphered and crystalline; his style "prouder than when blue Iris bends; " his spirit fiery, impatient, wayward, indefatigable. Instead of taking his impressions from without, in entire and almost unimpaired masses, he moulds them according to his own temperament, and heats the materials of his imagination in the furnace of his passions. —Lord Byron's verse glows like a flame, consuming every thing in its way; Sir Walter Scott's glides like a river, clear, gentle, harmless. The poetry of the first scorches, that of the last scarcely warms. The light of the one proceeds from an internal source, ensanguined, sullen, fixed; the other reflects the hues of Heaven, or the face of nature, glancing vivid and various. The productions of the Northern Bard have the rust and the freshness of antiquity about them; those of the Noble Poet cease to startle from their extreme ambition of novelty, both in style and matter. Sir Walter's rhymes are "silly sooth" —

> "And dally with the innocence of thought,
> Like the old age" —

his Lordship's Muse spurns *the olden time*, and affects all the supercilious airs of a modern fine lady and an upstart. The object of the one writer is to restore us to truth and nature: the other chiefly thinks how he shall display his own power, or vent his spleen, or astonish the reader either by starting new subjects and trains of speculation, or by expressing old ones in a more striking and emphatic manner than they have been expressed before. He cares little what it is he says, so that he can say it differently from others. This may account for the charges of plagiarism which have been repeatedly brought against the Noble Poet—if he can borrow an image or sentiment from another, and heighten it by an epithet or an allusion of greater force and beauty than is to be found in the original passage, he thinks he shews his superiority of execution in this in a more marked manner than if the first suggestion had been his own. It is not the value of the observation itself he is solicitous about; but he wishes to shine by contrast—even nature only serves as a foil to set off his style. He therefore takes the thoughts of others (whether contemporaries or not) out of their mouths, and is content to make them his own, to set his stamp upon them, by imparting to them a more meretricious gloss, a higher relief, a greater loftiness of tone, and a characteristic inveteracy of purpose. Even in those collateral ornaments of modern style, slovenliness, abruptness, and eccentricity (as well as in terseness and significance), Lord Byron, when he pleases, defies competition and surpasses all his contemporaries. Whatever he does, he must do in a more decided and daring manner than any one else—he lounges with extravagance, and yawns so as to alarm the reader! Self-will, passion, the love of singularity, a disdain of himself and of others (with a conscious sense that this is among the ways and means of procuring admiration) are the proper categories of his mind: he is a lordly writer, is above his own reputation, and condescends to the Muses with a scornful grace!

Lord Byron, who in his politics is a *liberal*, in his genius is haughty and aristocratic: Walter Scott, who is an aristocrat in principle, is popular in his writings, and is (as it were) equally *servile* to nature and to opinion. The genius of Sir Walter is essentially imitative, or "denotes a foregone conclusion: " that of Lord Byron is self-dependent; or at least requires no aid, is governed by no law, but the impulses of its own will. We confess, however much we may admire independence of feeling and erectness of spirit in general or practical questions, yet in works of genius we prefer him who bows to the authority of nature, who appeals to actual objects, to mouldering superstitions, to history, observation, and tradition, before him who only consults the pragmatical and restless workings of his own breast, and gives them out as oracles to the world. We like a writer (whether poet or prose-writer) who takes in (or is willing to take in) the range of half the universe in feeling, character, description, much better than we do one who obstinately and invariably shuts himself up in the Bastile of his own ruling passions. In short, we had rather be Sir Walter Scott (meaning thereby the Author of Waverley) than Lord Byron, a hundred times over. And for the reason just given, namely, that he casts his descriptions in the mould of nature, ever-varying, never tiresome, always interesting and always instructive, instead of casting them constantly in the mould of his own individual impressions. He gives us man as he is, or as he was, in almost every variety of situation, action, and feeling. Lord Byron makes man after his own image, woman after his own heart; the one is a capricious tyrant, the other a yielding slave; he gives us the misanthrope and the voluptuary by turns; and with these two characters, burning or melting in their own fires, he makes out everlasting centos of himself. He hangs the cloud, the film of his existence over all outward things—sits in the centre of his thoughts, and enjoys dark night, bright day, the glitter and the gloom "in cell monastic"—we see the mournful pall, the crucifix, the death's heads, the faded chaplet of flowers, the gleaming tapers, the agonized brow of genius, the wasted form of beauty—but we are still imprisoned in a dungeon, a curtain intercepts our view, we do not breathe freely the air of nature or of our own thoughts—the other admired author draws aside the curtain, and the veil of egotism is rent, and he shews us the crowd of living men and women, the endless groups, the landscape back-ground, the cloud and the rainbow, and enriches our imaginations and relieves one passion by another, and expands and lightens reflection, and takes away that tightness at the breast which arises from thinking or wishing to think that there is nothing in the world out of a man's self! —In this point of view, the Author of Waverley is one of the greatest teachers of morality that ever lived, by emancipating the mind from petty, narrow, and bigotted prejudices: Lord Byron is the greatest pamperer of those prejudices, by seeming to think there is nothing else worth encouraging but the seeds or the full luxuriant growth of dogmatism and self-conceit. In reading the *Scotch Novels*, we never think about the author, except from a feeling of curiosity respecting our unknown benefactor: in reading Lord Byron's works, he himself is never absent from our minds. The colouring of Lord Byron's style, however rich and dipped in Tyrian dyes, is nevertheless opaque, is in itself an object of delight and wonder: Sir Walter Scott's is perfectly transparent. In studying the one, you seem to gaze at the figures cut in stained glass, which exclude the view beyond, and where the pure light of Heaven is only a means of setting off the gorgeousness of art: in reading the other, you look through a noble window at the clear and varied landscape without. Or to sum up the distinction in one word, Sir Walter Scott is the most *dramatic* writer now living; and Lord Byron is the least so. It would be difficult to imagine that the Author of Waverley is in the smallest degree a pedant; as it would be hard to persuade ourselves that the author of Childe Harold and Don Juan is not a coxcomb, though a provoking and sublime one. In this decided preference given to Sir Walter Scott over Lord Byron, we distinctly include the prose-works of the former; for we do not think his poetry alone by any means entitles him to that precedence. Sir Walter in his poetry, though pleasing and natural, is a comparative trifler: it is in his anonymous productions that he has shewn himself for what he is! —

Intensity is the great and prominent distinction of Lord Byron's writings. He seldom gets beyond force of style, nor has he produced any regular work or masterly whole. He does not prepare any plan beforehand, nor revise and retouch what he has written with polished accuracy. His only object seems to be to stimulate himself and his readers for the moment—to keep both alive, to drive away *ennui*, to substitute a feverish and irritable state of excitement for listless indolence or even calm enjoyment. For this purpose he pitches on any subject at random without much thought or delicacy—he is only impatient to begin—and takes care to adorn and enrich it as he proceeds with "thoughts that breathe and words that burn. " He composes (as he himself has said) whether he is in the bath, in his study, or on horseback—he writes as habitually as others talk or think—and whether we have the inspiration of the Muse or not, we always find the spirit of the man of genius breathing from his verse. He grapples with his subject, and moves, penetrates, and animates it by the electric force of his own feelings. He is often monotonous, extravagant, offensive; but he is never dull, or tedious, but when he writes prose. Lord Byron does not exhibit a new view of nature, or raise insignificant objects into importance by the romantic associations with which he surrounds them; but generally (at least) takes common-place thoughts and events, and endeavours to express them in stronger and statelier language than others. His poetry stands like a Martello tower by the side of his subject. He does not, like Mr. Wordsworth, lift poetry from the ground, or create a sentiment out of nothing. He does not describe a daisy or a periwinkle, but the cedar or the cypress: not "poor men's cottages, but princes' palaces. " His Childe Harold contains a lofty and impassioned review of the great events of history, of the mighty objects left as wrecks of time, but he dwells chiefly on what is familiar to the mind of every school-boy; has brought out few new traits of feeling or thought; and has done no more than justice to the reader's preconceptions by the sustained force and brilliancy of his style and imagery. Lord Byron's earlier productions, *Lara*, the *Corsair*, &c. were wild and gloomy romances, put into rapid and shining verse. They discover the madness of poetry, together with the inspiration: sullen, moody, capricious, fierce, inexorable, gloating on beauty, thirsting for revenge, hurrying from the extremes of pleasure to pain, but with nothing permanent, nothing healthy or natural. The gaudy decorations and the morbid sentiments remind one of flowers strewed over the face of death! In his *Childe Harold* (as has been just observed) he assumes a lofty and philosophic tone, and "reasons high of providence, fore-knowledge, will, and fate. " He takes the highest points in the history of the world, and comments on them from a more commanding eminence: he shews us the crumbling monuments of time, he invokes the great names, the mighty spirit of antiquity. The universe is changed into a stately mausoleum: —in solemn measures he chaunts a hymn to fame. Lord Byron has strength and elevation enough to fill up the moulds of our classical and time-hallowed recollections, and to rekindle the earliest aspirations of the mind after greatness and true glory with a pen of fire. The names of Tasso, of Ariosto, of Dante, of Cincinnatus, of Caesar, of Scipio, lose nothing of their pomp or their lustre in his hands, and when he begins and continues a strain of panegyric on such subjects, we indeed sit down with him to a banquet of rich praise, brooding over imperishable glories,

"Till Contemplation has her fill. "

Lord Byron seems to cast himself indignantly from "this bank and shoal of time, " or the frail tottering bark that bears up modern reputation, into the huge sea of ancient renown, and to revel there with untired, outspread plume. Even this in him is spleen—his contempt of his contemporaries makes him turn back to the lustrous past, or project himself forward to the dim future! —Lord Byron's tragedies, Faliero, [B] Sardanapalus, &c. are not equal to his other works. They want the essence of the drama. They abound in speeches and descriptions, such as he himself might make either to himself or others, lolling on his couch of a morning, but do not carry the reader out of the poet's mind to the scenes and events recorded. They have neither action, character, nor interest, but are a sort of *gossamer* tragedies, spun out, and glittering, and spreading a flimsy veil over the face of nature. Yet he spins them on. Of all that he has done in this way the *Heaven and Earth* (the same subject as Mr. Moore's *Loves of the Angels*) is the best. We prefer it even to *Manfred*. *Manfred* is merely himself, with a fancy-drapery on: but in the dramatic fragment published in the *Liberal*, the space between Heaven and Earth, the stage on which his characters have to pass to and fro, seems to fill his Lordship's imagination; and the Deluge, which he has so finely described, may be said to have drowned all his own idle humours.

We must say we think little of our author's turn for satire. His "English Bards and Scotch Reviewers" is dogmatical and insolent, but without refinement or point. He calls people names, and tries to transfix a character with an epithet, which does not stick, because it has no other foundation than his own petulance and spite; or he endeavours to degrade by alluding to some circumstance of external situation. He says of Mr. Wordsworth's poetry, that "it is his aversion. " That may be: but whose fault is it? This is the satire of a lord, who is accustomed to have all his whims or dislikes taken for gospel, and who cannot be at the pains to do more than signify his contempt or displeasure. If a great man meets with a rebuff which he does not like, he turns on his heel, and this passes for a repartee. The Noble Author says of a celebrated barrister and critic, that he was "born in a garret sixteen stories high. " The insinuation is not true; or if it were, it is low. The allusion degrades the person who makes, not him to whom it is applied. This is also the satire of a person of birth and quality, who measures all merit by external rank, that is, by his own standard. So his Lordship, in a "Letter to the Editor of My Grandmother's Review, " addresses him fifty times as "*my dear Robarts;* " nor is there any other wit in the article. This is surely a mere assumption of superiority from his Lordship's rank, and is the sort of *quizzing* he might use to a person who came to hire himself as a valet to him at *Long's*—the waiters might laugh, the public will not. In like manner, in the controversy about Pope, he claps Mr. Bowles on the back with a coarse facetious familiarity, as if he were his chaplain whom he had invited to dine with him, or was about to present to a benefice. The reverend divine might submit to the obligation, but he has no occasion to subscribe to the jest. If it is a jest that Mr. Bowles should be a parson, and Lord Byron a peer, the world knew this before; there was no need to write a pamphlet to prove it.

The *Don Juan* indeed has great power; but its power is owing to the force of the serious writing, and to the oddity of the contrast between that and the flashy passages with which it is interlarded. From the sublime to the ridiculous there is but one step. You laugh and are surprised that any one should turn round and *travestie* himself: the drollery is in the utter discontinuity of ideas and feelings. He makes virtue serve as a foil to vice; *dandyism* is (for want of any other) a variety of genius. A classical intoxication is followed by the splashing of soda-water, by frothy effusions of ordinary bile. After the lightning and the hurricane, we are introduced to the interior of the cabin and the contents of wash-hand basins. The solemn hero of tragedy plays *Scrub* in the farce. This is "very tolerable and not to be endured. " The Noble Lord is almost the only writer who has prostituted his talents in this way. He hallows in order to desecrate; takes a pleasure in defacing the images of beauty his hands have wrought; and raises our hopes and our belief in goodness to Heaven only to dash them to the earth again, and break them in pieces the more effectually from the very height they have fallen. Our enthusiasm for genius or virtue is thus turned into a jest by the very person who has kindled it, and who thus fatally quenches the sparks of both. It is not that Lord Byron is sometimes serious and sometimes trifling, sometimes profligate, and sometimes moral—but when he is most serious and most moral, he is only preparing to mortify the unsuspecting reader by putting a pitiful *hoax* upon him. This is a most unaccountable anomaly. It is as if the eagle were to build its eyry in a common sewer, or the owl were seen soaring to the midday sun. Such a sight might make one laugh, but one would not wish or expect it to occur more than once! [C]

In fact, Lord Byron is the spoiled child of fame as well as fortune. He has taken a surfeit of popularity, and is not contented to delight, unless he can shock the public. He would force them to admire in spite of decency and common sense—he would have them read what they would read in no one but himself, or he would not give a rush for their applause. He is to be "a chartered libertine, " from whom insults are favours, whose contempt is to be a new incentive to admiration. His Lordship is hard to please: he is equally averse to notice or neglect, enraged at censure and scorning praise. He tries the patience of the town to the very utmost, and when they shew signs of weariness or disgust, threatens to *discard* them. He says he will write on, whether he is read or not. He would never write another page, if it were not to court popular applause, or to affect a superiority over it. In this respect also, Lord Byron presents a striking contrast to Sir Walter Scott. The latter takes what part of the public favour falls to his share, without grumbling (to be sure he has no reason to complain) the former is always quarrelling with the world about his *modicum* of applause, the *spolia opima* of vanity, and ungraciously throwing the offerings of incense heaped on his shrine back in the faces of his admirers. Again, there is no taint in the writings of the Author of Waverley, all is fair and natural and *above-board*: he never outrages the public mind. He introduces no anomalous character: broaches no staggering opinion. If he goes back to old prejudices and superstitions as a relief to the modern reader, while Lord Byron floats on swelling paradoxes—

"Like proud seas under him; "

if the one defers too much to the spirit of antiquity, the other panders to the spirit of the age, goes to the very edge of extreme and licentious speculation, and breaks his neck over it. Grossness and levity are the playthings of his pen. It is a ludicrous circumstance that he should have dedicated his *Cain* to the worthy Baronet! Did the latter ever acknowledge the obligation? We are not nice, not very nice; but we do not particularly approve those subjects that shine chiefly from their rottenness: nor do we wish to see the Muses drest out in the flounces of a false or questionable philosophy, like *Portia* and *Nerissa* in the garb of Doctors of Law. We like metaphysics as well as Lord Byron; but not to see them making flowery speeches, nor dancing a measure in the fetters of verse. We have as good as hinted, that his Lordship's poetry consists mostly of a tissue of superb common-places; even his paradoxes are *common-place*. They are familiar in the schools: they are only new and striking in his dramas and stanzas, by being out of place. In a word, we think that poetry moves best within the circle of nature and received opinion: speculative theory and subtle casuistry are forbidden ground to it. But Lord Byron often wanders into this ground wantonly, wilfully, and unwarrantably. The only apology we can conceive for the spirit of some of Lord Byron's writings, is the spirit of some of those opposed to him. They would provoke a man to write any thing. "Farthest from them is best. " The extravagance and license of the one seems a proper antidote to the bigotry and narrowness of the other. The first *Vision of Judgment* was a set-off to the second, though

"None but itself could be its parallel. "

Perhaps the chief cause of most of Lord Byron's errors is, that he is that anomaly in letters and in society, a Noble Poet. It is a double privilege, almost too much for humanity. He has all the pride of birth and genius. The strength of his imagination leads him to indulge in fantastic opinions; the elevation of his rank sets censure at defiance. He becomes a pampered egotist. He has a seat in the House of Lords, a niche in the Temple of Fame. Every-day mortals, opinions, things are not good enough for him to touch or think of. A mere nobleman is, in his estimation, but "the tenth transmitter of a foolish face: " a mere man of genius is no better than a worm. His Muse is also a lady of quality. The people are not polite enough for him: the Court not sufficiently intellectual. He hates the one and despises the other. By hating and despising others, he does not learn to be satisfied with himself. A fastidious man soon grows querulous and splenetic. If there is nobody but ourselves to come up to our idea of fancied perfection, we easily get tired of our idol. When a man is tired of what he is, by a natural perversity he sets up for what he is not. If he is a poet, he pretends to be a metaphysician: if he is a patrician in rank and feeling, he would fain be one of the people. His ruling motive is not the love of the people, but of distinction not of truth, but of singularity. He patronizes men of letters out of vanity, and deserts them from caprice, or from the advice of friends. He embarks in an obnoxious publication to provoke censure, and leaves it to shift for itself for fear of scandal. We do not like Sir Walter's gratuitous servility: we like Lord Byron's preposterous *liberalism* little better. He may affect the principles of equality, but he resumes his privilege of peerage, upon occasion. His Lordship has made great offers of service to the Greeks—money and horses. He is at present in Cephalonia, waiting the event!

* * * * *

We had written thus far when news came of the death of Lord Byron, and put an end at once to a strain of somewhat peevish invective, which was intended to meet his eye, not to insult his memory. Had we known that we were writing his epitaph, we must have done it with a different feeling. As it is, we think it better and more like himself, to let what we had written stand, than to take up our leaden shafts, and try to melt them into "tears of sensibility, " or mould them into dull praise, and an affected shew of candour. We were not silent during the author's life-time, either for his reproof or encouragement (such us we could give, and *he* did not disdain to accept) nor can we now turn undertakers' men to fix the glittering plate upon his coffin, or fall into the procession of popular woe. — Death cancels every thing but truth; and strips a man of every thing but genius and virtue. It is a sort of natural canonization. It makes the meanest of us sacred—it installs the poet in his immortality, and lifts him to the skies. Death is the great assayer of the sterling ore of talent. At his touch the drossy particles fall off, the irritable, the personal, the gross, and mingle with the dust—the finer and more ethereal part mounts with the winged spirit to watch over our latest memory and protect our bones from insult. We consign the least worthy qualities to oblivion, and cherish the nobler and imperishable nature with double pride and fondness. Nothing could shew the real superiority of genius in a more striking point of view than the idle contests and the public indifference about the place of Lord Byron's interment, whether in Westminster-Abbey or his own family-vault. A king must have a coronation—a nobleman a funeral-procession. —The man is nothing without the pageant. The poet's cemetery is the human mind, in which he sows the seeds of never ending thought—his monument is to be found in his works:

> "Nothing can cover his high fame but Heaven;
> No pyramids set off his memory,
> But the eternal substance of his greatness. "

Lord Byron is dead: he also died a martyr to his zeal in the cause of freedom, for the last, best hopes of man. Let that be his excuse and his epitaph!

[Footnote A: This Essay was written just before Lord Byron's death.]

[Footnote B:

> "Don Juan was my Moscow, and Faliero
> My Leipsic, and my Mont St. Jean seems Cain, "
> *Don Juan*, Canto. XI.]

[Footnote C: This censure applies to the first Cantos of DON JUAN much more than to the last. It has been called a TRISTRAM SHANDY in rhyme: it is rather a poem written about itself.]

* * * * *

MR. CAMPBELL AND MR. CRABBE.

"Mr. Campbell may be said to hold a place (among modern poets) between Lord Byron and Mr. Rogers. With much of the glossy splendour, the pointed vigour, and romantic interest of the one, he possesses the fastidious refinement, the classic elegance of the other. Mr. Rogers, as a writer, is too effeminate, Lord Byron too extravagant: Mr. Campbell is neither. The author of the *Pleasures of Memory* polishes his lines till they sparkle with the most exquisite finish; he attenuates them into the utmost degree of trembling softness: but we may complain, in spite of the delicacy and brilliancy of the execution, of a want of strength and solidity. The author of the *Pleasures of Hope*, with a richer and deeper vein of thought and imagination, works it out into figures of equal grace and dazzling beauty, avoiding on the one hand the tinsel of flimsy affectation, and on the other the vices of a rude and barbarous negligence. His Pegasus is not a rough, skittish colt, running wild among the mountains, covered with bur-docks and thistles, nor a tame, sleek pad, unable to get out of the same ambling pace, but a beautiful *manege*-horse, full of life and spirit in itself, and subject to the complete controul of the rider. Mr. Campbell gives scope to his feelings and his fancy, and embodies them in a noble and naturally interesting subject; and he at the same time conceives himself called upon (in these days of critical nicety) to pay the exactest attention to the expression of each thought, and to modulate each line into the most faultless harmony. The character of his mind is a lofty and self-scrutinising ambition, that strives to reconcile the integrity of general design with the perfect elaboration of each component part, that aims at striking effect, but is jealous of the means by which this is to be produced. Our poet is not averse to popularity (nay, he is tremblingly alive to it)—but self-respect is the primary law, the indispensable condition on which it must be obtained. We should dread to point out (even if we could) a false concord, a mixed metaphor, an imperfect rhyme in any of Mr. Campbell's productions; for we think that all his fame would hardly compensate to him for the discovery. He seeks for perfection, and nothing evidently short of it can satisfy his mind. He is a *high finisher* in poetry, whose every work must bear inspection, whose slightest touch is precious—not a coarse dauber who is contented to impose on public wonder and credulity by some huge, ill-executed design, or who endeavours to wear out patience and opposition together by a load of lumbering, feeble, awkward, improgressive lines—on the contrary, Mr. Campbell labours to lend every grace of execution to his subject, while he borrows his ardour and inspiration from it, and to deserve the laurels he has earned, by true genius and by true pains. There is an apparent consciousness of this in most of his writings. He has attained to great excellence by aiming at the greatest, by a cautious and yet daring selection of topics, and by studiously (and with a religious horror) avoiding all those faults which arise from grossness, vulgarity, haste, and disregard of public opinion. He seizes on the highest point of eminence, and strives to keep it to himself—he "snatches a grace beyond the reach of art, " and will not let it go—he steeps a single thought or image so deep in the Tyrian dyes of a gorgeous imagination, that it throws its lustre over a whole page—every where vivid *ideal* forms hover (in intense conception) over the poet's verse, which ascends, like the aloe, to the clouds, with pure flowers at its top. Or to take an humbler comparison (the pride of genius must sometimes stoop to the lowliness of criticism) Mr. Campbell's poetry often reminds us of the purple gilliflower, both for its colour and its scent, its glowing warmth, its rich, languid, sullen hue,

"Yet sweeter than the lids of Juno's eyes,
Or Cytherea's breath! "

There are those who complain of the little that Mr. Campbell has done in poetry, and who seem to insinuate that he is deterred by his own reputation from making any further or higher attempts. But after having produced two poems that have gone to the heart of a nation, and are gifts to a world, he may surely linger out the rest of his life in a dream of immortality. There are moments in our lives so exquisite that all that remains of them afterwards seems useless and barren; and there are lines and stanzas in our author's early writings in which he may be thought to have exhausted all the sweetness and all the essence of poetry, so that nothing farther was left to his efforts or his ambition. Happy is it for those few and fortunate worshippers of the Muse (not a subject of grudging or envy to others) who already enjoy in their life-time a foretaste of their future fame, who see their names accompanying them, like a cloud of glory, from youth to age,

"And by the vision splendid,
Are on their way attended" —

and who know that they have built a shrine for the thoughts and feelings, that were most dear to them, in the minds and memories of other men, till the language which they lisped in childhood is forgotten, or the human heart shall beat no more!

The *Pleasures of Hope* alone would not have called forth these remarks from us; but there are passages in the *Gertrude of Wyoming* of so rare and ripe a beauty, that they challenge, as they exceed all praise. Such, for instance, is the following peerless description of Gertrude's childhood: —

> "A loved bequest—and I may half impart
> To those that feel the strong paternal tie,
> How like a new existence in his heart
> That living flow'r uprose beneath his eye,
> Dear as she was, from cherub infancy,
> From hours when she would round his garden play,
> To time when as the ripening years went by,
> Her lovely mind could culture well repay,
> And more engaging grew from pleasing day to day.
>
> "I may not paint those thousand infant charms
> (Unconscious fascination, undesign'd!)
> The orison repeated in his arms,
> For God to bless her sire and all mankind;
> The book, the bosom on his knee reclined,
> Or how sweet fairy-lore he heard her con
> (The play-mate ere the teacher of her mind)
> All uncompanion'd else her years had gone,
> Till now in Gertrude's eyes their ninth blue summer shone.
>
> "And summer was the tide, and sweet the hour,
> When sire and daughter saw, with fleet descent,
> An Indian from his bark approach their bower,
> Of buskin'd limb and swarthy lineament;
> The red wild feathers on his brow were blent,
> And bracelets bound the arm that help'd to light
> A boy, who seem'd, as he beside him went,
> Of Christian vesture and complexion bright,
> Led by his dusty guide, like morning brought by night. "

In the foregoing stanzas we particularly admire the line—

"Till now in Gertrude's eyes their ninth blue summer shone. "

It appears to us like the ecstatic union of natural beauty and poetic fancy, and in its playful sublimity resembles the azure canopy mirrored in the smiling waters, bright, liquid, serene, heavenly! A great outcry, we know, has prevailed for some time past against poetic diction and affected conceits, and, to a certain degree, we go along with it; but this must not prevent us from feeling the thrill of pleasure when we see beauty linked to beauty, like kindred flame to flame, or from applauding the voluptuous fancy that raises and adorns the fairy fabric of thought, that nature has begun! Pleasure is "scattered in stray-gifts o'er the earth"—beauty streaks the "famous poet's page" in occasional lines of inconceivable brightness; and wherever this is the case, no splenetic censures or "jealous leer malign, " no idle theories or cold indifference should hinder us from greeting it with rapture. —There are other parts of this poem equally delightful, in which there is a light startling as the red-bird's wing; a perfume like that of the magnolia; a music like the murmuring of pathless woods or of the everlasting ocean. We conceive, however, that Mr. Campbell excels chiefly in sentiment and imagery. The story moves slow, and is mechanically conducted, and rather resembles a Scotch canal carried over lengthened aqueducts and with a number of *locks* in it, than one of those rivers that sweep in their majestic course, broad and full, over Transatlantic plains and lose themselves in rolling gulfs, or thunder down lofty precipices. But in the centre, the inmost recesses of our poet's heart, the pearly dew of sensibility is distilled and collects, like the diamond in the mine, and the structure of his fame rests on the crystal columns of a polished imagination. We prefer the *Gertrude* to the *Pleasures of Hope*, because with perhaps less brilliancy, there is more of tenderness and natural imagery in the former. In the *Pleasures of Hope* Mr. Campbell had not completely emancipated himself from the trammels of the more artificial style of poetry—from epigram, and antithesis, and hyperbole. The best line in it, in which earthly joys are said to be—

"Like angels' visits, few and far between"—

is a borrowed one. [A] But in the Gertrude of Wyoming "we perceive a softness coming over the heart of the author, and the scales and crust of formality that fence in his couplets and give them a somewhat glittering and rigid appearance, fall off, " and he has succeeded in engrafting the wild and more expansive interest of the romantic school of poetry on classic elegance and precision. After the poem we have just named, Mr. Campbell's SONGS are the happiest efforts of his Muse: —breathing freshness, blushing like the morn, they seem, like clustering roses, to weave a chaplet for love and liberty; or their bleeding words gush out in mournful and hurried succession, like "ruddy drops that visit the sad heart" of thoughtful Humanity. The *Battle of Hohenlinden* is of all modern compositions the most lyrical in spirit and in sound. To justify this encomium, we need only recall the lines to the reader's memory.

"On Linden, when the sun was low,
All bloodless lay th' untrodden snow,
And dark as winter was the flow
Of Iser, rolling rapidly.

But Linden saw another sight,
When the drum beat at dead of night,
Commanding fires of death to light
The darkness of her scenery.

By torch and trumpet fast array'd,
Each horseman drew his battle blade,
And furious every charger neigh'd,
To join the dreadful revelry.

Then shook the hills with thunder riv'n,
Then rush'd the steed to battle driv'n,
And louder than the bolts of heav'n
Far flash'd the red artillery.

But redder yet that light shall glow
On Linden's hills of stained snow,
And bloodier yet the torrent flow
Of Iser, rolling rapidly.

'Tis morn, but scarce yon level sun
Can pierce the war-clouds, rolling[B] dun,
Where furious Frank and fiery Hun
Shout in their sulph'rous canopy.

The combat deepens. On, ye brave,
Who rush to glory, or the grave!
Wave, Munich! all thy banners wave!
And charge with all thy chivalry!

Few, few shall part, where many meet!
The snow shall be their winding-sheet,
And every turf beneath their feet
Shall be a soldier's sepulchre. "

Mr. Campbell's prose-criticisms on contemporary and other poets (which have appeared in the New Monthly Magazine) are in a style at once chaste, temperate, guarded, and just.

Mr. Crabbe presents an entire contrast to

Mr. Campbell: —the one is the most ambitious and aspiring of living poets, the other the most humble and prosaic. If the poetry of the one is like the arch of the rainbow, spanning and adorning the earth, that of the other is like a dull, leaden cloud hanging over it. Mr. Crabbe's style might be cited as an answer to Audrey's question—"Is poetry a true thing? " There are here no ornaments, no flights of fancy, no illusions of sentiment, no tinsel of words. His song is one sad reality, one unraised, unvaried note of unavailing woe. Literal fidelity serves him in the place of invention; he assumes importance by a number of petty details; he rivets attention by being tedious. He not only deals in incessant matters of fact, but in matters of fact of the most familiar, the least animating, and the most unpleasant kind; but he relies for the effect of novelty on the microscopic minuteness with which he dissects the most trivial objects—and for the interest he excites, on the unshrinking determination with which he handles the most painful. His poetry has an official and professional air. He is called in to cases of difficult births, of fractured limbs, or breaches of the peace; and makes out a parochial list of accidents and offences. He takes the most trite, the most gross and obvious and revolting part of nature, for the subject of his elaborate descriptions; but it is Nature still, and Nature is a great and mighty Goddess! It is well for the Reverend Author that it is so. Individuality is, in his theory, the only definition of poetry. Whatever *is*, he hitches into rhyme. Whoever makes an exact image of any thing on the earth, however deformed or insignificant, according to him, must succeed—and he himself has succeeded. Mr. Crabbe is one of the most popular and admired of our living authors. That he is so, can be accounted for on no other principle than the strong ties that bind us to the world about us, and our involuntary yearnings after whatever in any manner powerfully and directly reminds us of it. His Muse is not one of *the Daughters of Memory*, but the old toothless, mumbling dame herself, doling out the gossip and scandal of the neighbourhood, recounting *totidem verbis et literis,* what happens in every place of the kingdom every hour in the year, and fastening always on the worst as the most palatable morsels. But she is a circumstantial old lady, communicative, scrupulous, leaving nothing to the imagination, harping on the smallest grievances, a village-oracle and critic, most veritable, most identical, bringing us acquainted with persons and things just as they chanced to exist, and giving us a local interest in all she knows and tells. Mr. Crabbe's Helicon is choked up with weeds and corruption; it reflects no light from heaven, it emits no cheerful sound: no flowers of love, of hope, or joy spring up near it, or they bloom only to wither in a moment. Our poet's verse does not put a spirit of youth in every thing, but a spirit of fear, despondency, and decay: it is not an electric spark to kindle or expand, but acts like the torpedo's touch to deaden or contract. It lends no dazzling tints to fancy, it aids no soothing feelings in the heart, it gladdens no prospect, it stirs no wish; in its view the current of life runs slow, dull, cold, dispirited, half under ground, muddy, and clogged with all creeping things. The world is one vast infirmary; the hill of Parnassus is a penitentiary, of which our author is the overseer: to read him is a penance, yet we read on! Mr. Crabbe, it must be confessed, is a repulsive writer. He contrives to "turn diseases to commodities, " and makes a virtue of necessity. He puts us out of conceit with this world, which perhaps a severe divine should do; yet does not, as a charitable divine ought, point to another. His morbid feelings droop and cling to the earth, grovel where they should soar; and throw a dead weight on every aspiration of the soul after the good or beautiful. By degrees we submit, and are reconciled to our fate, like patients to the physician, or prisoners in the condemned cell. We can only explain this by saying, as we said before, that Mr. Crabbe gives us one part of nature, the mean, the little, the disgusting, the distressing; that he does this thoroughly and like a master, and we forgive all the rest.

Mr. Crabbe's first poems were published so long ago as the year 1782, and received the approbation of Dr. Johnson only a little before he died. This was a testimony from an enemy; for Dr. Johnson was not an admirer of the simple in style or minute in description. Still he was an acute, strong-minded man, and could see truth when it was presented to him, even through the mist of his prejudices and his foibles. There was something in Mr. Crabbe's intricate points that did not, after all, so ill accord with the Doctor's purblind vision; and he knew quite enough of the petty ills of life to judge of the merit of our poet's descriptions, though he himself chose to slur them over in high-sounding dogmas or general invectives. Mr. Crabbe's earliest poem of the *Village* was recommended to the notice of Dr. Johnson by Sir Joshua Reynolds; and we cannot help thinking that a taste for that sort of poetry, which leans for support on the truth and fidelity of its imitations of nature, began to display itself much about that time, and, in a good measure, in consequence of the direction of the public taste to the subject of painting. Book-learning, the accumulation of wordy common-places, the gaudy pretensions of poetical fiction, had enfeebled and perverted our eye for nature. The study of the fine arts, which came into fashion about forty years ago, and was then first considered as a polite accomplishment, would tend imperceptibly to restore it. Painting is essentially an imitative art; it cannot subsist for a moment on empty generalities: the critic, therefore, who had been used to this sort of substantial entertainment, would be disposed to read poetry with the eye of a connoisseur, would be little captivated with smooth, polished, unmeaning periods, and would turn with double eagerness and relish to the force and precision of individual details, transferred, as it were, to the page from the canvas. Thus an admirer of Teniers or Hobbima might think little of the pastoral sketches of Pope or Goldsmith; even Thompson describes not so much the naked object as what he sees in his mind's eye, surrounded and glowing with the mild, bland, genial vapours of his brain: —but the adept in Dutch interiors, hovels, and pig-styes must find in Mr. Crabbe a man after his own heart. He is the very thing itself; he paints in words, instead of colours: there is no other difference. As Mr. Crabbe is not a painter, only because he does not use a brush and colours, so he is for the most part a poet, only because he writes in lines of ten syllables. All the rest might be found in a newspaper, an old magazine, or a county-register. Our author is himself a little jealous of the prudish fidelity of his homely Muse, and tries to justify himself by precedents. He brings as a parallel instance of merely literal description, Pope's lines on the gay Duke of Buckingham, beginning "In the worst inn's worst room see Villiers lies! " But surely nothing can be more dissimilar. Pope describes what is striking, Crabbe would have described merely what was there. The objects in Pope stand out to the fancy from the mixture of the mean with the gaudy, from the contrast of the scene and the character. There is an appeal to the imagination; you see what is passing in a poetical point of view. In Crabbe there is no foil, no contrast, no impulse given to the mind. It is all on a level and of a piece. In fact, there is so little connection between the subject-matter of Mr. Crabbe's lines and the ornament of rhyme which is tacked to them, that many of his verses read like serious burlesque, and the parodies which have been made upon them are hardly so quaint as the originals.

Mr. Crabbe's great fault is certainly that he is a sickly, a querulous, a uniformly dissatisfied poet. He sings the country; and he sings it in a pitiful tone. He chooses this subject only to take the charm out of it, and to dispel the illusion, the glory, and the dream, which had hovered over it in golden verse from Theocritus to Cowper. He sets out with professing to overturn the theory which had hallowed a shepherd's life, and made the names of grove and valley music to our ears, in order to give us truth in its stead; but why not lay aside the fool's cap and bells at once? Why not insist on the unwelcome reality in plain prose? If our author is a poet, why trouble himself with statistics? If he is a statistic writer, why set his ill news to harsh and grating verse? The philosopher in painting the dark side of human nature may have reason on his side, and a moral lesson or remedy in view. The tragic poet, who shews the sad vicissitudes of things and the disappointments of the passions, at least strengthens our yearnings after imaginary good, and lends wings to our desires, by which we, "at one bound, high overleap all bound" of actual suffering. But Mr. Crabbe does neither. He gives us discoloured paintings of life; helpless, repining, unprofitable, unedifying distress. He is not a philosopher, but a sophist, a misanthrope in verse; a *namby-pamby* Mandeville, a Malthus turned metrical romancer. He professes historical fidelity; but his vein is not dramatic; nor does he give us the *pros* and *cons* of that versatile gipsey, Nature. He does not indulge his fancy, or sympathise with us, or tell us how the poor feel; but how he should feel in their situation, which we do not want to know. He does not weave the web of their lives of a mingled yarn, good and ill together, but clothes them all in the same dingy linsey-woolsey, or tinges them with a green and yellow melancholy. He blocks out all possibility of good, cancels the hope, or even the wish for it as a weakness; check-mates Tityrus and Virgil at the game of pastoral cross-purposes, disables all his adversary's white pieces, and leaves none but black ones on the board. The situation of a country clergyman is not necessarily favourable to the cultivation of the Muse. He is set down, perhaps, as he thinks, in a small curacy for life, and he takes his revenge by imprisoning the reader's imagination in luckless verse. Shut out from social converse, from learned colleges and halls, where he passed his youth, he has no cordial fellow-feeling with the unlettered manners of the *Village* or the *Borough*; and he describes his neighbours as more uncomfortable and discontented than himself. All this while he dedicates successive volumes to rising generations of noble patrons; and while he desolates a line of coast with sterile, blighting lines, the only leaf of his books where honour, beauty, worth, or pleasure bloom, is that inscribed to the Rutland family! We might adduce instances of what we have said from every page of his works: let one suffice —

> "Thus by himself compelled to live each day,
> To wait for certain hours the tide's delay;
> At the same times the same dull views to see,
> The bounding marsh-bank and the blighted tree;
> The water only when the tides were high,
> When low, the mud half-covered and half-dry;
> The sun-burnt tar that blisters on the planks,
> And bank-side stakes in their uneven ranks;
> Heaps of entangled weeds that slowly float,
> As the tide rolls by the impeded boat.
> When tides were neap, and in the sultry day,
> Through the tall bounding mud-banks made their way,
> Which on each side rose swelling, and below
> The dark warm flood ran silently and slow;
> There anchoring, Peter chose from man to hide,
> There hang his head, and view the lazy tide
> In its hot slimy channel slowly glide;
> Where the small eels, that left the deeper way
> For the warm shore, within the shallows play;
> Where gaping muscles, left upon the mud,
> Slope their slow passage to the fall'n flood:
> Here dull and hopeless he'd lie down and trace
> How side-long crabs had crawled their crooked race;
> Or sadly listen to the tuneless cry
> Of fishing gull or clanging golden-eye;
> What time the sea-birds to the marsh would come,
> And the loud bittern, from the bull-rush home,
> Gave from the salt ditch-side the bellowing boom:
> He nursed the feelings these dull scenes produce
> And loved to stop beside the opening sluice;
> Where the small stream, confined in narrow bound,
> Ran with a dull, unvaried, saddening sound;
> Where all, presented to the eye or ear,
> Oppressed the soul with misery, grief, and fear. "

This is an exact *fac-simile* of some of the most unlovely parts of the creation. Indeed the whole of Mr. Crabbe's *Borough*, from which the above passage is taken, is done so to the life, that it seems almost like some sea-monster, crawled out of the neighbouring slime, and harbouring a breed of strange vermin, with a strong local scent of tar and bulge-water. Mr. Crabbe's *Tales* are more readable than his *Poems*; but in proportion as the interest increases, they become more oppressive. They turn, one and all, upon the same sort of teazing, helpless, mechanical, unimaginative distress; —and though it is not easy to lay them down, you never wish to take them up again. Still in this way, they are highly finished, striking, and original portraits, worked out with an eye to nature, and an intimate knowledge of the small and intricate folds of the human heart. Some of the best are the *Confidant*, the story of *Silly Shore*, the *Young Poet*, the *Painter*. The episode of *Phoebe Dawson* in the *Village*, is one of the most tender and pensive; and the character of the methodist parson who persecutes the sailor's widow with his godly, selfish love, is one of the most profound. In a word, if Mr. Crabbe's writings do not add greatly to the store of entertaining and delightful fiction, yet they will remain "as a thorn in the side of poetry, " perhaps for a century to come!

[Footnote A:

"Like angels' visits, short and far between. " —.
Blair's Grave.]

[Footnote B: Is not this word, which occurs in the last line but one, (as well as before) an instance of that repetition, which we so often meet with in the most correct and elegant writers?]

* * * * *

SIR JAMES MACKINTOSH.

The subject of the present article is one of the ablest and most accomplished men of the age, both as a writer, a speaker, and a converser. He is, in fact, master of almost every known topic, whether of a passing or of a more recondite nature. He has lived much in society, and is deeply conversant with books. He is a man of the world and a scholar; but the scholar gives the tone to all his other acquirements and pursuits. Sir James is by education and habit, and we were going to add, by the original turn of his mind, a college-man; and perhaps he would have passed his time most happily and respectably, had he devoted himself entirely to that kind of life. The strength of his faculties would have been best developed, his ambition would have met its proudest reward, in the accumulation and elaborate display of grave and useful knowledge. As it is, it may be said, that in company he talks well, but too much; that in writing he overlays the original subject and spirit of the composition, by an appeal to authorities and by too formal a method; that in public speaking the logician takes place of the orator, and that he fails to give effect to a particular point or to urge an immediate advantage home upon his adversary from the enlarged scope of his mind, and the wide career he takes in the field of argument.

To consider him in the last point of view, first. As a political partisan, he is rather the lecturer than the advocate. He is able to instruct and delight an impartial and disinterested audience by the extent of his information, by his acquaintance with general principles, by the clearness and aptitude of his illustrations, by vigour and copiousness of style; but where he has a prejudiced or unfair antagonist to contend with, he is just as likely to put weapons into his enemy's hands as to wrest them from him, and his object seems to be rather to deserve than to obtain success. The characteristics of his mind are retentiveness and comprehension, with facility of production: but he is not equally remarkable for originality of view, or warmth of feeling, or liveliness of fancy. His eloquence is a little rhetorical; his reasoning chiefly logical: he can bring down the account of knowledge on a vast variety of subjects to the present moment, he can embellish any cause he undertakes by the most approved and graceful ornaments, he can support it by a host of facts and examples, but he cannot advance it a step forward by placing it on a new and triumphant 'vantage-ground, nor can he overwhelm and break down the artificial fences and bulwarks of sophistry by the irresistible tide of manly enthusiasm. Sir James Mackintosh is an accomplished debater, rather than a powerful orator: he is distinguished more as a man of wonderful and variable talent than as a man of commanding intellect. His mode of treating a question is critical, and not parliamentary. It has been formed in the closet and the schools, and is hardly fitted for scenes of active life, or the collisions of party-spirit. Sir James reasons on the square; while the arguments of his opponents are loaded with iron or gold. He makes, indeed, a respectable ally, but not a very formidable opponent. He is as likely, however, to prevail on a neutral, as he is almost certain to be baffled on a hotly contested ground. On any question of general policy or legislative improvement, the Member for Nairn is heard with advantage, and his speeches are attended with effect: and he would have equal weight and influence at other times, if it were the object of the House to hear reason, as it is his aim to speak it. But on subjects of peace or war, of political rights or foreign interference, where the waves of party run high, and the liberty of nations or the fate of mankind hangs trembling in the scales, though he probably displays equal talent, and does full and heaped justice to the question (abstractedly speaking, or if it were to be tried before an impartial assembly), yet we confess we have seldom heard him, on such occasions, without pain for the event. He did not slur his own character and pretensions, but he compromised the argument. He spoke *the truth, the whole truth, and nothing but the truth*; but the House of Commons (we dare aver it) is not the place where the truth, the whole truth, and nothing but the truth can be spoken with safety or with advantage. The judgment of the House is not a balance to weigh scruples and reasons to the turn of a fraction: another element, besides the love of truth, enters into the composition of their decisions, the reaction of which must be calculated upon and guarded against. If our philosophical statesman had to open the case before a class of tyros, or a circle of grey-beards, who wished to form or to strengthen their judgments upon fair and rational grounds, nothing could be more satisfactory, more luminous, more able or more decisive than the view taken of it by Sir James Mackintosh. But the House of Commons, as a collective body, have not the docility of youth, the calm wisdom of age; and often only want an excuse to do wrong, or to adhere to what they have already determined upon; and Sir James, in detailing the inexhaustible stores of his memory and reading, in unfolding the wide range of his theory and practice, in laying down the rules and the exceptions, in insisting upon the advantages and the objections with equal explicitness, would be sure to let something drop that a dextrous and watchful adversary would easily pick up and turn against him, if this were found necessary; or if with so many *pros* and *cons*, doubts and difficulties, dilemmas and alternatives thrown into it, the scale, with its natural bias to interest and power, did not already fly up and kick the beam. There wanted unity of purpose, impetuosity of feeling to break through the phalanx of hostile and inveterate prejudice arrayed against him. He gave a handle to his enemies; threw stumbling-blocks in the way of his friends. He raised so many objections for the sake of answering them, proposed so many doubts for the sake of solving them, and made so many concessions where none were demanded, that his reasoning had the effect of neutralizing itself; it became a mere exercise of the understanding without zest or spirit left in it; and the provident engineer who was to shatter in pieces the strong-holds of corruption and oppression, by a well-directed and unsparing discharge of artillery, seemed to have brought not only his own cannon-balls, but his own wool-packs along with him to ward off the threatened mischief. This was a good deal the effect of his maiden speech on the transfer of Genoa, to which Lord Castlereagh did not deign an answer, and which another Honourable Member called "a *finical* speech. " It was a most able, candid, closely argued, and philosophical exposure of that unprincipled transaction; but for this very reason it was a solecism in the place where it was delivered. Sir James has, since this period, and with the help of practice, lowered himself to the tone of the House; and has also applied himself to questions more congenial to his habits of mind, and where the success would be more likely to be proportioned to his zeal and his exertions.

There was a greater degree of power, or of dashing and splendid effect (we wish we could add, an equally humane and liberal spirit) in the *Lectures on the Law of Nature and Nations*, formerly delivered by Sir James (then Mr.) Mackintosh, in Lincoln's-Inn Hall. He shewed greater confidence; was more at home there. The effect was more electrical and instantaneous, and this elicited a prouder display of intellectual riches, and a more animated and imposing mode of delivery. He grew wanton with success. Dazzling others by the brilliancy of his acquirements, dazzled himself by the admiration they excited, he lost fear as well as prudence; dared every thing, carried every thing before him. The Modern Philosophy, counterscarp, outworks, citadel, and all, fell without a blow, by "the whiff and wind of his fell *doctrine*, " as if it had been a pack of cards. The volcano of the French Revolution was seen expiring in its own flames, like a bon-fire made of straw: the principles of Reform were scattered in all directions, like chaff before the keen northern blast. He laid about him like one inspired; nothing could withstand his envenomed tooth. Like some savage beast got into the garden of the fabled Hesperides, he made clear work of it, root and branch, with white, foaming tusks—

"Laid waste the borders, and o'erthrew the bowers. "

The havoc was amazing, the desolation was complete. As to our visionary sceptics and Utopian philosophers, they stood no chance with our lecturer—he did not "carve them as a dish fit for the Gods, but hewed them as a carcase fit for hounds. " Poor Godwin, who had come, in the *bonhommie* and candour of his nature, to hear what new light had broken in upon his old friend, was obliged to quit the field, and slunk away after an exulting taunt thrown out at "such fanciful chimeras as a golden mountain or a perfect man. " Mr. Mackintosh had something of the air, much of the dexterity and self-possession, of a political and philosophical juggler; and an eager and admiring audience gaped and greedily swallowed the gilded bait of sophistry, prepared for their credulity and wonder. Those of us who attended day after day, and were accustomed to have all our previous notions confounded and struck out of our hands by some metaphysical legerdemain, were at last at some loss to know *whether two and two made four*, till we had heard the lecturer's opinion on that head. He might have some mental reservation on the subject, some pointed ridicule to pour upon the common supposition, some learned authority to quote against it. To anticipate the line of argument he might pursue, was evidently presumptuous and premature. One thing only appeared certain, that whatever opinion he chose to take up, he was able to make good either by the foils or the cudgels, by gross banter or nice distinctions, by a well-timed mixture of paradox and common-place, by an appeal to vulgar prejudices or startling scepticism. It seemed to be equally his object, or the tendency of his Discourses, to unsettle every principle of reason or of common sense, and to leave his audience at the mercy of the *dictum* of a lawyer, the nod of a minister, or the shout of a mob. To effect this purpose, he drew largely on the learning of antiquity, on modern literature, on history, poetry, and the belles-lettres, on the Schoolmen and on writers of novels, French, English, and Italian. In mixing up the sparkling julep, that by its potent operation was to scour away the dregs and feculence and peccant humours of the body politic, he seemed to stand with his back to the drawers in a metaphysical dispensary, and to take out of them whatever ingredients suited his purpose. In this way he had an antidote for every error, an answer to every folly. The writings of Burke, Hume, Berkeley, Paley, Lord Bacon, Jeremy Taylor, Grotius, Puffendorf, Cicero, Aristotle, Tacitus, Livy, Sully, Machiavel, Guicciardini, Thuanus, lay open beside him, and he could instantly lay his hand upon the passage, and quote them chapter and verse to the clearing up of all difficulties, and the silencing of all oppugners. Mr. Mackintosh's Lectures were after all but a kind of philosophical centos. They were profound, brilliant, new to his hearers; but the profundity, the brilliancy, the novelty were not his own. He was like Dr. Pangloss (not Voltaire's, but Coleman's) who speaks only in quotations; and the pith, the marrow of Sir James's reasoning and rhetoric at that memorable period might be put within inverted commas. It, however, served its purpose and the loud echo died away. We remember an excellent man and a sound critic[A] going to hear one of these elaborate effusions; and on his want of enthusiasm being accounted for from its not being one of the orator's brilliant days, he replied, "he did not think a man of genius could speak for two hours without saying something by which he would have been electrified. " We are only sorry, at this distance of time, for one thing in these Lectures—the tone and spirit in which they seemed to have been composed and to be delivered. If all that body of opinions and principles of which the orator read his recantation was unfounded, and there was an end of all those views and hopes that pointed to future improvement, it was not a matter of triumph or exultation to the lecturer or any body else, to the young or the old, the wise or the foolish; on the contrary, it was a subject of regret, of slow, reluctant, painful admission—

"Of lamentation loud heard through the rueful air. "

The immediate occasion of this sudden and violent change in Sir James's views and opinions was attributed to a personal interview which he had had a little before his death with Mr. Burke, at his house at Beaconsfield. In the latter end of the year 1796, appeared the *Regicide Peace*, from the pen of the great apostate from liberty and betrayer of his species into the hands of those who claimed it as their property by divine right—a work imposing, solid in many respects, abounding in facts and admirable reasoning, and in which all flashy ornaments were laid aside for a testamentary gravity, (the eloquence of despair resembling the throes and heaving and muttered threats of an earthquake, rather than the loud thunder-bolt)—and soon after came out a criticism on it in *The Monthly Review*, doing justice to the author and the style, and combating the inferences with force and at much length; but with candour and with respect, amounting to deference. It was new to Mr. Burke not to be called names by persons of the opposite party; it was an additional triumph to him to be spoken well of, to be loaded with well-earned praise by the author of the *Vindiciæ Gallicæ*. It was a testimony from an old, a powerful, and an admired antagonist. [B] He sent an invitation to the writer to come and see him; and in the course of three days' animated discussion of such subjects, Mr. Mackintosh became a convert not merely to the graces and gravity of Mr. Burke's style, but to the liberality of his views, and the solidity of his opinions. —The Lincoln's-Inn Lectures were the fruit of this interview: such is the influence exercised by men of genius and imaginative power over those who have nothing to oppose to their unforeseen flashes of thought and invention, but the dry, cold, formal deductions of the understanding. Our politician had time, during a few years of absence from his native country, and while the din of war and the cries of party-spirit "were lost over a wide and unhearing ocean, " to recover from his surprise and from a temporary alienation of mind; and to return in spirit, and in the mild and mellowed maturity of age, to the principles and attachments of his early life.

The appointment of Sir James Mackintosh to a Judgeship in India was one, which, however flattering to his vanity or favourable to his interests, was entirely foreign to his feelings and habits. It was an honourable exile. He was out of his element among black slaves and sepoys, and Nabobs and cadets, and writers to India. He had no one to exchange ideas with. The "unbought grace of life, " the charm of literary conversation was gone. It was the habit of his mind, his ruling passion to enter into the shock and conflict of opinions on philosophical, political, and critical questions—not to dictate to raw tyros or domineer over persons in subordinate situations—but to obtain the guerdon and the laurels of superior sense and information by meeting with men of equal standing, to have a fair field pitched, to argue, to distinguish, to reply, to hunt down the game of intellect with eagerness and skill, to push an advantage, to cover a retreat, to give and take a fall—

"And gladly would he learn, and gladly teach. "

It is no wonder that this sort of friendly intellectual gladiatorship is Sir James's greatest pleasure, for it is his peculiar *forte*. He has not many equals, and scarcely any superior in it. He is too indolent for an author; too unimpassioned for an orator: but in society he is just vain enough to be pleased with immediate attention, good-humoured enough to listen with patience to others, with great coolness and self-possession, fluent, communicative, and with a manner equally free from violence and insipidity. Few subjects can be started, on which he is not qualified to appear to advantage as the gentleman and scholar. If there is some tinge of pedantry, it is carried off by great affability of address and variety of amusing and interesting topics. There is scarce an author that he has not read; a period of history that he is not conversant with; a celebrated name of which he has not a number of anecdotes to relate; an intricate question that he is not prepared to enter upon in a popular or scientific manner. If an opinion in an abstruse metaphysical author is referred to, he is probably able to repeat the passage by heart, can tell the side of the page on which it is to be met with, can trace it back through various descents to Locke, Hobbes, Lord Herbert of Cherbury, to a place in some obscure folio of the School-men or a note in one of the commentators on Aristotle or Plato, and thus give you in a few moments' space, and without any effort or previous notice, a chronological table of the progress of the human mind in that particular branch of inquiry. There is something, we think, perfectly admirable and delightful in an exhibition of this kind, and which is equally creditable to the speaker and gratifying to the hearer. But this kind of talent was of no use in India: the intellectual wares, of which the Chief Judge delighted to make a display, were in no request there. He languished after the friends and the society he had left behind; and wrote over incessantly for books from England. One that was sent him at this time was an *Essay on the Principles of Human Action*; and the way in which he spoke of that dry, tough, metaphysical *choke-pear*, shewed the dearth of intellectual intercourse in which he lived, and the craving in his mind after those studies which had once been his pride, and to which he still turned for consolation in his remote solitude. —Perhaps to another, the novelty of the scene, the differences of mind and manners might have atoned for a want of social and literary *agrèmens*: but Sir James is one of those who see nature through the spectacles of books. He might like to read an account of India; but India itself with its burning, shining face would be a mere blank, an endless waste to him. To persons of this class of mind things must be translated into words, visible images into abstract propositions to meet their refined apprehensions, and they have no more to say to a matter-of-fact staring them in the face without a label in its mouth, than they would to a hippopotamus! —We may add, before we quit this point, that we cannot conceive of any two persons more different in colloquial talents, in which they both excel, than Sir James Mackintosh and Mr. Coleridge. They have nearly an equal range of reading and of topics of conversation: but in the mind of the one we see nothing but *fixtures*, in the other every thing is fluid. The ideas of the one are as formal and tangible, as those of the other are shadowy and evanescent. Sir James Mackintosh walks over the ground, Mr. Coleridge is always flying off from it. The first knows all that has been said upon a subject; the last has something to say that was never said before. If the one deals too much in learned *common-places*, the other teems with idle fancies. The one has a good deal of the *caput mortuum* of genius, the other is all volatile salt. The conversation of Sir James Mackintosh has the effect of reading a well-written book, that of his friend is like hearing a bewildered dream. The one is an Encyclopedia of knowledge, the other is a succession of *Sybilline Leaves*!

As an author, Sir James Mackintosh may claim the foremost rank among those who pride themselves on artificial ornaments and acquired learning, or who write what may be termed a *composite* style. His *Vindciae Gallicae* is a work of great labour, great ingenuity, great brilliancy, and great vigour. It is a little too antithetical in the structure of its periods, too dogmatical in the announcement of its opinions. Sir James has, we believe, rejected something of the *false brilliant* of the one, as he has retracted some of the abrupt extravagance of the other. We apprehend, however, that our author is not one of those who draw from their own resources and accumulated feelings, or who improve with age. He belongs to a class (common in Scotland and elsewhere) who get up school-exercises on any given subject in a masterly manner at twenty, and who at forty are either where they were—or retrograde, if they are men of sense and modesty. The reason is, their vanity is weaned, after the first hey-day and animal spirits of youth are flown, from making an affected display of knowledge, which, however useful, is not their own, and may be much more simply stated; they are tired of repeating the same arguments over and over again, after having exhausted and rung the changes on their whole stock for a number of times. Sir James Mackintosh is understood to be a writer in the Edinburgh Review; and the articles attributed to him there are full of matter of great pith and moment. But they want the trim, pointed expression, the ambitious ornaments, the ostentatious display and rapid volubility of his early productions. We have heard it objected to his later compositions, that his style is good as far as single words and phrases are concerned, but that his sentences are clumsy and disjointed, and that these make up still more awkward and sprawling paragraphs. This is a nice criticism, and we cannot speak to its truth: but if the fact be so, we think we can account for it from the texture and obvious process of the author's mind. All his ideas may be said to be given preconceptions. They do not arise, as it were, out of the subject, or out of one another at the moment, and therefore do not flow naturally and gracefully from one another. They have been laid down beforehand in a sort of formal division or frame-work of the understanding; and the connexion between the premises and the conclusion, between one branch of a subject and another, is made out in a bungling and unsatisfactory manner. There is no principle of fusion in the work: he strikes after the iron is cold, and there is a want of malleability in the style. Sir James is at present said to be engaged in writing a *History of England* after the downfall of the house of Stuart. May it be worthy of the talents of the author, and of the principles of the period it is intended to illustrate!

[Footnote A: The late Rev. Joseph Fawcett, of Walthamstow.]

[Footnote B: At the time when the *Vindiciae Gallicae* first made its appearance, as a reply to the *Reflections on the French Revolution*, it was cried up by the partisans of the new school, as a work superior in the charms of composition to its redoubted rival: in acuteness, depth, and soundness of reasoning, of course there was supposed to be no comparison.]

* * * * *

MR. WORDSWORTH.

Mr. Wordsworth's genius is a pure emanation of the Spirit of the Age. Had he lived in any other period of the world, he would never have been heard of. As it is, he has some difficulty to contend with the hebetude of his intellect, and the meanness of his subject. With him "lowliness is young ambition's ladder: " but he finds it a toil to climb in this way the steep of Fame. His homely Muse can hardly raise her wing from the ground, nor spread her hidden glories to the sun. He has "no figures nor no fantasies, which busy *passion* draws in the brains of men: " neither the gorgeous machinery of mythologic lore, nor the splendid colours of poetic diction. His style is vernacular: he delivers household truths. He sees nothing loftier than human hopes; nothing deeper than the human heart. This he probes, this he tampers with, this he poises, with all its incalculable weight of thought and feeling, in his hands; and at the same time calms the throbbing pulses of his own heart, by keeping his eye ever fixed on the face of nature. If he can make the life-blood flow from the wounded breast, this is the living colouring with which he paints his verse: if he can assuage the pain or close up the wound with the balm of solitary musing, or the healing power of plants and herbs and "skyey influences, " this is the sole triumph of his art. He takes the simplest elements of nature and of the human mind, the mere abstract conditions inseparable from our being, and tries to compound a new system of poetry from them; and has perhaps succeeded as well as any one could. *"Nihil humani a me alienum puto"* —is the motto of his works. He thinks nothing low or indifferent of which this can be affirmed: every thing that professes to be more than this, that is not an absolute essence of truth and feeling, he holds to be vitiated, false, and spurious. In a word, his poetry is founded on setting up an opposition (and pushing it to the utmost length) between the natural and the artificial: between the spirit of humanity, and the spirit of fashion and of the world!

It is one of the innovations of the time. It partakes of, and is carried along with, the revolutionary movement of our age: the political changes of the day were the model on which he formed and conducted his poetical experiments. His Muse (it cannot be denied, and without this we cannot explain its character at all) is a levelling one. It proceeds on a principle of equality, and strives to reduce all things to the same standard. It is distinguished by a proud humility. It relies upon its own resources, and disdains external shew and relief. It takes the commonest events and objects, as a test to prove that nature is always interesting from its inherent truth and beauty, without any of the ornaments of dress or pomp of circumstances to set it off. Hence the unaccountable mixture of seeming simplicity and real abstruseness in the *Lyrical Ballads*. Fools have laughed at, wise men scarcely understand them. He takes a subject or a story merely as pegs or loops to hang thought and feeling on; the incidents are trifling, in proportion to his contempt for imposing appearances; the reflections are profound, according to the gravity and the aspiring pretensions of his mind. His popular, inartificial style gets rid (at a blow) of all the trappings of verse, of all the high places of poetry: "the cloud-capt towers, the solemn temples, the gorgeous palaces, " are swept to the ground, and "like the baseless fabric of a vision, leave not a wreck behind. " All the traditions of learning, all the superstitions of age, are obliterated and effaced. We begin *de novo*, on a *tabula rasa* of poetry. The purple pall, the nodding plume of tragedy are exploded as mere pantomime and trick, to return to the simplicity of truth and nature. Kings, queens, priests, nobles, the altar and the throne, the distinctions of rank, birth, wealth, power, "the judge's robe, the marshall's truncheon, the ceremony that to great ones 'longs, " are not to be found here. The author tramples on the pride of art with greater pride. The Ode and Epode, the Strophe and the Antistrophe, he laughs to scorn. The harp of Homer, the trump of Pindar and of Alcaeus are still. The decencies of costume, the decorations of vanity are stripped off without mercy as barbarous, idle, and Gothic. The jewels in the crisped hair, the diadem on the polished brow are thought meretricious, theatrical, vulgar; and nothing contents his fastidious taste beyond a simple garland of flowers. Neither does he avail himself of the advantages which nature or accident holds out to him. He chooses to have his subject a foil to his invention, to owe nothing but to himself. He gathers manna in the wilderness, he strikes the barren rock for the gushing moisture. He elevates the mean by the strength of his own aspirations; he clothes the naked with beauty and grandeur from the store of his own recollections. No cypress-grove loads his verse with perfumes: but his imagination lends a sense of joy

> "To the bare trees and mountains bare,
> And grass in the green field. "

No storm, no shipwreck startles us by its horrors: but the rainbow lifts its head in the cloud, and the breeze sighs through the withered fern. No sad vicissitude of fate, no overwhelming catastrophe in nature deforms his page: but the dew-drop glitters on the bending flower, the tear collects in the glistening eye.

"Beneath the hills, along the flowery vales,
The generations are prepared; the pangs,
The internal pangs are ready; the dread strife
Of poor humanity's afflicted will,
Struggling in vain with ruthless destiny. "

As the lark ascends from its low bed on fluttering wing, and salutes the morning skies; so Mr. Wordsworth's unpretending Muse, in russet guise, scales the summits of reflection, while it makes the round earth its footstool, and its home!

Possibly a good deal of this may be regarded as the effect of disappointed views and an inverted ambition. Prevented by native pride and indolence from climbing the ascent of learning or greatness, taught by political opinions to say to the vain pomp and glory of the world, "I hate ye, " seeing the path of classical and artificial poetry blocked up by the cumbrous ornaments of style and turgid *common-places*, so that nothing more could be achieved in that direction but by the most ridiculous bombast or the tamest servility; he has turned back partly from the bias of his mind, partly perhaps from a judicious policy—has struck into the sequestered vale of humble life, sought out the Muse among sheep-cotes and hamlets and the peasant's mountain-haunts, has discarded all the tinsel pageantry of verse, and endeavoured (not in vain) to aggrandise the trivial and add the charm of novelty to the familiar. No one has shewn the same imagination in raising trifles into importance: no one has displayed the same pathos in treating of the simplest feelings of the heart. Reserved, yet haughty, having no unruly or violent passions, (or those passions having been early suppressed,) Mr. Wordsworth has passed his life in solitary musing, or in daily converse with the face of nature. He exemplifies in an eminent degree the power of *association*; for his poetry has no other source or character. He has dwelt among pastoral scenes, till each object has become connected with a thousand feelings, a link in the chain of thought, a fibre of his own heart. Every one is by habit and familiarity strongly attached to the place of his birth, or to objects that recal the most pleasing and eventful circumstances of his life. But to the author of the *Lyrical Ballads*, nature is a kind of home; and he may be said to take a personal interest in the universe. There is no image so insignificant that it has not in some mood or other found the way into his heart: no sound that does not awaken the memory of other years. —

"To him the meanest flower that blows can give
Thoughts that do often lie too deep for tears. "

The daisy looks up to him with sparkling eye as an old acquaintance: the cuckoo haunts him with sounds of early youth not to be expressed: a linnet's nest startles him with boyish delight: an old withered thorn is weighed down with a heap of recollections: a grey cloak, seen on some wild moor, torn by the wind, or drenched in the rain, afterwards becomes an object of imagination to him: even the lichens on the rock have a life and being in his thoughts. He has described all these objects in a way and with an intensity of feeling that no one else had done before him, and has given a new view or aspect of nature. He is in this sense the most original poet now living, and the one whose writings could the least be spared: for they have no substitute elsewhere. The vulgar do not read them, the learned, who see all things through books, do not understand them, the great despise, the fashionable may ridicule them: but the author has created himself an interest in the heart of the retired and lonely student of nature, which can never die. Persons of this class will still continue to feel what he has felt: he has expressed what they might in vain wish to express, except with glistening eye and faultering tongue! There is a lofty philosophic tone, a thoughtful humanity, infused into his pastoral vein. Remote from the passions and events of the great world, he has communicated interest and dignity to the primal movements of the heart of man, and ingrafted his own conscious reflections on the casual thoughts of hinds and shepherds. Nursed amidst the grandeur of mountain scenery, he has stooped to have a nearer view of the daisy under his feet, or plucked a branch of white-thorn from the spray: but in describing it, his mind seems imbued with the majesty and solemnity of the objects around him— the tall rock lifts its head in the erectness of his spirit; the cataract roars in the sound of his verse; and in its dim and mysterious meaning, the mists seem to gather in the hollows of Helvellyn, and the forked Skiddaw hovers in the distance. There is little mention of mountainous scenery in Mr. Wordsworth's poetry; but by internal evidence one might be almost sure that it was written in a mountainous country, from its bareness, its simplicity, its loftiness and its depth!

His later philosophic productions have a somewhat different character. They are a departure from, a dereliction of his first principles. They are classical and courtly. They are polished in style, without being gaudy; dignified in subject, without affectation. They seem to have been composed not in a cottage at Grasmere, but among the half-inspired groves and stately recollections of Cole-Orton. We might allude in particular, for examples of what we mean, to the lines on a Picture by Claude Lorraine, and to the exquisite poem, entitled *Laodamia*. The last of these breathes the pure spirit of the finest fragments of antiquity—the sweetness, the gravity, the strength, the beauty and the langour of death—

"Calm contemplation and majestic pains. "

Its glossy brilliancy arises from the perfection of the finishing, like that of careful sculpture, not from gaudy colouring—the texture of the thoughts has the smoothness and solidity of marble. It is a poem that might be read aloud in Elysium, and the spirits of departed heroes and sages would gather round to listen to it! Mr. Wordsworth's philosophic poetry, with a less glowing aspect and less tumult in the veins than Lord Byron's on similar occasions, bends a calmer and keener eye on mortality; the impression, if less vivid, is more pleasing and permanent; and we confess it (perhaps it is a want of taste and proper feeling) that there are lines and poems of our author's, that we think of ten times for once that we recur to any of Lord Byron's. Or if there are any of the latter's writings, that we can dwell upon in the same way, that is, as lasting and heart-felt sentiments, it is when laying aside his usual pomp and pretension, he descends with Mr. Wordsworth to the common ground of a disinterested humanity. It may be considered as characteristic of our poet's writings, that they either make no impression on the mind at all, seem mere *nonsense-verses*, or that they leave a mark behind them that never wears out. They either

"Fall blunted from the indurated breast" —

without any perceptible result, or they absorb it like a passion. To one class of readers he appears sublime, to another (and we fear the largest) ridiculous. He has probably realised Milton's wish, —"and fit audience found, though few: " but we suspect he is not reconciled to the alternative. There are delightful passages in the EXCURSION, both of natural description and of inspired reflection (passages of the latter kind that in the sound of the thoughts and of the swelling language resemble heavenly symphonies, mournful *requiems* over the grave of human hopes); but we must add, in justice and in sincerity, that we think it impossible that this work should ever become popular, even in the same degree as the *Lyrical Ballads*. It affects a system without having any intelligible clue to one; and instead of unfolding a principle in various and striking lights, repeats the same conclusions till they become flat and insipid. Mr. Wordsworth's mind is obtuse, except as it is the organ and the receptacle of accumulated feelings: it is not analytic, but synthetic; it is reflecting, rather than theoretical. The EXCURSION, we believe, fell stillborn from the press. There was something abortive, and clumsy, and ill-judged in the attempt. It was long and laboured. The personages, for the most part, were low, the fare rustic: the plan raised expectations which were not fulfilled, and the effect was like being ushered into a stately hall and invited to sit down to a splendid banquet in the company of clowns, and with nothing but successive courses of apple-dumplings served up. It was not even *toujours perdrix*!

Mr. Wordsworth, in his person, is above the middle size, with marked features, and an air somewhat stately and Quixotic. He reminds one of some of Holbein's heads, grave, saturnine, with a slight indication of sly humour, kept under by the manners of the age or by the pretensions of the person. He has a peculiar sweetness in his smile, and great depth and manliness and a rugged harmony, in the tones of his voice. His manner of reading his own poetry is particularly imposing; and in his favourite passages his eye beams with preternatural lustre, and the meaning labours slowly up from his swelling breast. No one who has seen him at these moments could go away with an impression that he was a "man of no mark or likelihood. " Perhaps the comment of his face and voice is necessary to convey a full idea of his poetry. His language may not be intelligible, but his manner is not to be mistaken. It is clear that he is either mad or inspired. In company, even in a *tête-à-tête*, Mr. Wordsworth is often silent, indolent, and reserved. If he is become verbose and oracular of late years, he was not so in his better days. He threw out a bold or an indifferent remark without either effort or pretension, and relapsed into musing again. He shone most (because he seemed most roused and animated) in reciting his own poetry, or in talking about it. He sometimes gave striking views of his feelings and trains of association in composing certain passages; or if one did not always understand his distinctions, still there was no want of interest — there was a latent meaning worth inquiring into, like a vein of ore that one Cannot exactly hit upon at the moment, but of which there are sure indications. His standard of poetry is high and severe, almost to exclusiveness. He admits of nothing below, scarcely of any thing above himself. It is fine to hear him talk of the way in which certain subjects should have been treated by eminent poets, according to his notions of the art. Thus he finds fault with Dryden's description of Bacchus in the *Alexander's Feast*, as if he were a mere good-looking youth, or boon companion—

> "Flushed with a purple grace,
> He shews his honest face" —

instead of representing the God returning from the conquest of India, crowned with vine-leaves, and drawn by panthers, and followed by troops of satyrs, of wild men and animals that he had tamed. You would thank, in hearing him speak on this subject, that you saw Titian's picture of the meeting of *Bacchus and Ariadne*—so classic were his conceptions, so glowing his style. Milton is his great idol, and he sometimes dares to compare himself with him. His Sonnets, indeed, have something of the same high-raised tone and prophetic spirit. Chaucer is another prime favourite of his, and he has been at the pains to modernise some of the Canterbury Tales. Those persons who look upon Mr. Wordsworth as a merely puerile writer, must be rather at a loss to account for his strong predilection for such geniuses as Dante and Michael Angelo. We do not think our author has any very cordial sympathy with Shakespear. How should he? Shakespear was the least of an egotist of any body in the world. He does not much relish the variety and scope of dramatic composition. "He hates those interlocutions between Lucius and Caius. " Yet Mr. Wordsworth himself wrote a tragedy when he was young; and we have heard the following energetic lines quoted from it, as put into the mouth of a person smit with remorse for some rash crime:

> ——"Action is momentary,
> The motion of a muscle this way or that;
> Suffering is long, obscure, and infinite! "

Perhaps for want of light and shade, and the unshackled spirit of the drama, this performance was never brought forward. Our critic has a great dislike to Gray, and a fondness for Thomson and Collins. It is mortifying to hear him speak of Pope and Dryden, whom, because they have been supposed to have all the possible excellences of poetry, he will allow to have none. Nothing, however, can be fairer, or more amusing, than the way in which he sometimes exposes the unmeaning verbiage of modern poetry. Thus, in the beginning of Dr. Johnson's *Vanity of Human Wishes*—

> "Let observation with extensive view
> Survey mankind from China to Peru"—

he says there is a total want of imagination accompanying the words, the same idea is repeated three times under the disguise of a different phraseology: it comes to this—"let *observation*, with extensive *observation, observe* mankind; " or take away the first line, and the second,

> "Survey mankind from China to Peru, "

literally conveys the whole. Mr. Wordsworth is, we must say, a perfect Drawcansir as to prose writers. He complains of the dry reasoners and matter-of-fact people for their want of *passion*; and he is jealous of the rhetorical declaimers and rhapsodists as trenching on the province of poetry. He condemns all French writers (as well of poetry as prose) in the lump. His list in this way is indeed small. He approves of Walton's Angler, Paley, and some other writers of an inoffensive modesty of pretension. He also likes books of voyages and travels, and Robinson Crusoe. In art, he greatly esteems Bewick's wood-cuts, and Waterloo's sylvan etchings. But he sometimes takes a higher tone, and gives his mind fair play. We have known him enlarge with a noble intelligence and enthusiasm on Nicolas Poussin's fine landscape-compositions, pointing out the unity of design that pervades them, the superintending mind, the imaginative principle that brings all to bear on the same end; and declaring he would not give a rush for any landscape that did not express the time of day, the climate, the period of the world it was meant to illustrate, or had not this character of *wholeness* in it. His eye also does justice to Rembrandt's fine and masterly effects. In the way in which that artist works something out of nothing, and transforms the stump of a tree, a common figure into an *ideal* object, by the gorgeous light and shade thrown upon it, he perceives an analogy to his own mode of investing the minute details of nature with an atmosphere of sentiment; and in pronouncing Rembrandt to be a man of genius, feels that he strengthens his own claim to the title. It has been said of Mr. Wordsworth, that "he hates conchology, that he hates the Venus of Medicis. " But these, we hope, are mere epigrams and *jeux-d'esprit*, as far from truth as they are free from malice; a sort of running satire or critical clenches—

"Where one for sense and one for rhyme
Is quite sufficient at one time. "

We think, however, that if Mr. Wordsworth had been a more liberal and candid critic, he would have been a more sterling writer. If a greater number of sources of pleasure had been open to him, he would have communicated pleasure to the world more frequently. Had he been less fastidious in pronouncing sentence on the works of others, his own would have been received more favourably, and treated more leniently. The current of his feelings is deep, but narrow; the range of his understanding is lofty and aspiring rather than discursive. The force, the originality, the absolute truth and identity with which he feels some things, makes him indifferent to so many others. The simplicity and enthusiasm of his feelings, with respect to nature, renders him bigotted and intolerant in his judgments of men and things. But it happens to him, as to others, that his strength lies in his weakness; and perhaps we have no right to complain. We might get rid of the cynic and the egotist, and find in his stead a common-place man. We should "take the good the Gods provide us: " a fine and original vein of poetry is not one of their most contemptible gifts, and the rest is scarcely worth thinking of, except as it may be a mortification to those who expect perfection from human nature; or who have been idle enough at some period of their lives, to deify men of genius as possessing claims above it. But this is a chord that jars, and we shall not dwell upon it.

Lord Byron we have called, according to the old proverb, "the spoiled child of fortune: " Mr. Wordsworth might plead, in mitigation of some peculiarities, that he is "the spoiled child of disappointment. " We are convinced, if he had been early a popular poet, he would have borne his honours meekly, and would have been a person of great *bonhommie* and frankness of disposition. But the sense of injustice and of undeserved ridicule sours the temper and narrows the views. To have produced works of genius, and to find them neglected or treated with scorn, is one of the heaviest trials of human patience. We exaggerate our own merits when they are denied by others, and are apt to grudge and cavil at every particle of praise bestowed on those to whom we feel a conscious superiority. In mere self-defence we turn against the world, when it turns against us; brood over the undeserved slights we receive; and thus the genial current of the soul is stopped, or vents itself in effusions of petulance and self-conceit. Mr. Wordsworth has thought too much of contemporary critics and criticism; and less than he ought of the award of posterity, and of the opinion, we do not say of private friends, but of those who were made so by their admiration of his genius. He did not court popularity by a conformity to established models, and he ought not to have been surprised that his originality was not understood as a matter of course. He has *gnawed too much on the bridle*; and has often thrown out crusts to the critics, in mere defiance or as a point of honour when he was challenged, which otherwise his own good sense would have withheld. We suspect that Mr. Wordsworth's feelings are a little morbid in this respect, or that he resents censure more than he is gratified by praise. Otherwise, the tide has turned much in his favour of late years—he has a large body of determined partisans—and is at present sufficiently in request with the public to save or relieve him from the last necessity to which a man of genius can be reduced—that of becoming the God of his own idolatry!

* * * * *

MR. MALTHUS.

Mr. Malthus may be considered as one of those rare and fortunate writers who have attained a *scientific* reputation in questions of moral and political philosophy. His name undoubtedly stands very high in the present age, and will in all probability go down to posterity with more or less of renown or obloquy. It was said by a person well qualified to judge both from strength and candour of mind, that "it would take a thousand years at least to answer his work on Population. " He has certainly thrown a new light on that question, and changed the aspect of political economy in a decided and material point of view — whether he has not also endeavoured to spread a gloom over the hopes and more sanguine speculations of man, and to cast a slur upon the face of nature, is another question. There is this to be said for Mr. Malthus, that in speaking of him, one knows what one is talking about. He is something beyond a mere name — one has not to *beat the bush* about his talents, his attainments, his vast reputation, and leave off without knowing what it all amounts to — he is not one of those great men, who set themselves off and strut and fret an hour upon the stage, during a day-dream of popularity, with the ornaments and jewels borrowed from the common stock, to which nothing but their vanity and presumption gives them the least individual claim — he has dug into the mine of truth, and brought up ore mixed with dross! In weighing his merits we come at once to the question of what he has done or failed to do. It is a specific claim that he sets up. When we speak of Mr. Malthus, we mean the *Essay on Population*; and when we mention the Essay on Population, we mean a distinct leading proposition, that stands out intelligibly from all trashy pretence, and is a ground on which to fix the levers that may move the world, backwards or forwards. He has not left opinion where he found it; he has advanced or given it a wrong bias, or thrown a stumbling-block in its way. In a word, his name is not stuck, like so many others, in the firmament of reputation, nobody knows why, inscribed in great letters, and with a transparency of TALENTS, GENIUS, LEARNING blazing round it — it is tantamount to an idea, it is identified with a principle, it means that *the population cannot go on perpetually increasing without pressing on the limits of the means of subsistence, and that a check of some kind or other must, sooner or later, be opposed to it.* This is the essence of the doctrine which Mr. Malthus has been the first to bring into general notice, and as we think, to establish beyond the fear of contradiction. Admitting then as we do the prominence and the value of his claims to public attention, it yet remains a question, how far those claims are (as to the talent displayed in them) strictly original; how far (as to the logical accuracy with which he has treated the subject) he has introduced foreign and doubtful matter into it; and how far (as to the spirit in which he has conducted his inquiries, and applied a general principle to particular objects) he has only drawn fair and inevitable conclusions from it, or endeavoured to tamper with and wrest it to sinister and servile purposes. A writer who shrinks from following up a well-founded principle into its untoward consequences from timidity or false delicacy, is not worthy of the name of a philosopher: a writer who assumes the garb of candour and an inflexible love of truth to garble and pervert it, to crouch to power and pander to prejudice, deserves a worse title than that of a sophist!

Mr. Malthus's first octavo volume on this subject (published in the year 1798) was intended as an answer to Mr. Godwin's *Enquiry concerning Political Justice*. It was well got up for the purpose, and had an immediate effect. It was what in the language of the ring is called *a facer*. It made Mr. Godwin and the other advocates of Modern Philosophy look about them. It may be almost doubted whether Mr. Malthus was in the first instance serious in many things that he threw out, or whether he did not hazard the whole as an amusing and extreme paradox, which might puzzle the reader as it had done himself in an idle moment, but to which no practical consequence whatever could attach. This state of mind would probably continue till the irritation of enemies and the encouragement of friends convinced him that what he had at first exhibited as an idle fancy was in fact a very valuable discovery, or "like the toad ugly and venomous, had yet a precious jewel in its head. " Such a supposition would at least account for some things in the original Essay, which scarcely any writer would venture upon, except as professed exercises of ingenuity, and which have been since in part retracted. But a wrong bias was thus given, and the author's theory was thus rendered warped, disjointed, and sophistical from the very outset.

Nothing could in fact be more illogical (not to say absurd) than the whole of Mr. Malthus's reasoning applied as an answer (*par excellence*) to Mr. Godwin's book, or to the theories of other Utopian philosophers. Mr. Godwin was not singular, but was kept in countenance by many authorities, both ancient and modern, in supposing a state of society possible in which the passions and wills of individuals would be conformed to the general good, in which the

111

knowledge of the best means of promoting human welfare and the desire of contributing to it would banish vice and misery from the world, and in which, the stumbling-blocks of ignorance, of selfishness, and the indulgence of gross appetite being removed, all things would move on by the mere impulse of wisdom and virtue, to still higher and higher degrees of perfection and happiness. Compared with the lamentable and gross deficiencies of existing institutions, such a view of futurity as barely possible could not fail to allure the gaze and tempt the aspiring thoughts of the philanthropist and the philosopher: the hopes and the imaginations of speculative men could not but rush forward into this ideal world as into a *vacuum* of good; and from "the mighty stream of tendency" (as Mr. Wordsworth in the cant of the day calls it,) there was danger that the proud monuments of time-hallowed institutions, that the strong-holds of power and corruption, that "the Corinthian capitals of polished society, " with the base and pediments, might be overthrown and swept away as by a hurricane. There were not wanting persons whose ignorance, whose fears, whose pride, or whose prejudices contemplated such an alternative with horror; and who would naturally feel no small obligation to the man who should relieve their apprehensions from the stunning roar of this mighty change of opinion that thundered at a distance, and should be able, by some logical apparatus or unexpected turn of the argument, to prevent the vessel of the state from being hurried forward with the progress of improvement, and dashed in pieces down the tremendous precipice of human perfectibility. Then comes Mr. Malthus forward with the geometrical and arithmetical ratios in his hands, and holds them out to his affrighted contemporaries as the only means of salvation. "For" (so argued the author of the Essay) "let the principles of Mr. Godwin's Enquiry and of other similar works be carried literally and completely into effect; let every corruption and abuse of power be entirely got rid of; let virtue, knowledge, and civilization be advanced to the greatest height that these visionary reformers would suppose; let the passions and appetites be subjected to the utmost control of reason and influence of public opinion: grant them, in a word, all that they ask, and the more completely their views are realized, the sooner will they be overthrown again, and the more inevitable and fatal will be the catastrophe. For the principle of population will still prevail, and from the comfort, ease, and plenty that will abound, will receive an increasing force and *impetus*; the number of mouths to be fed will have no limit, but the food that is to supply them cannot keep pace with the demand for it; we must come to a stop somewhere, even though each square yard, by extreme improvements in cultivation, could maintain its man: in this state of things there will be no remedy, the wholesome checks of vice and misery (which have hitherto kept this principle within bounds) will have been done away; the voice of reason will be unheard; the passions only will bear sway; famine, distress, havoc, and dismay will spread around; hatred, violence, war, and bloodshed will be the infallible consequence, and from the pinnacle of happiness, peace, refinement, and social advantage, we shall be hurled once more into a profounder abyss of misery, want, and barbarism than ever, by the sole operation of the principle of population! "—Such is a brief abstract of the argument of the Essay. Can any thing be less conclusive, a more complete fallacy and *petitio principii*? Mr. Malthus concedes, he assumes a state of perfectibility, such as his opponents imagined, in which the general good is to obtain the entire mastery of individual interests, and reason of gross appetites and passions; and then he argues that such a perfect structure of society will fall by its own weight, or rather be undermined by the principle of population, because in the highest possible state of the subjugation of the passions to reason, they will be absolutely lawless and unchecked, and because as men become enlightened, quick sighted and public-spirited, they will shew themselves utterly blind to the consequences of their actions, utterly indifferent to their own well-being and that of all succeeding generations, whose fate is placed in their hands. This we conceive to be the boldest paralogism that ever was offered to the world, or palmed upon willing credulity. Against whatever other scheme of reform this objection might be valid, the one it was brought expressly to overturn was impregnable against it, invulnerable to its slightest graze. Say that the Utopian reasoners are visionaries, unfounded; that the state of virtue and knowledge they suppose, in which reason shall have become all-in-all, can never take place, that it is inconsistent with the nature of man and with all experience, well and good—but to say that society will have attained this high and "palmy state, " that reason will have become the master- key to all our motives, and that when arrived at its greatest power it will cease to act at all, but will fall down dead, inert, and senseless before the principle of population, is an opinion which one would think few people would choose to advance or assent to, without strong inducements for maintaining or believing it.

The fact, however, is, that Mr. Malthus found this argument entire (the principle and the application of it) in an obscure and almost forgotten work published about the middle of the last century, entitled *Various Prospects of Mankind, Nature, and Providence,* by a Scotch gentleman of the name of Wallace. The chapter in this work on the Principle of Population, considered as a bar to all ultimate views of human improvement, was probably written to amuse an idle hour, or read as a paper to exercise the wits of some literary society in the Northern capital, and no farther responsibility or importance annexed to it. Mr. Malthus, by adopting and setting his name to it, has given it sufficient currency and effect. It sometimes happens that one writer is the first to discover a certain principle or lay down a given observation, and that another makes an application of, or draws a remote or an immediate inference from it, totally unforeseen by the first, and from which, in all probability, he might have widely dissented. But this is not so in the present instance. Mr. Malthus has borrowed (perhaps without consciousness, at any rate without acknowledgment) both the preliminary statement, that the increase in the supply of food "from a limited earth and a limited fertility" must have an end, while the tendency to increase in the principle of population has none, without some external and forcible restraint on it, and the subsequent use made of this statement as an insuperable bar to all schemes of Utopian or progressive improvement—both these he has borrowed (whole) from Wallace, with all their imperfections on their heads, and has added more and greater ones to them out of his own store. In order to produce something of a startling and dramatic effect, he has strained a point or two. In order to quell and frighten away the bugbear of Modern Philosophy, he was obliged to make a sort of monster of the principle of population, which was brought into the field against it, and which was to swallow it up quick. No half-measures, no middle course of reasoning would do. With a view to meet the highest possible power of reason in the new order of things, Mr. Malthus saw the necessity of giving the greatest possible physical weight to the antagonist principle, and he accordingly lays it down that its operation is mechanical and irresistible. He premises these two propositions as the basis of all his reasoning, 1. *That food is necessary to man*; 2. *That the desire to propagate the species is an equally indispensable law of our existence*: —thus making it appear that these two wants or impulses are equal and coordinate principles of action. If this double statement had been true, the whole scope and structure of his reasoning (as hostile to human hopes and sanguine speculations) would have been irrefragable; but as it is not true, the whole (in that view) falls to the ground. According to Mr. Malthus's octavo edition, the sexual passion is as necessary to be gratified as the appetite of hunger, and a man can no more exist without propagating his species than he can live without eating. Were it so, neither of these passions would admit of any excuses, any delay, any restraint from reason or foresight; and the only checks to the principle of population must be vice and misery. The argument would be triumphant and complete. But there is no analogy, no parity in the two cases, such as our author here assumes. No man can live for any length of time without food; many persons live all their lives without gratifying the other sense. The longer the craving after food is unsatisfied, the more violent, imperious, and uncontroulable the desire becomes; whereas the longer the gratification of the sexual passion is resisted, the greater force does habit and resolution acquire over it; and, generally speaking, it is a well-known fact, attested by all observation and history, that this latter passion is subject more or less to controul from personal feelings and character, from public opinions and the institutions of society, so as to lead either to a lawful and regulated indulgence, or to partial or total abstinence, according to the dictates of *moral restraint*, which latter check to the inordinate excesses and unheard-of consequences of the principle of population, our author, having no longer an extreme case to make out, admits and is willing to patronize in addition to the two former and exclusive ones of *vice and misery*, in the second and remaining editions of his work. Mr. Malthus has shewn some awkwardness or even reluctance in softening down the harshness of his first peremptory decision. He sometimes grants his grand exception cordially, proceeds to argue stoutly, and to try conclusions upon it; at other times he seems disposed to cavil about or retract it: — "the influence of moral restraint is very inconsiderable, or none at all. " It is indeed difficult (more particularly for so formal and nice a reasoner as Mr. Malthus) to piece such contradictions plausibly or gracefully together. We wonder how *he* manages it—how *any one* should attempt it! The whole question, the *gist* of the argument of his early volume turned upon this, "Whether vice and misery were the *only* actual or possible checks to the principle of population? " He then said they were, and farewell to building castles in the air: he now says that *moral restraint* is to be coupled with these, and that its influence depends greatly on the state of laws and manners—and Utopia stands where it did, a great way off indeed, but not turned *topsy-turvy* by our magician's wand! Should we ever arrive there, that is, attain to a state of *perfect moral restraint*, we shall not be driven headlong back into Epicurus's stye for want of the only possible checks to population, *vice and misery*; and in proportion as we advance that way, that is, as the influence of moral restraint is extended, the necessity for vice and misery will be diminished, instead of being increased according to the first alarm given by the Essay. Again, the advance of civilization and of population in consequence with the same degree of moral restraint (as there exists in England at this present time, for instance) is a good, and not an evil—but this does not appear from the Essay. The Essay shews that population is not (as had been sometimes taken for granted) an abstract and unqualified good; but it led many persons to suppose that it was an abstract and unqualified evil, to be checked only by vice and misery, and producing, according to its encouragement a greater quantity of vice and misery; and this error the author has not been at sufficient pains to do away. Another thing, in which Mr. Malthus attempted to *clench* Wallace's argument, was in giving to the disproportionate power of increase in the principle of population and the supply of food a mathematical form, or reducing it to the arithmetical and geometrical ratios, in which we believe Mr. Malthus is now generally admitted, even by his friends and admirers, to have been wrong. There is evidently no inherent difference in the principle of increase in food or population; since a grain of corn, for example, will propagate and multiply itself much faster even than the human species. A bushel of wheat will sow a field; that field will furnish seed for twenty others. So that the limit to the means of subsistence is only the want of room to raise it in, or, as Wallace expresses it, "a limited fertility and a limited earth. " Up to the point where the earth or any given country is fully occupied or cultivated, the means of subsistence naturally increase in a geometrical ratio, and will more than keep pace with the natural and unrestrained progress of population; and beyond that point, they do not go on increasing even in Mr. Malthus's arithmetical ratio, but are stationary or nearly so. So far, then, is this proportion from being universally and mathematically true, that in no part of the world or state of society does it hold good. But our theorist, by laying down this double ratio as a law of nature, gains this advantage, that at all times it seems as if, whether in new or old-peopled countries, in fertile or barren soils, the population was pressing hard on the means of subsistence; and again, it seems as if the evil increased with the progress of improvement and civilization; for if you cast your eye at the scale which is supposed to be calculated upon true and infallible *data*, you find that when the population is at 8, the means of subsistence are at 4; so that here there is only a *deficit* of one half; but when it is at 32, they have only got to 6, so that here there is a difference of 26 in 32, and so on in proportion; the farther we proceed, the more enormous is the mass of vice and misery we must undergo, as a consequence of the natural excess of the population over the means of subsistence and as a salutary check to its farther desolating progress. The mathematical Table, placed at the front of the Essay, therefore leads to a secret suspicion or a bare-faced assumption, that we ought in mere kindness and compassion to give every sort of indirect and under-hand encouragement (to say the least) to the providential checks of vice and misery; as the sooner we arrest this formidable and paramount evil in its course, the less opportunity we leave it of doing incalculable mischief. Accordingly, whenever there is the least talk of colonizing new countries, of extending the population, or adding to social comforts and improvements, Mr. Malthus conjures up his double ratios, and insists on the alarming results of advancing them a single step forward in the series. By the same rule, it would be better to return at once to a state of barbarism; and to take the benefit of acorns and scuttle-fish, as a security against the luxuries and wants of civilized life. But it is not our ingenious author's wish to hint at or recommend any alterations in existing institutions; and he is therefore silent on that unpalatable part of the subject and natural inference from his principles.

Mr. Malthus's "gospel is preached to the poor. " He lectures them on economy, on morality, the regulation of their passions (which, he says, at other times, are amenable to no restraint) and on the ungracious topic, that "the laws of nature, which are the laws of God, have doomed them and their families to starve for want of a right to the smallest portion of food beyond what their labour will supply, or some charitable hand may hold out in compassion. " This is illiberal, and it is not philosophical. The laws of nature or of God, to which the author appeals, are no other than a limited fertility and a limited earth. Within those bounds, the rest is regulated by the laws of man. The division of the produce of the soil, the price of labour, the relief afforded to the poor, are matters of human arrangement: while any charitable hand can extend relief, it is a proof that the means of subsistence are not exhausted in themselves, that "the tables are not full! " Mr. Malthus says that the laws of nature, which are the laws of God, have rendered that relief physically impossible; and yet he would abrogate the poor-laws by an act of the legislature, in order to take away that *impossible* relief, which the laws of God deny, and which the laws of man *actually* afford. We cannot think that this view of his subject, which is prominent and dwelt on at great length and with much pertinacity, is dictated either by rigid logic or melting charity! A labouring man is not allowed to knock down a hare or a partridge that spoils his garden: a country-squire keeps a pack of hounds: a lady of quality rides out with a footman behind her, on two sleek, well-fed horses. We have not a word to say against all this as exemplifying the spirit of the English Constitution, as a part of the law of the land, or as an artful distribution of light and shade in the social picture; but if any one insists at the same time that "the laws of nature, which are the laws of God, have doomed the poor and their families to starve, " because the principle of population has encroached upon and swallowed up the means of subsistence, so that not a mouthful of food is left *by the grinding law of necessity* for the poor, we beg leave to deny both fact and inference—and we put it to Mr. Malthus whether we are not, in strictness, justified in doing so?

We have, perhaps, said enough to explain our feeling on the subject of Mr. Malthus's merits and defects. We think he had the opportunity and the means in his hands of producing a great work on the principle of population; but we believe he has let it slip from his having an eye to other things besides that broad and unexplored question. He wished not merely to advance to the discovery of certain great and valuable truths, but at the same time to overthrow certain unfashionable paradoxes by exaggerated statements—to curry favour with existing prejudices and interests by garbled representations. He has, in a word, as it appears to us on a candid retrospect and without any feelings of controversial asperity rankling in our minds, sunk the philosopher and the friend of his species (a character to which he might have aspired) in the sophist and party-writer. The period at which Mr. Malthus came forward teemed with answers to Modern Philosophy, with antidotes to liberty and humanity, with abusive Histories of the Greek and Roman republics, with fulsome panegyrics on the Roman Emperors (at the very time when we were reviling Buonaparte for his strides to universal empire) with the slime and offal of desperate servility— and we cannot but consider the Essay as one of the poisonous ingredients thrown into the cauldron of Legitimacy "to make it thick and slab. " Our author has, indeed, so far done service to the cause of truth, that he has counteracted many capital errors formerly prevailing as to the universal and indiscriminate encouragement of population under all circumstances; but he has countenanced opposite errors, which if adopted in theory and practice would be even more mischievous, and has left it to future philosophers to follow up the principle, that some check must be provided for the unrestrained progress of population, into a set of wiser and more humane consequences. Mr. Godwin has lately attempted an answer to the Essay (thus giving Mr. Malthus a *Roland for his Oliver*) but we think he has judged ill in endeavouring to invalidate the principle, instead of confining himself to point out the misapplication of it. There is one argument introduced in this Reply, which will, perhaps, amuse the reader as a sort of metaphysical puzzle.

"It has sometimes occurred to me whether Mr. Malthus did not catch the first hint of his geometrical ratio from a curious passage of Judge Blackstone, on consanguinity, which is as follows: —

"The doctrine of lineal consanguinity is sufficiently plain and obvious; but it is at the first view astonishing to consider the number of lineal ancestors which every man has within no very great number of degrees: and so many different bloods is a man said to contain in his veins, as he hath lineal ancestors. Of these he hath two in the first ascending degree, his own parents; he hath four in the second, the parents of his father and the parents of his mother; he hath eight in the third, the parents of his two grandfathers and two grandmothers; and by the same rule of progression, he hath an hundred and twenty-eight in the seventh; a thousand and twenty-four in the tenth; and at the twentieth degree, or the distance of twenty generations, every man hath above a million of ancestors, as common arithmetic will demonstrate.

"This will seem surprising to those who are unacquainted with the increasing power of progressive numbers; but is palpably evident from the following table of a geometrical progression, in which the first term is 2, and the denominator also 2; or, to speak more intelligibly, it is evident, for that each of us has two ancestors in the first degree; the number of which is doubled at every remove, because each of our ancestors had also two ancestors of his own.

Lineal Degrees.				*Number of Ancestors.*
1	..	..	..	2
2	..	..	..	4
3	..	..	..	8
4	..	..	..	16
5	..	..	..	32
6	..	..	..	64
7	..	..	..	128
8	..	..	..	256
9	..	..	..	512

10	..	..	..	1024
11	..	..	..	2048
12	..	..	..	4096
13	..	..	..	8192
14	..	..	..	16,384
15	..	..	..	32,768
16	..	..	..	65,536
17	..	..	..	131,072
18	..	..	..	262,144
19	..	..	..	524,288
20	..	..	..	1,048,576

"This argument, however, " (proceeds Mr. Godwin) "from Judge Blackstone of a geometrical progression would much more naturally apply to Montesquieu's hypothesis of the depopulation of the world, and prove that the human species is hastening fast to extinction, than to the purpose for which Mr. Malthus has employed it. An ingenious sophism might be raised upon it, to shew that the race of mankind will ultimately terminate in unity. Mr. Malthus, indeed, should have reflected, that it is much more certain that every man has had ancestors than that he will have posterity, and that it is still more doubtful, whether he will have posterity to twenty or to an indefinite number of generations. "—ENQUIRY CONCERNING POPULATION, p. 100.

Mr. Malthus's style is correct and elegant; his tone of controversy mild and gentlemanly; and the care with which he has brought his facts and documents together, deserves the highest praise. He has lately quitted his favourite subject of population, and broke a lance with Mr. Ricardo on the question of rent and value. The partisans of Mr. Ricardo, who are also the admirers of Mr. Malthus, say that the usual sagacity of the latter has here failed him, and that he has shewn himself to be a very illogical writer. To have said this of him formerly on another ground, was accounted a heresy and a piece of presumption not easily to be forgiven. Indeed Mr. Malthus has always been a sort of "darling in the public eye, " whom it was unsafe to meddle with. He has contrived to make himself as many friends by his attacks on the schemes of *Human Perfectibility* and on the *Poor-Laws*, as Mandeville formerly procured enemies by his attacks on *Human Perfections* and on *Charity-Schools*; and among other instances that we might mention, *Plug* Pulteney, the celebrated miser, of whom Mr. Burke said on his having a large estate left him, "that now it was to be hoped he would *set up a pocket-handkerchief*, " was so enamoured with the saving schemes and humane economy of the Essay, that he desired a friend to find out the author and offer him a church living! This liberal intention was (by design or accident) unhappily frustrated.

* * * * *

MR. GIFFORD.

Mr. Gifford was originally bred to some handicraft: he afterwards contrived to learn Latin, and was for some time an usher in a school, till he became a tutor in a nobleman's family. The low-bred, self-taught man, the pedant, and the dependant on the great contribute to form the Editor of the *Quarterly Review*. He is admirably qualified for this situation, which he has held for some years, by a happy combination of defects, natural and acquired; and in the event of his death, it will be difficult to provide him a suitable successor.

Mr. Gifford has no pretensions to be thought a man of genius, of taste, or even of general knowledge. He merely understands the mechanical and instrumental part of learning. He is a critic of the last age, when the different editions of an author, or the dates of his several performances were all that occupied the inquiries of a profound scholar, and the spirit of the writer or the beauties of his style were left to shift for themselves, or exercise the fancy of the light and superficial reader. In studying an old author, he has no notion of any thing beyond adjusting a point, proposing a different reading, or correcting, by the collation of various copies, an error of the press. In appreciating a modern one, if it is an enemy, the first thing he thinks of is to charge him with bad grammar—he scans his sentences instead of weighing his sense; or if it is a friend, the highest compliment he conceives it possible to pay him is, that his thoughts and expressions are moulded on some hackneyed model. His standard of *ideal* perfection is what he himself now is, a person of *mediocre* literary attainments: his utmost contempt is shewn by reducing any one to what he himself once was, a person without the ordinary advantages of education and learning. It is accordingly assumed, with much complacency in his critical pages, that Tory writers are classical and courtly as a matter of course; as it is a standing jest and evident truism, that Whigs and Reformers must be persons of low birth and breeding—imputations from one of which he himself has narrowly escaped, and both of which he holds in suitable abhorrence. He stands over a contemporary performance with all the self-conceit and self-importance of a country schoolmaster, tries it by technical rules, affects not to understand the meaning, examines the hand-writing, the spelling, shrugs up his shoulders and chuckles over a slip of the pen, and keeps a sharp look-out for a false concord and—a flogging. There is nothing liberal, nothing humane in his style of judging: it is altogether petty, captious, and literal. The Editor's political subserviency adds the last finishing to his ridiculous pedantry and vanity. He has all his life been a follower in the train of wealth and power—strives to back his pretensions on Parnassus by a place at court, and to gild his reputation as a man of letters by the smile of greatness. He thinks his works are stamped with additional value by having his name in the *Red-Book*. He looks up to the distinctions of rank and station as he does to those of learning, with the gross and overweening adulation of his early origin. All his notions are low, upstart, servile. He thinks it the highest honour to a poet to be patronised by a peer or by some dowager of quality. He is prouder of a court-livery than of a laurel-wreath; and is only sure of having established his claims to respectability by having sacrificed those of independence. He is a retainer to the Muses; a door-keeper to learning; a lacquey in the state. He believes that modern literature should wear the fetters of classical antiquity; that truth is to be weighed in the scales of opinion and prejudice; that power is equivalent to right; that genius is dependent on rules; that taste and refinement of language consist in *word-catching*. Many persons suppose that Mr. Gifford knows better than he pretends; and that he is shrewd, artful, and designing. But perhaps it may be nearer the mark to suppose that his dulness is guarantee for his sincerity; or that before he is the tool of the profligacy of others, he is the dupe of his own jaundiced feelings, and narrow, hoodwinked perceptions.

> "Destroy his fib or sophistry: in vain—
> The creature's at his dirty work again! "

But this is less from choice or perversity, than because he cannot help it and can do nothing else. He damns a beautiful expression less out of spite than because he really does not understand it: any novelty of thought or sentiment gives him a shock from which he cannot recover for some time, and he naturally takes his revenge for the alarm and uneasiness occasioned him, without referring to venal or party motives. He garbles an author's meaning, not so much wilfully, as because it is a pain to him to enlarge his microscopic view to take in the context, when a particular sentence or passage has struck him as quaint and out of the way: he fly-blows an author's style, and picks out detached words and phrases for cynical reprobation, simply because he feels himself at home, or takes a pride and pleasure in this sort of petty warfare. He is tetchy and impatient of contradiction; sore with wounded pride; angry at obvious faults, more angry at unforeseen beauties. He has the *chalk-*

stones in his understanding, and from being used to long confinement, cannot bear the slightest jostling or irregularity of motion. He may call out with the fellow in the *Tempest*—"I am not Stephano, but a cramp! " He would go back to the standard of opinions, style, the faded ornaments, and insipid formalities that came into fashion about forty years ago. Flashes of thought, flights of fancy, idiomatic expressions, he sets down among the signs of the times—the extraordinary occurrences of the age we live in. They are marks of a restless and revolutionary spirit: they disturb his composure of mind, and threaten (by implication) the safety of the state. His slow, snail-paced, bed-rid habits of reasoning cannot keep up with the whirling, eccentric motion, the rapid, perhaps extravagant combinations of modern literature. He has long been stationary himself, and is determined that others shall remain so. The hazarding a paradox is like letting off a pistol close to his ear: he is alarmed and offended. The using an elliptical mode of expression (such as he did not use to find in Guides to the English Tongue) jars him like coming suddenly to a step in a flight of stairs that you were not aware of. He *pishes* and *pshaws* at all this, exercises a sort of interjectional criticism on what excites his spleen, his envy, or his wonder, and hurls his meagre anathemas *ex cathedrâ* at all those writers who are indifferent alike to his precepts and his example!

Mr. Gifford, in short, is possessed of that sort of learning which is likely to result from an over-anxious desire to supply the want of the first rudiments of education; that sort of wit, which is the offspring of ill-humour or bodily pain; that sort of sense, which arises from a spirit of contradiction and a disposition to cavil at and dispute the opinions of others; and that sort of reputation, which is the consequence of bowing to established authority and ministerial influence. He dedicates to some great man, and receives his compliments in return. He appeals to some great name, and the Under-graduates of the two Universities look up to him as an oracle of wisdom. He throws the weight of his verbal criticism and puny discoveries in *black-letter* reading into the gap, that is supposed to be making in the Constitution by Whigs and Radicals, whom he qualifies without mercy as dunces and miscreants; and so entitles himself to the protection of Church and State. The character of his mind is an utter want of independence and magnanimity in all that he attempts. He cannot go alone, he must have crutches, a go-cart and trammels, or he is timid, fretful, and helpless as a child. He cannot conceive of any thing different from what he finds it, and hates those who pretend to a greater reach of intellect or boldness of spirit than himself. He inclines, by a natural and deliberate bias, to the traditional in laws and government; to the orthodox in religion; to the safe in opinion; to the trite in imagination; to the technical in style; to whatever implies a surrender of individual judgment into the hands of authority, and a subjection of individual feeling to mechanic rules. If he finds any one flying in the face of these, or straggling from the beaten path, he thinks he has them at a notable disadvantage, and falls foul of them without loss of time, partly to soothe his own sense of mortified self-consequence, and as an edifying spectacle to his legitimate friends. He takes none but unfair advantages. He *twits* his adversaries (that is, those who are not in the leading-strings of his school or party) with some personal or accidental defect. If a writer has been punished for a political libel, he is sure to hear of it in a literary criticism. If a lady goes on crutches and is out of favour at court, she is reminded of it in Mr. Gilford's manly satire. He sneers at people of low birth or who have not had a college-education, partly to hide his own want of certain advantages, partly as well-timed flattery to those who possess them. He has a right to laugh at poor, unfriended, untitled genius from wearing the livery of rank and letters, as footmen behind a coronet-coach laugh at the rabble. He keeps good company, and forgets himself. He stands at the door of Mr. Murray's shop, and will not let any body pass but the well-dressed mob, or some followers of the court. To edge into the *Quarterly* Temple of Fame the candidate must have a diploma from the Universities, a passport from the Treasury. Otherwise, it is a breach of etiquette to let him pass, an insult to the better sort who aspire to the love of letters—and may chance to drop in to the *Feast of the Poets*. Or, if he cannot manage it thus, or get rid of the claim on the bare ground of poverty or want of school-learning, he *trumps* up an excuse for the occasion, such as that "a man was confined in Newgate a short time before"—it is not a *lie* on the part of the critic, it is only an amiable subserviency to the will of his betters, like that of a menial who is ordered to deny his master, a sense of propriety, a knowledge of the world, a poetical and moral license. Such fellows (such is his cue from his employers) should at any rate be kept out of privileged places: persons who have been convicted of prose-libels ought not to be suffered to write poetry—if the fact was not exactly as it was stated, it was something of the kind, or it *ought* to have been so, the assertion was a pious fraud, — the public, the court, the prince himself might read the work, but for this mark of opprobrium set upon it—it was not to be endured that an insolent plebeian should aspire to elegance, taste, fancy—it was throwing down the barriers which ought to separate the higher and the lower classes, the loyal and the disloyal—the paraphrase of the story of Dante was therefore to perform quarantine, it was to seem not yet recovered from the gaol infection, there was to be a taint upon it, as there was none in it—and all this was performed by a single slip of Mr. Gifford's pen! We would willingly believe (if we could) that in this case there was as much weakness and prejudice as there was malice and cunning. —Again, we do not think it possible that under any circumstances the writer of the *Verses to Anna* could enter into the spirit or delicacy of Mr. Keats's poetry. The fate of the latter somewhat resembled that of

> —"a bud bit by an envious worm,
> Ere it could spread its sweet leaves to the air,
> Or dedicate its beauty to the sun. "

Mr. Keats's ostensible crime was that he had been praised in the *Examiner Newspaper*: a greater and more unpardonable offence probably was, that he was a true poet, with all the errors and beauties of youthful genius to answer for. Mr. Gifford was as insensible to the one as he was inexorable to the other. Let the reader judge from the two subjoined specimens how far the one writer could ever, without a presumption equalled only by a want of self-knowledge, set himself in judgment on the other.

> "Out went the taper as she hurried in;
> Its little smoke in pallid moonshine died:
> She closed the door, she panted, all akin
> To spirits of the air and visions wide:
> No utter'd syllable, or woe betide!
> But to her heart, her heart was voluble,
> Paining with eloquence her balmy side;
> As though a tongueless nightingale should swell
> Her heart in vain, and die, heart-stifled, in her dell.

> "A casement high and triple-arch'd there was,
> All garlanded with carven imag'ries
> Of fruits, and flowers, and bunches of knot-grass,
> And diamonded with panes of quaint device,
> Innumerable of stains and splendid dyes,
> As are the tiger-moth's deep-damask'd wings;
> And in the midst, 'mong thousand heraldries,
> And twilight saints and dim emblazonings,
> A shielded scutcheon blush'd with blood of queens and kings.

"Full on this casement shone the wintry moon,
And threw warm gules on Madeline's fair breast,
As down she knelt for Heaven's grace and boon;
Rose-bloom fell on her hands, together prest,
And on her silver cross soft amethyst,
And on her hair a glory, like a Saint:
She seem'd a splendid angel, newly drest,
Save wings, for heaven: —Porphyro grew faint:
She knelt, so pure a thing, so free from mortal taint.

"Anon his heart revives: her vespers done,
Of all its wreathed pearls her hair she frees;
Unclasps her warmed jewels one by one;
Loosens her fragrant boddice; by degrees
Her rich attire creeps rustling to her knees:
Half-hidden, like a mermaid in sea-weed,
Pensive awhile she dreams awake, and sees,
In fancy, fair St. Agnes in her bed,
But dares not look behind, or all the charm is fled.

"Soon trembling in her soft and chilly nest,
In sort of wakeful swoon, perplex'd she lay,
Until the poppied warmth of sleep oppress'd
Her soothed limbs, and soul fatigued away
Flown, like a thought, until the morrow-day:
Blissfully haven'd both from joy and pain;
Clasp'd like a missal where swart Paynims pray;
Blinded alike from sunshine and from rain,
As though a rose should shut, and be a bud again. "
EVE OF ST. AGNES.

With the rich beauties and the dim obscurities of lines like these, let us contrast the Verses addressed *To a Tuft of early Violets* by the fastidious author of the Baviad and Mæviad. —

"Sweet flowers! that from your humble beds
Thus prematurely dare to rise,
And trust your unprotected heads
To cold Aquarius' watery skies.

"Retire, retire! *These* tepid airs A
re not the genial brood of May;
That sun with light malignant glares,

And flatters only to betray.

"Stern Winter's reign is not yet past—
Lo! while your buds prepare to blow,
On icy pinions comes the blast,
And nips your root, and lays you low.

"Alas, for such ungentle doom!
But I will shield you; and supply
A kindlier soil on which to bloom,
A nobler bed on which to die.

"Come then—'ere yet the morning ray
Has drunk the dew that gems your crest,
And drawn your balmiest sweets away;
O come and grace my Anna's breast.

"Ye droop, fond flowers! But did ye know
What worth, what goodness there reside,
Your cups with liveliest tints would glow;
And spread their leaves with conscious pride.

"For there has liberal Nature joined
Her riches to the stores of Art,
And added to the vigorous mind
The soft, the sympathising heart.

"Come, then—'ere yet the morning ray
Has drunk the dew that gems your crest,
And drawn your balmiest sweets away;
O come and grace my Anna's breast.

"O! I should think—*that fragrant bed*
Might I but hope with you to share—
[A] Years of anxiety repaid
By one short hour of transport there.

"More blest than me, thus shall ye live
Your little day; and when ye die,
Sweet flowers! the grateful Muse shall give
A verse; the sorrowing maid, a sigh.

"While I alas! no distant date,

Mix with the dust from whence I came,
Without a friend to weep my fate,
Without a stone to tell my name. "

We subjoin one more specimen of these "wild strains"[B] said to be
"Written two years after the preceding. " ECCE ITERUM CRISPINUS.

"I wish I was where Anna lies;
For I am sick of lingering here,
And every hour Affection cries,
Go, and partake her humble bier.

"I wish I could! for when she died
I lost my all; and life has prov'd
Since that sad hour a dreary void,
A waste unlovely and unlov'd.

"But who, when I am turn'd to clay,
Shall duly to her grave repair,
And pluck the ragged moss away,
And weeds that have "no business there? "

"And who, with pious hand, shall bring
The flowers she cherish'd, snow-drops cold,
And violets that unheeded spring,
To scatter o'er her hallow'd mould?

"And who, while Memory loves to dwell
Upon her name for ever dear,
Shall feel his heart with passion swell,
And pour the bitter, bitter tear?

"I did it; and would fate allow,
Should visit still, should still deplore—
But health and strength have left me now,
But I, alas! can weep no more.

"Take then, sweet maid! this simple strain,
The last I offer at thy shrine;
Thy grave must then undeck'd remain,
And all thy memory fade with mine.

"And can thy soft persuasive look,

That voice that might with music vie,
Thy air that every gazer took,
Thy matchless eloquence of eye,

"Thy spirits, frolicsome as good,
Thy courage, by no ills dismay'd,
Thy patience, by no wrongs subdued,
Thy gay good-humour—can they "fade? "

"Perhaps—but sorrow dims my eye:
Cold turf, which I no more must view,
Dear name, which I no more must sigh,
A long, a last, a sad adieu! "

It may be said in extenuation of the low, mechanic vein of these impoverished lines, that they were written at an early age—they were the inspired production of a youthful lover! Mr. Gifford was thirty when he wrote them, Mr. Keats died when he was scarce twenty! Farther it may be said, that Mr. Gifford hazarded his first poetical attempts under all the disadvantages of a neglected education: but the same circumstance, together with a few unpruned redundancies of fancy and quaintnesses of expression, was made the plea on which Mr. Keats was hooted out of the world, and his fine talents and wounded sensibilities consigned to an early grave. In short, the treatment of this heedless candidate for poetical fame might serve as a warning, and was intended to serve as a warning to all unfledged tyros, how they venture upon any such doubtful experiments, except under the auspices of some lord of the bedchamber or Government Aristarchus, and how they imprudently associate themselves with men of mere popular talent or independence of feeling! —It is the same in prose works. The Editor scorns to enter the lists of argument with any proscribed writer of the opposite party. He does not refute, but denounces him. He makes no concessions to an adversary, lest they should in some way be turned against him. He only feels himself safe in the fancied insignificance of others: he only feels himself superior to those whom he stigmatizes as the lowest of mankind. All persons are without common-sense and honesty who do not believe implicitly (with him) in the immaculateness of Ministers and the divine origin of Kings. Thus he informed the world that the author of TABLE-TALK was a person who could not write a sentence of common English and could hardly spell his own name, because he was not a friend to the restoration of the Bourbons, and had the assurance to write

Characters of Shakespears Plays in a style of criticism somewhat different from Mr. Gifford's. He charged this writer with imposing on the public by a flowery style; and when the latter ventured to refer to a work of his, called *An Essay on the Principles of Human Action,* which has not a single ornament in it, as a specimen of his original studies and the proper bias of his mind, the learned critic, with a shrug of great self-satisfaction, said, "It was amusing to see this person, sitting like one of Brouwer's Dutch boors over his gin and tobacco-pipes, and fancying himself a Leibnitz! " The question was, whether the subject of Mr. Gifford's censure had ever written such a work or not; for if he had, he had amused himself with something besides gin and tobacco-pipes. But our Editor, by virtue of the situation he holds, is superior to facts or arguments: he is accountable neither to the public nor to authors for what he says of them, but owes it to his employers to prejudice the work and vilify the writer, if the latter is not avowedly ready to range himself on the stronger side. —The *Quarterly Review,* besides the political *tirades* and denunciations of suspected writers, intended for the guidance of the heads of families, is filled up with accounts of books of Voyages and Travels for the amusement of the younger branches. The poetical department is almost a sinecure, consisting of mere summary decisions and a list of quotations. Mr. Croker is understood to contribute the St. Helena articles and the liberality, Mr. Canning the practical good sense, Mr. D'Israeli the good-nature, Mr. Jacob the modesty, Mr. Southey the consistency, and the Editor himself the chivalrous spirit and the attacks on Lady Morgan. It is a double crime, and excites a double portion of spleen in the Editor, when female writers are not advocates of passive obedience and non-resistance. This Journal, then, is a depository for every species of political sophistry and personal calumny. There is no abuse or corruption that does not there find a jesuitical palliation or a bare-faced vindication. There we meet the slime of hypocrisy, the varnish of courts, the cant of pedantry, the cobwebs of the law, the iron hand of power. Its object is as mischievous as the means by which it is pursued are odious. The intention is to poison the sources of public opinion and of individual fame—to pervert literature, from being the natural ally of freedom and humanity, into an engine of priestcraft and despotism, and to undermine the spirit of the English Constitution and the independence of the English character. The Editor and his friends systematically explode every principle of liberty, laugh patriotism and public spirit to scorn, resent every pretence to integrity as a piece of singularity or insolence, and strike at the root of all free inquiry or discussion, by running down every writer as a vile scribbler and a bad member of society, who is not a hireling and a slave. No means are stuck at in accomplishing this laudable end. Strong in patronage, they trample on truth, justice, and decency. They claim the privilege of court-favourites. They keep as little faith with the public, as with their opponents. No statement in the *Quarterly Review* is to be trusted: there is no fact that is not misrepresented in it, no quotation that is not garbled, no character that is not slandered, if it can answer the purposes of a party to do so. The weight of power, of wealth, of rank is thrown into the scale, gives its impulse to the machine; and the whole is under the guidance of Mr. Gifford's instinctive genius—of the inborn hatred of servility for independence, of dulness for talent, of cunning and impudence for truth and honesty. It costs him no effort to execute his disreputable task—in being the tool of a crooked policy, he but labours in his natural vocation. He patches up a rotten system as he would supply the chasms in a worm-eaten manuscript, from a grovelling incapacity to do any thing better; thinks that if a single iota in the claims of prerogative and power were lost, the whole fabric of society would fall upon his head and crush him; and calculates that his best chance for literary reputation is by *blackballing* one half of the competitors as Jacobins and levellers, and securing the suffrages of the other half in his favour as a loyal subject and trusty partisan!

Mr. Gifford, as a satirist, is violent and abrupt. He takes obvious or physical defects, and dwells upon them with much labour and harshness of invective, but with very little wit or spirit. He expresses a great deal of anger and contempt, but you cannot tell very well why—except that he seems to be sore and out of humour. His satire is mere peevishness and spleen, or something worse—personal antipathy and rancour. We are in quite as much pain for the writer, as for the object of his resentment. His address to Peter Pindar is laughable from its outrageousness. He denounces him as a wretch hateful to God and man, for some of the most harmless and amusing trifles that ever were written—and the very good- humour and pleasantry of which, we suspect, constituted their offence in the eyes of this Drawcansir. —His attacks on Mrs. Robinson were unmanly, and even those on Mr. Merry and the Della-Cruscan School were much more ferocious than the occasion warranted. A little affectation and quaintness of style did not merit such severity of castigation. [C] As a translator, Mr. Gifford's version of the Roman satirist is the baldest, and, in parts, the most offensive of all others. We do not know why he attempted it, unless he had got it in his head that he should thus follow in the steps of Dryden, as he had already done in those of Pope in the Baviad and Maeviad. As an editor of old authors, Mr. Gifford is entitled to considerable praise for the pains he has taken in revising the text, and for some improvements he has introduced into it. He had better have spared the notes, in which, though he has detected the blunders of previous commentators, he has exposed his own ill-temper and narrowness of feeling more. As a critic, he has thrown no light on the character and spirit of his authors. He has shewn no striking power of analysis nor of original illustration, though he has chosen to exercise his pen on writers most congenial to his own turn of mind, from their dry and caustic vein; Massinger, and Ben Jonson. What he will make of Marlowe, it is difficult to guess. He has none of "the fiery quality" of the poet. Mr. Gifford does not take for his motto on these occasions — *Spiritus precipitandus est!* — His most successful efforts in this way are barely respectable. In general, his observations are petty, ill-concocted, and discover as little *tact*, as they do a habit of connected reasoning. Thus, for instance, in attempting to add the name of Massinger to the list of Catholic poets, our minute critic insists on the profusion of crucifixes, glories, angelic visions, garlands of roses, and clouds of incense scattered through the *Virgin-Martyr*, as evidence of the theological sentiments meant to be inculcated by the play, when the least reflection might have taught him, that they proved nothing but the author's poetical conception of the character and *costume* of his subject. A writer might, with the same sinister, short-sighted shrewdness, be accused of Heathenism for talking of Flora and Ceres in a poem on the Seasons! What are produced as the exclusive badges and occult proofs of Catholic bigotry, are nothing but the adventitious ornaments and external symbols, the gross and sensible language, in a word, the *poetry* of Christianity in general. What indeed shews the frivolousness of the whole inference is that Deckar, who is asserted by our critic to have contributed some of the most passionate and fantastic of these devotional scenes, is not even suspected of a leaning to Popery. In like manner, he excuses Massinger for the grossness of one of his plots (that of the *Unnatural Combat*) by saying that it was supposed to take place before the Christian era; by this shallow common-place persuading himself, or fancying he could persuade others, that the crime in question (which yet on the very face of the story is made the ground of a tragic catastrophe) was first made *statutory* by the Christian religion.

The foregoing is a harsh criticism, and may be thought illiberal. But as Mr. Gifford assumes a right to say what he pleases of others—they may be allowed to speak the truth of him!

[Footnote A: What an awkward bed-fellow for a tuft of violets!]

[Footnote B:

> "How oft, O Dart! what time the faithful pair
> Walk'd forth, the fragrant hour of eve to share,
> On thy romantic banks, have my *wild strains*
> (Not yet forgot amidst my native plains)
> While thou hast sweetly gurgled down the vale.
> Filled up the pause of love's delightful tale!
> While, ever as she read, the conscious maid,
> By faultering voice and downcast looks betray'd,
> Would blushing on her lover's neck recline,
> And with her finger—point the tenderest line! "

Mæviad, pp. 194, 202.

Yet the author assures us just before, that in these "wild strains" "all was plain. "

> "Even then (admire, John Bell! my simple ways)
> No heaven and hell danced madly through my lays,
> No oaths, no execrations; *all was plain*;
> Yet trust me, while thy ever jingling train
> Chime their sonorous woes with frigid art,
> And shock the reason and revolt the heart;
> My hopes and fears, in nature's language drest,
> Awakened love in many a gentle breast. "

Ibid. v. 185-92.

If any one else had composed these "wild strains, " in which "all is plain, " Mr. Gifford would have accused them of three things, "1. Downright nonsense. 2. Downright frigidity. 3. Downright doggrel; " and proceeded to anatomise them very cordially in his way. As it is, he is thrilled with a very pleasing horror at his former scenes of tenderness, and "gasps at the recollection" *of watery Aquarius! he! jam satis est!* "Why rack a grub—a butterfly upon a wheel? "]

[Footnote C: Mr. Merry was even with our author in personality of abuse. See his Lines on the Story of the Ape that was given in charge to the ex-tutor.]

* * * * *

MR. JEFFREY

The *Quarterly Review* arose out of the *Edinburgh*, not as a corollary, but in contradiction to it. An article had appeared in the latter on Don Pedro Cevallos, which stung the Tories to the quick by the free way in which it spoke of men and things, and something must be done to check these *escapades* of the *Edinburgh*. It was not to be endured that the truth should *out* in this manner, even occasionally and half in jest. A startling shock was thus given to established prejudices, the mask was taken off from grave hypocrisy, and the most serious consequences were to be apprehended. The persons who wrote in this Review seemed "to have their hands full of truths", and now and then, in a fit of spleen or gaiety, let some of them fly; and while this practice continued, it was impossible to say that the Monarchy or the Hierarchy was safe. Some of the arrows glanced, others might stick, and in the end prove fatal. It was not the principles of the *Edinburgh Review*, but the spirit that was looked at with jealousy and alarm. The principles were by no means decidedly hostile to existing institutions: but the spirit was that of fair and free discussion; a field was open to argument and wit; every question was tried upon its own ostensible merits, and there was no foul play. The tone was that of a studied impartiality (which many called *trimming*) or of a sceptical indifference. This tone of impartiality and indifference, however, did not at all suit those who profited or existed by abuses, who breathed the very air of corruption. They know well enough that "those who are not *for* them are *against* them. " They wanted a publication impervious alike to truth and candour; that, hood-winked itself, should lead public opinion blindfold; that should stick at nothing to serve the turn of a party; that should be the exclusive organ of prejudice, the sordid tool of power; that should go the whole length of want of principle in palliating every dishonest measure, of want of decency in defaming every honest man; that should prejudge every question, traduce every opponent; that should give no quarter to fair inquiry or liberal sentiment; that should be "ugly all over with hypocrisy", and present one foul blotch of servility, intolerance, falsehood, spite, and ill-manners. The *Quarterly Review* was accordingly set up.

> "Sithence no fairy lights, no quickning ray,
> Nor stir of pulse, nor object to entice
> Abroad the spirits; but the cloister'd heart
> Sits squat at home, like Pagod in a niche

Obscure! "

This event was accordingly hailed (and the omen has been fulfilled!) as a great relief to all those of his Majesty's subjects who are firmly convinced that the only way to have things remain exactly as they are is to put a stop to all inquiries whether they are right or wrong, and that if you cannot answer a man's arguments, you may at least try to take away his character.

We do not implicitly bow to the political opinions, nor to the critical decisions of the *Edinburgh Review*; but we must do justice to the talent with which they are supported, and to the tone of manly explicitness in which they are delivered. [A] They are eminently characteristic of the Spirit of the Age; as it is the express object of the *Quarterly Review* to discountenance and extinguish that spirit, both in theory and practice. The *Edinburgh Review* stands upon the ground of opinion; it asserts the supremacy of intellect: the pre-eminence it claims is from an acknowledged superiority of talent and information and literary attainment, and it does not build one tittle of its influence on ignorance, or prejudice, or authority, or personal malevolence. It takes up a question, and argues it *pro* and *con* with great knowledge and boldness and skill; it points out an absurdity, and runs it down, fairly, and according to the evidence adduced. In the former case, its conclusions may be wrong, there may be a bias in the mind of the writer, but he states the arguments and circumstances on both sides, from which a judgment is to be formed—it is not his cue, he has neither the effrontery nor the meanness to falsify facts or to suppress objections. In the latter case, or where a vein of sarcasm or irony is resorted to, the ridicule is not barbed by some allusion (false or true) to private history; the object of it has brought the infliction on himself by some literary folly or political delinquency which is referred to as the understood and justifiable provocation, instead of being held up to scorn as a knave for not being a tool, or as a blockhead for thinking for himself. In the *Edinburgh Review* the talents of those on the opposite side are always extolled *pleno ore*—in the *Quarterly Review* they are denied altogether, and the justice that is in this way withheld from them is compensated by a proportionable supply of personal abuse. A man of genius who is a lord, and who publishes with Mr. Murray, may now and then stand as good a chance as a lord who is not a man of genius and who publishes with Messrs. Longman: but that is the utmost extent of the impartiality of the *Quarterly*. From its account you would take Lord Byron and Mr. Stuart Rose for two very pretty poets; but Mr. Moore's Magdalen Muse is sent to Bridewell without mercy, to beat hemp in silk-stockings. In the *Quarterly* nothing is regarded but the political creed or external circumstances of a writer: in the *Edinburgh* nothing is ever adverted to but his literary merits. Or if there is a bias of any kind, it arises from an affectation of magnanimity and candour in giving heaped measure to those on the aristocratic side in politics, and in being critically severe on others. Thus Sir Walter Scott is lauded to the skies for his romantic powers, without any allusion to his political demerits (as if this would be compromising the dignity of genius and of criticism by the introduction of party-spirit)—while Lord Byron is called to a grave moral reckoning. There is, however, little of the cant of morality in the *Edinburgh Review*—and it is quite free from that of religion. It keeps to its province, which is that of criticism—or to the discussion of debateable topics, and acquits itself in both with force and spirit. This is the natural consequence of the composition of the two Reviews. The one appeals with confidence to its own intellectual resources, to the variety of its topics, to its very character and existence as a literary journal, which depend on its setting up no pretensions but those which it can make good by the talent and ingenuity it can bring to bear upon them—it therefore meets every question, whether of a lighter or a graver cast, on its own grounds; the other *blinks* every question, for it has no confidence but in *the powers that be*—shuts itself up in the impregnable fastnesses of authority, or makes some paltry, cowardly attack (under cover of anonymous criticism) on individuals, or dispenses its award of merit entirely according to the rank or party of the writer. The faults of the *Edinburgh Review* arise out of the very consciousness of critical and logical power. In political questions it relies too little on the broad basis of liberty and humanity, enters too much into mere dry formalities, deals too often in *moot-points*, and descends too readily to a sort of special-pleading in defence of *home* truths and natural feelings: in matters of taste and criticism, its tone is sometimes apt to be supercilious and *cavalier* from its habitual faculty of analysing defects and beauties according to given principles, from its quickness in deciding, from its facility in illustrating its views. In this latter department it has been guilty of some capital oversights. The chief was in its treatment of the *Lyrical Ballads* at their first appearance— not in its ridicule of their puerilities, but in its denial of their beauties, because they were included in no school, because they were reducible to no previous standard or theory of poetical excellence. For this, however, considerable reparation has been made by the prompt and liberal spirit that has been shewn in bringing forward other examples of poetical genius. Its capital sin, in a doctrinal point of view, has been (we shrewdly suspect) in the uniform and unqualified encouragement it has bestowed on Mr. Malthus's system. We do not mean that the *Edinburgh Review* was to join in the general *hue and cry* that was raised against this writer; but while it asserted the soundness of many of his arguments, and yielded its assent to the truths he has divulged, it need not have screened his errors. On this subject alone we think the *Quarterly* has the advantage of it. But as the *Quarterly Review* is a mere mass and tissue of prejudices on all subjects, it is the foible of the *Edinburgh Review* to affect a somewhat fastidious air of superiority over prejudices of all kinds, and a determination not to indulge in any of the amiable weaknesses of our nature, except as it can give a reason for the faith that is in it. Luckily, it is seldom reduced to this alternative: "reasons" are with it "as plenty as blackberries! "

Mr. Jeffrey is the Editor of the *Edinburgh Review,* and is understood to have contributed nearly a fourth part of the articles from its commencement. No man is better qualified for this situation; nor indeed so much so. He is certainly a person in advance of the age, and yet perfectly fitted both from knowledge and habits of mind to put a curb upon its rash and headlong spirit. He is thoroughly acquainted with the progress and pretensions of modern literature and philosophy; and to this he adds the natural acuteness and discrimination of the logician with the habitual caution and coolness of his profession. If the *Edinburgh Review* may be considered as the organ of or at all pledged to a party, that party is at least a respectable one, and is placed in the middle between two extremes. The Editor is bound to lend a patient hearing to the most paradoxical opinions and extravagant theories which have resulted in our times from the "infinite agitation of wit", but he is disposed to qualify them by a number of practical objections, of speculative doubts, of checks and drawbacks, arising out of actual circumstances and prevailing opinions, or the frailties of human nature. He has a great range of knowledge, an incessant activity of mind; but the suspension of his judgment, the well-balanced moderation of his sentiments, is the consequence of the very discursiveness of his reason. What may be considered as *a commonplace* conclusion is often the result of a comprehensive view of all the circumstances of a case. Paradox, violence, nay even originality of conception is not seldom owing to our dwelling long and pertinaciously on some one part of a subject, instead of attending to the whole. Mr. Jeffrey is neither a bigot nor an enthusiast. He is not the dupe of the prejudices of others, nor of his own. He is not wedded to any dogma, he is not long the sport of any whim; before he can settle in any fond or fantastic opinion, another starts up to match it, like beads on sparkling wine. A too restless display of talent, a too undisguised statement of all that can be said for and against a question, is perhaps the great fault that is to be attributed to him. Where there is so much power and prejudice to contend with in the opposite scale, it may be thought that the balance of truth can hardly be held with a slack or an even hand; and that the infusion of a little more visionary speculation, of a little more popular indignation into the great Whig Review would be an advantage both to itself and to the cause of freedom. Much of this effect is chargeable less on an Epicurean levity of feeling or on party-trammels, than on real sanguineness of disposition, and a certain fineness of professional tact. Our sprightly Scotchman is not of a desponding and gloomy turn of mind. He argues well for the future hopes of mankind from the smallest beginnings, watches the slow, gradual, reluctant growth of liberal views, and smiling sees the aloe of Reform blossom at the end of a hundred years; while the habitual subtlety of his mind makes him perceive decided advantages where vulgar ignorance or passion sees only doubts and difficulty; and a flaw in an adversary's argument stands him instead of the shout of a mob, the votes of a majority, or the fate of a pitched battle. The Editor is satisfied with his own conclusions, and does not make himself uneasy about the fate of mankind. The issue, he thinks, will verify his moderate and well-founded expectations. —We believe also that late events have given a more decided turn to Mr. Jeffrey's mind, and that he feels that as in the struggle between liberty and slavery, the views of the one party have been laid bare with their success, so the exertions on the other side should become more strenuous, and a more positive stand be made against the avowed and appalling encroachments of priestcraft and arbitrary power.

The characteristics of Mr. Jeffrey's general style as a writer correspond, we think, with what we have here stated as the characteristics of his mind. He is a master of the foils; he makes an exulting display of the dazzling fence of wit and argument. His strength consists in great range of knowledge, an equal familiarity with the principles and the details of a subject, and in a glancing brilliancy and rapidity of style. Indeed, we doubt whether the brilliancy of his manner does not resolve itself into the rapidity, the variety and aptness of his illustrations. His pen is never at a loss, never stands still; and would dazzle for this reason alone, like an eye that is ever in motion. Mr. Jeffrey is far from a flowery or affected writer; he has few tropes or figures, still less any odd startling thoughts or quaint innovations in expression: —but he has a constant supply of ingenious solutions and pertinent examples; he never proses, never grows dull, never wears an argument to tatters; and by the number, the liveliness and facility of his transitions, keeps up that appearance of vivacity, of novel and sparkling effect, for which others are too often indebted to singularity of combination or tinsel ornaments.

It may be discovered, by a nice observer, that Mr. Jeffrey's style of composition is that of a person accustomed to public speaking. There is no pause, no meagreness, no inanimateness, but a flow, a redundance and volubility like that of a stream or of a rolling-stone. The language is more copious than select, and sometimes two or three words perform the office of one. This copiousness and facility is perhaps an advantage in *extempore* speaking, where no stop or break is allowed in the discourse, and where any word or any number of words almost is better than coming to a dead stand; but in written compositions it gives an air of either too much carelessness or too much labour. Mr. Jeffrey's excellence, as a public speaker, has betrayed him into this peculiarity. He makes fewer *blots* in addressing an audience than any one we remember to have heard. There is not a hair's-breadth space between any two of his words, nor is there a single expression either ill-chosen or out of its place. He speaks without stopping to take breath, with ease, with point, with elegance, and without "spinning the thread of his verbosity finer than the staple of his argument. " He may be said to weave words into any shapes he pleases for use or ornament, as the glass-blower moulds the vitreous fluid with his breath; and his sentences shine like glass from their polished smoothness, and are equally transparent. His style of eloquence, indeed, is remarkable for neatness, for correctness, and epigrammatic point; and he has applied this as a standard to his written compositions, where the very same degree of correctness and precision produces, from the contrast between writing and speaking, an agreeable diffuseness, freedom, and animation. Whenever the Scotch advocate has appeared at the bar of the English House of Lords, he has been admired by those who were in the habit of attending to speeches there, as having the greatest fluency of language and the greatest subtlety of distinction of any one of the profession. The law-reporters were as little able to follow him from the extreme rapidity of his utterance as from the tenuity and evanescent nature of his reasoning.

Mr. Jeffrey's conversation is equally lively, various, and instructive. There is no subject on which he is not *au fait*: no company in which he is not ready to scatter his pearls for sport. Whether it be politics, or poetry, or science, or anecdote, or wit, or raillery, he takes up his cue without effort, without preparation, and appears equally incapable of tiring himself or his hearers. His only difficulty seems to be not to speak, but to be silent. There is a constitutional buoyancy and elasticity of mind about him that cannot subside into repose, much less sink into dulness. There may be more original talkers, persons who occasionally surprise or interest you more; few, if any, with a more uninterrupted flow of cheerfulness and animal spirits, with a greater fund of information, and with fewer specimens of the *bathos* in their conversation. He is never absurd, nor has he any favourite points which he is always bringing forward. It cannot be denied that there is something bordering on petulance of manner, but it is of that least offensive kind which may be accounted for from merit and from success, and implies no exclusive pretensions nor the least particle of ill-will to others. On the contrary, Mr. Jeffrey is profuse of his encomiums and admiration of others, but still with a certain reservation of a right to differ or to blame. He cannot rest on one side of a question: he is obliged by a mercurial habit and disposition to vary his point of view. If he is ever tedious, it is from an excess of liveliness: he oppresses from a sense of airy lightness. He is always setting out on a fresh scent: there are always *relays* of topics; the harness is put to, and he rattles away as delightfully and as briskly as ever. New causes are called; he holds a brief in his hand for every possible question. This is a fault. Mr. Jeffrey is not obtrusive, is not impatient of opposition, is not unwilling to be interrupted; but what is said by another, seems to make no impression on him; he is bound to dispute, to answer it, as if he was in Court, or as if it were in a paltry Debating Society, where young beginners were trying their hands. This is not to maintain a character, or for want of good-nature—it is a thoughtless habit. He cannot help cross-examining a witness, or stating the adverse view of the question. He listens not to judge, but to reply. In consequence of this, you can as little tell the impression your observations make on him as what weight to assign to his. Mr. Jeffrey shines in mixed company; he is not good in a *tete-a-tete*. You can only shew your wisdom or your wit in general society: but in private your follies or your weaknesses are not the least interesting topics; and our critic has neither any of his own to confess, nor does he take delight in hearing those of others. Indeed in Scotland generally, the display of personal character, the indulging your whims and humours in the presence of a friend, is not much encouraged—every one there is looked upon in the light of a machine or a collection of topics. They turn you round like a cylinder to see what use they can make of you, and drag you into a dispute with as little ceremony as they would drag out an article from an Encyclopedia. They criticise every thing, analyse every thing, argue upon every thing, dogmatise upon every thing; and the bundle of your habits, feelings, humours, follies and pursuits is regarded by them no more than a bundle of old clothes. They stop you in a sentiment by a question or a stare, and cut you short in a narrative by the time of night. The accomplished and ingenious person of whom we speak, has been a little infected by the tone of his countrymen—he is too didactic, too pugnacious, too full of electrical shocks, too much like a voltaic battery, and reposes too little on his own excellent good sense, his own love of ease, his cordial frankness of disposition and unaffected candour. He ought to have belonged to us!

The severest of critics (as he has been sometimes termed) is the best-natured of men. Whatever there may be of wavering or indecision in Mr. Jeffrey's reasoning, or of harshness in his critical decisions, in his disposition there is nothing but simplicity and kindness. He is a person that no one knows without esteeming, and who both in his public connections and private friendships, shews the same manly uprightness and unbiassed independence of spirit. At a distance, in his writings, or even in his manner, there may be something to excite a little uneasiness and apprehension: in his conduct there is nothing to except against. He is a person of strict integrity himself, without pretence or affectation; and knows how to respect this quality in others, without prudery or intolerance. He can censure a friend or a stranger, and serve him effectually at the same time. He expresses his disapprobation, but not as an excuse for closing up the avenues of his liberality. He is a Scotchman without one particle of hypocrisy, of cant, of servility, or selfishness in his composition. He has not been spoiled by fortune—has not been tempted by power—is firm without violence, friendly without weakness—a critic and even-tempered, a casuist and an honest man—and amidst the toils of his profession and the distractions of the world, retains the gaiety, the unpretending carelessness and simplicity of youth. Mr. Jeffrey in his person is slight, with a countenance of much expression, and a voice of great flexibility and acuteness of tone.

[Footnote A: The style of philosophical criticism, which has been the boast of the Edinburgh Review, was first introduced into the

Monthly Review about the year 1796, in a series of articles by Mr. William Taylor, of Norwich.]

* * * * *

MR. BROUGHAM—SIR F. BURDETT.

There is a class of eloquence which has been described and particularly insisted on, under the style and title of *Irish Eloquence*: there is another class which it is not absolutely unfair to oppose to this, and that is the Scotch. The first of these is entirely the offspring of *impulse*: the last of *mechanism*. The one is as full of fancy as it is bare of facts: the other excludes all fancy, and is weighed down with facts. The one is all fire, the other all ice: the one nothing but enthusiasm, extravagance, eccentricity; the other nothing but logical deductions, and the most approved postulates. The one without scruple, nay, with reckless zeal, throws the reins loose on the neck of the imagination: the other pulls up with a curbbridle, and starts at every casual object it meets in the way as a bug-bear. The genius of Irish oratory stands forth in the naked majesty of untutored nature, its eye glancing wildly round on all objects, its tongue darting forked fire: the genius of Scottish eloquence is armed in all the panoply of the schools; its drawling, ambiguous dialect seconds its circumspect dialectics; from behind the vizor that guards its mouth and shadows its pent-up brows, it sees no visions but its own set purpose, its own *data*, and its own dogmas. It "has no figures, nor no fantasies, " but "those which busy care draws in the brains of men, " or which set off its own superior acquirements and wisdom. It scorns to "tread the primrose path of dalliance"—it shrinks back from it as from a precipice, and keeps in the iron rail-way of the understanding. Irish oratory, on the contrary, is a sort of aeronaut: it is always going up in a balloon, and breaking its neck, or coming down in the parachute. It is filled full with gaseous matter, with whim and fancy, with alliteration and antithesis, with heated passion and bloated metaphors, that burst the slender, silken covering of sense; and the airy pageant, that glittered in empty space and rose in all the bliss of ignorance, flutters and sinks down to its native bogs! If the Irish orator riots in a studied neglect of his subject and a natural confusion of ideas, playing with words, ranging them into all sorts of fantastic combinations, because in the unlettered void or chaos of his mind there is no obstacle to their coalescing into any shapes they please, it must be confessed that the eloquence of the Scotch is encumbered with an excess of knowledge, that it cannot get on for a crowd of difficulties, that it staggers under a load of topics, that it is so environed in the forms of logic and rhetoric as to be equally precluded from originality or absurdity, from beauty or deformity: —the plea of humanity is lost by going through the process of law, the firm and manly tone of principle is exchanged for the wavering and pitiful cant of policy, the living bursts of passion are reduced to a defunct *common-place*, and all true imagination is buried under the dust and rubbish of learned models and imposing authorities. If the one is a bodiless phantom, the other is a lifeless skeleton: if the one in its feverish and hectic extravagance resembles a sick man's dream, the other is akin to the sleep of death—cold, stiff, unfeeling, monumental! Upon the whole, we despair less of the first than of the last, for the principle of life and motion is, after all, the primary condition of all genius. The luxuriant wildness of the one may be disciplined, and its excesses sobered down into reason; but the dry and rigid formality of the other can never burst the shell or husk of oratory. It is true that the one is disfigured by the puerilities and affectation of a Phillips; but then it is redeemed by the manly sense and fervour of a Plunket, the impassioned appeals and flashes of wit of a Curran, and by the golden tide of wisdom, eloquence, and fancy, that flowed from the lips of a Burke. In the other, we do not sink so low in the negative series; but we get no higher in the ascending scale than a Mackintosh or a Brougham. [A] It may be suggested that the late Lord Erskine enjoyed a higher reputation as an orator than either of these: but he owed it to a dashing and graceful manner, to presence of mind, and to great animation in delivering his sentiments. Stripped of these outward and personal advantages, the matter of his speeches, like that of his writings, is nothing, or perfectly inert and dead. Mr. Brougham is from the North of England, but he was educated in Edinburgh, and represents that school of politics and political economy in the House. He differs from Sir James Mackintosh in this, that he deals less in abstract principles, and more in individual details. He makes less use of general topics, and more of immediate facts. Sir James is better acquainted with the balance of an argument in old authors; Mr. Brougham with the balance of power in Europe. If the first is better versed in the progress of history, no man excels the last in a knowledge of the course of exchange. He is apprised of the exact state of our exports and imports, and scarce a ship clears out its cargo at Liverpool or Hull, but he has notice of the bill of lading. Our colonial policy, prison-discipline, the state of the Hulks, agricultural distress, commerce and manufactures, the Bullion question, the Catholic question, the Bourbons or the Inquisition, "domestic treason, foreign levy, " nothing can come amiss to him—he is at home in the crooked mazes of rotten boroughs, is not baffled by Scotch law, and can follow the meaning of one of Mr. Canning's speeches. With so many resources, with such variety and solidity of information, Mr. Brougham is rather a powerful and alarming, than an effectual debater. In so many details (which he himself goes through with unwearied and unshrinking resolution) the spirit of the question is lost to others who have not the same voluntary power of attention or the same interest in hearing that he has in speaking; the original impulse that urged him forward is forgotten in so wide a field, in so interminable a career. If he can, others *cannot* carry all he knows in their heads at the same time; a rope of circumstantial evidence does not hold well together, nor drag the unwilling mind along with it (the willing mind hurries on before it, and grows impatient and absent)—he moves in an unmanageable procession of facts and proofs, instead of coming to the point at once—and his premises (so anxious is he to proceed on sure and ample grounds) overlay and block up his conclusion, so that you cannot arrive at it, or not till the first fury and shock of the onset is over. The ball, from the too great width of the *calibre* from which it is sent, and from striking against such a number of hard, projecting points, is almost spent before it reaches its destination. He keeps a ledger or a debtor-and-creditor account between the Government and the Country, posts so much actual crime, corruption, and injustice against so much contingent advantage or sluggish prejudice, and at the bottom of the page brings in the balance of indignation and contempt, where it is due. But people are not to be *calculated into* contempt or indignation on abstract grounds; for however they may submit to this process where their own interests are concerned, in what regards the public good we believe they must see and feel instinctively, or not at all. There is (it is to be lamented) a good deal of froth as well as strength in the popular spirit, which will not admit of being *decanted* or served out in formal driblets; nor will spleen (the soul of Opposition) bear to be corked up in square patent bottles, and kept for future use! In a word, Mr. Brougham's is ticketed and labelled eloquence, registered and in numeros (like the successive parts of a Scotch Encyclopedia)—it is clever, knowing, imposing, masterly, an extraordinary display of clearness of head, of quickness and energy of thought, of application and industry; but it is not the eloquence of the imagination or the heart, and will never save a nation or an individual from perdition.

Mr. Brougham has one considerable advantage in debate: he is overcome by no false modesty, no deference to others. But then, by a natural consequence or parity of reasoning, he has little sympathy with other people, and is liable to be mistaken in the effect his arguments will have upon them. He relies too much, among other things, on the patience of his hearers, and on his ability to turn every thing to his own advantage. He accordingly goes to the full length of *his tether* (in vulgar phrase) and often overshoots the mark. *C'est dommage.* He has no reserve of discretion, no retentiveness of mind or check upon himself. He needs, with so much wit,

"As much again to govern it. "

He cannot keep a good thing or a shrewd piece of information in his possession, though the letting it out should mar a cause. It is not that he thinks too much of himself, too little of his cause: but he is absorbed in the pursuit of truth as an abstract inquiry, he is led away by the headstrong and over-mastering activity of his own mind. He is borne along, almost involuntarily, and not impossibly against his better judgment, by the throng and restlessness of his ideas as by a crowd of people in motion. His perceptions are literal, tenacious, *epileptic*—his understanding voracious of facts, and equally communicative of them—and he proceeds to

" — — — —Pour out all as plain
As downright Shippen or as old Montaigne" —

without either the virulence of the one or the *bonhommie* of the other. The repeated, smart, unforeseen discharges of the truth jar those that are next him. He does not dislike this state of irritation and collision, indulges his curiosity or his triumph, till by calling for more facts or hazarding some extreme inference, he urges a question to the verge of a precipice, his adversaries urge it *over*, and he himself shrinks back from the consequence —

"Scared at the sound himself has made! "

Mr. Brougham has great fearlessness, but not equal firmness; and after going too far on the *forlorn hope*, turns short round without due warning to others or respect for himself. He is adventurous, but easily panic-struck; and sacrifices the vanity of self-opinion to the necessity of self-preservation. He is too improvident for a leader, too petulant for a partisan; and does not sufficiently consult those with whom he is supposed to act in concert. He sometimes leaves them in the lurch, and is sometimes left in the lurch by them. He wants the principle of co-operation. He frequently, in a fit of thoughtless levity, gives an unexpected turn to the political machine, which alarms older and more experienced heads: if he was not himself the first to get out of harm's way and escape from the danger, it would be well! —We hold, indeed, as a general rule, that no man born or bred in Scotland can be a great orator, unless he is a mere quack; or a great statesman unless he turns plain knave. The national gravity is against the first: the national caution is against the last. To a Scotchman if a thing *is*, *it is*; there is an end of the question with his opinion about it. He is positive and abrupt, and is not in the habit of conciliating the feelings or soothing the follies of others. His only way therefore to produce a popular effect is to sail with the stream of prejudice, and to vent common dogmas, "the total grist, unsifted, husks and all, " from some evangelical pulpit. This may answer, and it has answered. On the other hand, if a Scotchman, born or bred, comes to think at all of the feelings of others, it is not as they regard them, but as their opinion reacts on his own interest and safety. He is therefore either pragmatical and offensive, or if he tries to please, he becomes cowardly and fawning. His public spirit wants pliancy; his selfish compliances go all lengths. He is as impracticable as a popular partisan, as he is mischievous as a tool of Government. We do not wish to press this argument farther, and must leave it involved in some degree of obscurity, rather than bring the armed intellect of a whole nation on our heads.

Mr. Brougham speaks in a loud and unmitigated tone of voice, sometimes almost approaching to a scream. He is fluent, rapid, vehement, full of his subject, with evidently a great deal to say, and very regardless of the manner of saying it. As a lawyer, he has not hitherto been remarkably successful. He is not profound in cases and reports, nor does he take much interest in the peculiar features of a particular cause, or shew much adroitness in the management of it. He carries too much weight of metal for ordinary and petty occasions: he must have a pretty large question to discuss, and must make *thorough-stitch* work of it. He, however, had an encounter with Mr. Phillips the other day, and shook all his tender blossoms, so that they fell to the ground, and withered in an hour; but they soon bloomed again! Mr. Brougham writes almost, if not quite, as well as he speaks. In the midst of an Election contest he comes out to address the populace, and goes back to his study to finish an article for the Edinburgh Review; sometimes indeed wedging three or four articles (in the shape of *refaccimentos* of his own pamphlets or speeches in parliament) into a single number. Such indeed is the activity of his mind that it appears to require neither repose, nor any other stimulus than a delight in its own exercise. He can turn his hand to any thing, but he cannot be idle. There are few intellectual accomplishments which he does not possess, and possess in a very high degree. He speaks French (and, we believe, several other modern languages) fluently: is a capital mathematician, and obtained an introduction to the celebrated Carnot in this latter character, when the conversation turned on squaring the circle, and not on the propriety of confining France within the natural boundary of the Rhine. Mr. Brougham is, in fact, a striking instance of the versatility and strength of the human mind, and also in one sense of the length of human life, if we make a good use of our time. There is room enough to crowd almost every art and science into it. If we pass "no day without a line, " visit no place without the company of a book, we may with ease fill libraries or empty them of their contents. Those who complain of the shortness of life, let it slide by them without wishing to seize and make the most of its golden minutes. The more we do, the more we can do; the more busy we are, the more leisure we have. If any one possesses any advantage in a considerable degree, he may make himself master of nearly as many more as he pleases, by employing his spare time and cultivating the waste faculties of his mind. While one person is determining on the choice of a profession or study, another shall have made a fortune or gained a merited reputation. While one person is dreaming over the meaning of a word, another will have learnt several languages. It is not incapacity, but indolence, indecision, want of imagination, and a proneness to a sort of mental tautology, to repeat the same images and tread the same circle, that leaves us so poor, so dull, and inert as we are, so naked of acquirement, so barren of resources! While we are walking backwards and forwards between Charing-Cross and Temple-Bar, and sitting in the same coffee-house every day, we might make the grand tour of Europe, and visit the Vatican and the Louvre. Mr. Brougham, among other means of strengthening and enlarging his views, has visited, we believe, most of the courts, and turned his attention to most of the Constitutions of the continent. He is, no doubt, a very accomplished, active-minded, and admirable person.

Sir Francis Burdett, in many respects, affords a contrast to the foregoing character. He is a plain, unaffected, unsophisticated English gentleman. He is a person of great reading too and considerable information, but he makes very little display of these, unless it be to quote Shakespear, which he does often with extreme aptness and felicity. Sir Francis is one of the most pleasing speakers in the House, and is a prodigious favourite of the English people. So he ought to be: for he is one of the few remaining examples of the old

English understanding and old English character. All that he pretends to is common sense and common honesty; and a greater compliment cannot be paid to these than the attention with which he is listened to in the House of Commons. We cannot conceive a higher proof of courage than the saying things which he has been known to say there; and we have seen him blush and appear ashamed of the truths he has been obliged to utter, like a bashful novice. He could not have uttered what he often did there, if, besides his general respectability, he had not been a very honest, a very good-tempered, and a very good-looking man. But there was evidently no wish to shine, nor any desire to offend: it was painful to him to hurt the feelings of those who heard him, but it was a higher duty in him not to suppress his sincere and earnest convictions. It is wonderful how much virtue and plain-dealing a man may be guilty of with impunity, if he has no vanity, or ill-nature, or duplicity to provoke the contempt or resentment of others, and to make them impatient of the superiority he sets up over them. We do not recollect that Sir Francis ever endeavoured to atone for any occasional indiscretions or intemperance by giving the Duke of York credit for the battle of Waterloo, or congratulating Ministers on the confinement of Buonaparte at St. Helena. There is no honest cause which he dares not avow: no oppressed individual that he is not forward to succour. He has the firmness of manhood with the unimpaired enthusiasm of youthful feeling about him. His principles are mellowed and improved, without having become less sound with time: for at one period he sometimes appeared to come charged to the House with the petulance and caustic sententiousness he had imbibed at Wimbledon Common. He is never violent or in extremes, except when the people or the parliament happen to be out of their senses; and then he seems to regret the necessity of plainly telling them he thinks so, instead of pluming himself upon it or exulting over impending calamities. There is only one error he seems to labour under (which, we believe, he also borrowed from Mr. Horne Tooke or Major Cartwright), the wanting to go back to the early times of our Constitution and history in search of the principles of law and liberty. He might as well

"Hunt half a day for a forgotten dream. "

Liberty, in our opinion, is but a modern invention (the growth of books and printing)—and whether new or old, is not the less desirable. A man may be a patriot, without being an antiquary. This is the only point on which Sir Francis is at all inclined to a tincture of pedantry. In general, his love of liberty is pure, as it is warm and steady: his humanity is unconstrained and free. His heart does not ask leave of his head to feel; nor does prudence always keep a guard upon his tongue or his pen. No man writes a better letter to his Constituents than the member for Westminster; and his compositions of that kind ought to be good, for they have occasionally cost him dear. He is the idol of the people of Westminster: few persons have a greater number of friends and well-wishers; and he has still greater reason to be proud of his enemies, for his integrity and independence have made them so. Sir Francis Burdett has often been left in a Minority in the House of Commons, with only one or two on his side. We suspect, unfortunately for his country, that History will be found to enter its protest on the same side of the question!

[Footnote A: Mr. Brougham is not a Scotchman literally, but by adoption.]

* * * * *

LORD ELDON AND MR. WILBERFORCE.

Lord Eldon is an exceedingly good-natured man; but this does not prevent him, like other good-natured people, from consulting his own ease or interest. The character of *good-nature*, as it is called, has been a good deal mistaken; and the present Chancellor is not a bad illustration of the grounds of the prevailing error. When we happen to see an individual whose countenance is "all tranquillity and smiles; " who is full of good-humour and pleasantry; whose manners are gentle and conciliating; who is uniformly temperate in his expressions, and punctual and just in his every-day dealings; we are apt to conclude from so fair an outside, that

"All is conscience and tender heart"

within also, and that such a one would not hurt a fly. And neither would he without a motive. But mere good-nature (or what passes in the world for such) is often no better than indolent selfishness. A person distinguished and praised for this quality will not needlessly offend others, because they may retaliate; and besides, it ruffles his own temper. He likes to enjoy a perfect calm, and to live in an interchange of kind offices. He suffers few things to irritate or annoy him. He has a fine oiliness in his disposition, which smooths the waves of passion as they rise. He does not enter into the quarrels or enmities of others; bears their calamities with patience; he listens to the din and clang of war, the earthquake and the hurricane of the political and moral world with the temper and spirit of a philosopher; no act of injustice puts him beside himself, the follies and absurdities of mankind never give him a moment's uneasiness, he has none of the ordinary causes of fretfulness or chagrin that torment others from the undue interest they take in the conduct of their neighbours or in the public good. None of these idle or frivolous sources of discontent, that make such havoc with the peace of human life, ever discompose his features or alter the serenity of his pulse. If a nation is robbed of its rights,

"If wretches hang that Ministers may dine, " —

the laughing jest still collects in his eye, the cordial squeeze of the hand is still the same. But tread on the toe of one of these amiable and imperturbable mortals, or let a lump of soot fall down the chimney and spoil their dinners, and see how they will bear it. All their patience is confined to the accidents that befal others: all their good-humour is to be resolved into giving themselves no concern about any thing but their own ease and self-indulgence. Their charity begins and ends at home. Their being free from the common infirmities of temper is owing to their indifference to the common feelings of humanity; and if you touch the sore place, they betray more resentment, and break out (like spoiled children) into greater fractiousness than others, partly from a greater degree of selfishness, and partly because they are taken by surprise, and mad to think they have not guarded every point against annoyance or attack, by a habit of callous insensibility and pampered indolence.

An instance of what we mean occurred but the other day. An allusion was made in the House of Commons to something in the proceedings in the Court of Chancery, and the Lord Chancellor comes to his place in the Court, with the statement in his hand, fire in his eyes, and a direct charge of falsehood in his mouth, without knowing any thing certain of the matter, without making any inquiry into it, without using any precaution or putting the least restraint upon himself, and all on no better authority than a common newspaper report. The thing was (not that we are imputing any strong blame in this case, we merely bring it as an illustration) it touched himself, his office, the inviolability of his jurisdiction, the unexceptionableness of his proceedings, and the wet blanket of the Chancellor's temper instantly took fire like tinder! All the fine balancing was at an end; all the doubts, all the delicacy, all the candour real or affected, all the chances that there might be a mistake in the report, all the decencies to be observed towards a Member of the House, are overlooked by the blindness of passion, and the wary Judge pounces upon the paragraph without mercy, without a moment's delay, or the smallest attention to forms! This was indeed serious business, there was to be no trifling here; every instant was an age till the Chancellor had discharged his sense of indignation on the head of the indiscreet interloper on his authority. Had it been another person's case, another person's dignity that had been compromised, another person's conduct that had been called in question, who doubts but that the matter might have stood over till the next term, that the Noble Lord would have taken the Newspaper home in his pocket, that he would have compared it carefully with other newspapers, that he would have written in the most mild and gentlemanly terms to the Honourable Member to inquire into the truth of the statement, that he would have watched a convenient opportunity good-humouredly to ask other Honourable Members what all this was about, that the greatest caution and fairness would have been observed, and that to this hour the lawyers' clerks and the junior counsel would have been in the greatest admiration of the Chancellor's nicety of discrimination, and the utter inefficacy of the heats, importunities, haste, and passions of others to influence his judgment? This would have been true; yet his readiness to decide and to condemn where he himself is concerned, shews that passion is not dead in him, nor subject to the controul of reason; but that self-love is the main-spring that moves it, though on all beyond that limit he looks with the most perfect calmness and philosophic indifference.

> "Resistless passion sways us to the mood
> Of what it likes or loaths. "

All people are passionate in what concerns themselves, or in what they take an interest in. The range of this last is different in different persons; but the want of passion is but another name for the want of sympathy and imagination.

The Lord Chancellor's impartiality and conscientious exactness is proverbial; and is, we believe, as inflexible as it is delicate in all cases that occur in the stated routine of legal practice. The impatience, the irritation, the hopes, the fears, the confident tone of the applicants move him not a jot from his intended course, he looks at their claims with the "lack lustre eye" of prefessional indifference. Power and influence apart, his next strongest passion is to indulge in the exercise of professional learning and skill, to amuse himself with the dry details and intricate windings of the law of equity. He delights to balance a straw, to see a feather turn the scale, or make it even again; and divides and subdivides a scruple to the smallest fraction. He unravels the web of argument and pieces it together again; folds it up and lays it aside, that he may examine it more at his leisure. He hugs indecision to his breast, and takes home a modest doubt or a nice point to solace himself with it in protracted, luxurious dalliance. Delay seems, in his mind, to be of the very essence of justice. He no more hurries through a question than if no one was waiting for the result, and he was merely a *dilettanti*, fanciful judge, who played at my Lord Chancellor, and busied himself with quibbles and punctilios as an idle hobby and harmless illusion. The phlegm of the Chancellor's disposition gives one almost a surfeit of impartiality and candour: we are sick of the eternal poise of childish dilatoriness; and would wish law and justice to be decided at once by a cast of the dice (as they were in Rabelais) rather than be kept in frivolous and tormenting suspense. But there is a limit even to this extreme refinement and scrupulousness of the Chancellor. The understanding acts only in the absence of the passions. At the approach of the loadstone, the needle trembles, and points to it. The air of a political question has a wonderful tendency to brace and quicken the learned Lord's faculties. The breath of a court speedily oversets a thousand objections, and scatters the cobwebs of his brain. The secret wish of power is a thumping *make-weight,* where all is so nicely-balanced beforehand. In the case of a celebrated beauty and heiress, and the brother of a Noble Lord, the Chancellor hesitated long, and went through the forms, as usual: but who ever doubted, where all this indecision would end? No man in his senses, for a single instant! We shall not press this point, which is rather a ticklish one. Some persons thought that from entertaining a fellow-feeling on the subject, the Chancellor would have been ready to favour the Poet-Laureat's application to the Court of Chancery for an injunction against Wat Tyler. His Lordship's sentiments on such points are not so variable, he has too much at stake. He recollected the year 1794, though Mr. Southey had forgotten it! —

The personal always prevails over the intellectual, where the latter is not backed by strong feeling and principle. Where remote and speculative objects do not excite a predominant interest and passion, gross and immediate ones are sure to carry the day, even in ingenuous and well-disposed minds. The will yields necessarily to some motive or other; and where the public good or distant consequences excite no sympathy in the breast, either from short-sightedness or an easiness of temperament that shrinks from any violent effort or painful emotion, self-interest, indolence, the opinion of others, a desire to please, the sense of personal obligation, come in and fill up the void of public spirit, patriotism, and humanity. The best men in the world in their own natural dispositions or in private life (for this reason) often become the most dangerous public characters, from their pliancy to the unruly passions of others, and from their having no set-off in strong moral *stamina* to the temptations that are held out to them, if, as is frequently the case, they are men of versatile talent or patient industry. —Lord Eldon has one of the best-natured faces in the world; it is pleasant to meet him in the street, plodding along with an umbrella under his arm, without one trace of pride, of spleen, or discontent in his whole demeanour, void of offence, with almost rustic simplicity and honesty of appearance—a man that makes friends at first sight, and could hardly make enemies, if he would; and whose only fault is that he cannot say *Nay* to power, or subject himself to an unkind word or look from a King or a Minister. He is a thorough-bred Tory. Others boggle or are at fault in their career, or give back at a pinch, they split into different factions, have various objects to distract them, their private friendships or antipathies stand in their way; but he has never flinched, never gone back, never missed his way, he is an *out-and-outer* in this respect, his allegiance has been without flaw, like "one entire and perfect chrysolite, " his implicit understanding is a kind of taffeta-lining to the Crown, his servility has assumed an air of the most determined independence, and he has

"Read his history in a Prince's eyes! " —

There has been no stretch of power attempted in his time that he has not seconded: no existing abuse, so odious or so absurd, that he has not sanctioned it. He has gone the whole length of the most unpopular designs of Ministers. When the heavy artillery of interest, power, and prejudice is brought into the field, the paper pellets of the brain go for nothing: his labyrinth of nice, lady-like doubts explodes like a mine of gun-powder. The Chancellor may weigh and palter—the courtier is decided, the politician is firm, and rivetted to his place in the Cabinet! On all the great questions that have divided party opinion or agitated the public mind, the Chancellor has been found uniformly and without a single exception on the side of prerogative and power, and against every proposal for the advancement of freedom. He was a strenuous supporter of the wars and coalitions against the principles of liberty abroad; he has been equally zealous in urging or defending every act and infringement of the Constitution, for abridging it at home: he at the same time opposes every amelioration of the penal laws, on the alleged ground of his abhorrence of even the shadow of innovation: he has studiously set his face against Catholic emancipation; he laboured hard in his vocation to prevent the abolition of the Slave Trade; he was Attorney General in the trials for High Treason in 1794; and the other day in giving his opinion on the Queen's Trial, shed tears and protested his innocence before God! This was natural and to be expected; but on all occasions he is to be found at his post, true to the call of prejudice, of power, to the will of others and to his own interest. In the whole of his public career, and with all the goodness of his disposition, he has not shewn "so small a drop of pity as a wren's eye. " He seems to be on his guard against every thing liberal and humane as his weak side. Others relax in their obsequiousness either from satiety or disgust, or a hankering after popularity, or a wish to be thought above narrow prejudices. The Chancellor alone is fixed and immoveable. Is it want of understanding or of principle? No—it is want of imagination, a phlegmatic habit, an excess of false complaisance and good-nature... Common humanity and justice are little better than vague terms to him: he acts upon his immediate feelings and least irksome impulses. The King's hand is velvet to the touch—the Woolsack is a seat of honour and profit! That is all he knows about the matter. As to abstract metaphysical calculations, the ox that stands staring at the corner of the street troubles his head as much about them as he does: yet this last is a very good sort of animal with no harm or malice in him, unless he is goaded on to mischief, and then it is necessary to keep out of his way, or warn others against him!

Mr. Wilberforce is a less perfect character in his way. He acts from mixed motives. He would willingly serve two masters, God and Mammon. He is a person of many excellent and admirable qualifications, but he has made a mistake in wishing to reconcile those that are incompatible. He has a most winning eloquence, specious, persuasive, familiar, silver-tongued, is amiable, charitable, conscientious, pious, loyal, humane, tractable to power, accessible to popularity, honouring the king, and no less charmed with the homage of his fellow-citizens. "What lacks he then? " Nothing but an economy of good parts. By aiming at too much, he has spoiled all, and neutralised what might have been an estimable character, distinguished by signal services to mankind. A man must take his choice not only between virtue and vice, but between different virtues. Otherwise, he will not gain his own approbation, or secure the respect of others. The graces and accomplishments of private life mar the man of business and the statesman. There is a severity, a sternness, a self-denial, and a painful sense of duty required in the one, which ill befits the softness and sweetness which should characterise the other. Loyalty, patriotism, friendship, humanity, are all virtues; but may they not sometimes clash? By being unwilling to forego the praise due to any, we may forfeit the reputation of all; and instead of uniting the suffrages of the whole world in our favour, we may end in becoming a sort of bye-word for affectation, cant, hollow professions, trimming, fickleness, and effeminate imbecility. It is best to choose and act up to some one leading character, as it is best to have some settled profession or regular pursuit in life.

We can readily believe that Mr. Wilberforce's first object and principle of action is to do what he thinks right: his next (and that we fear is of almost equal weight with the first) is to do what will be thought so by other people. He is always at a game of *hawk and buzzard* between these two: his "conscience will not budge, " unless the world goes with it. He does not seem greatly to dread the denunciation in Scripture, but rather to court it—"Woe unto you, when all men shall speak well of you! " We suspect he is not quite easy in his mind, because West-India planters and Guinea traders do not join in his praise. His ears are not strongly enough tuned to drink in the execrations of the spoiler and the oppressor as the sweetest music. It is not enough that one half of the human species (the images of God carved in ebony, as old Fuller calls them) shout his name as a champion and a saviour through vast burning zones, and moisten their parched lips with the gush of gratitude for deliverance from chains—he must have a Prime-Minister drink his health at a Cabinet-dinner for aiding to rivet on those of his country and of Europe! He goes hand and heart along with Government in all their notions of legitimacy and political aggrandizement, in the hope that they will leave him a sort of *no-man's ground* of humanity in the Great Desert, where his reputation for benevolence and public spirit may spring up and flourish, till its head touches the clouds, and it stretches out its branches to the farthest part of the earth. He has no mercy on those who claim a property in negro-slaves as so much live-stock on their estates; the country rings with the applause of his wit, his eloquence, and his indignant appeals to common sense and humanity on this subject—but not a word has he to say, not a whisper does he breathe against the claim set up by the Despots of the Earth over their Continental subjects, but does every thing in his power to confirm and sanction it! He must give no offence. Mr. Wilberforce's humanity will go all lengths that it can with safety and discretion: but it is not to be supposed that it should lose him his seat for Yorkshire, the smile of Majesty, or the countenance of the loyal and pious. He is anxious to do all the good he can without hurting himself or his fair fame. His conscience and his character compound matters very amicably. He rather patronises honesty than is a martyr to it. His patriotism, his philanthropy are not so ill-bred, as to quarrel with his loyalty or to banish him from the first circles. He preaches vital Christianity to untutored savages; and tolerates its worst abuses in civilized states. He thus shews his respect for religion without offending the clergy, or circumscribing the sphere of his usefulness. There is in all this an appearance of a good deal of cant and tricking. His patriotism may be accused of being servile; his humanity ostentatious; his loyalty conditional; his religion a mixture of fashion and fanaticism. "Out upon such half-faced fellowship! " Mr. Wilberforce has the pride of being familiar with the great; the vanity of being popular; the conceit of an approving conscience. He is coy in his approaches to power; his public spirit is, in a manner, *under the rose.* He thus reaps the credit of independence, without the obloquy; and secures the advantages of servility, without incurring any obligations. He has two strings to his bow: —he by no means neglects his worldly interests, while he expects a bright reversion in the skies. Mr. Wilberforce is far from being a hypocrite; but he is, we think, as fine a specimen of *moral equivocation* as can well be conceived. A hypocrite is one who is the very reverse of, or who despises the character he pretends to be: Mr. Wilberforce would be all that he pretends to be, and he is it in fact, as far as words, plausible theories, good inclinations, and easy services go, but not in heart and soul, or so as to give up the appearance of any one of his pretensions to preserve the reality of any other. He carefully chooses his ground to fight the battles of loyalty, religion, and humanity, and it is such as is always safe and advantageous to himself! This is perhaps hardly fair, and it is of dangerous or doubtful tendency. Lord Eldon, for instance, is known to be a thorough-paced ministerialist: his opinion is only that of his party. But Mr. Wilberforce is not a party-man. He is the more looked up to on this account, but not with sufficient reason. By tampering with different temptations and personal projects, he has all the air of the most perfect independence, and gains a character for impartiality and candour, when he is only striking a balance in his mind between the *éclat* of differing from a Minister on some 'vantage ground, and the risk or odium that may attend it. He carries all the weight of his artificial popularity over to the Government on vital points and hard-run questions; while they, in return, lend him a little of the gilding of court-favour to set off his disinterested philanthropy and tramontane enthusiasm. As a leader or a follower, he makes an odd jumble of interests. By virtue of religious sympathy, he has brought the Saints over to the side of the abolition of Negro slavery. This his adversaries think hard and stealing a march upon them. What have the SAINTS to do with freedom or reform of any kind? —Mr. Wilberforce's style of speaking is not quite *parliamentary*, it is halfway between that and *evangelical.* He is altogether a *double-entendre:* the very tone of his voice is a *double-entendre.* It winds, and undulates, and glides up and down on texts of Scripture, and scraps from Paley, and trite sophistry, and pathetic appeals to his hearers in a faltering, inprogressive, sidelong way, like those birds of weak wing, that are borne from their strait-forward course

"By every little breath that under heaven is blown. "

Something of this fluctuating, time-serving principle was visible even in the great question of the Abolition of the Slave Trade. He was, at one time, half inclined to surrender it into Mr. Pitt's dilatory hands, and seemed to think the gloss of novelty was gone from it, and the gaudy colouring of popularity sunk into the *sable* ground from which it rose! It was, however, persisted in and carried to a triumphant conclusion. Mr. Wilberforce said too little on this occasion of one, compared with whom he was but the frontispiece to that great chapter in the history of the world—the mask, the varnishing, and painting—the man that effected it by Herculean labours of body, and equally gigantic labours of mind was Clarkson, the true Apostle of human Redemption on that occasion, and who, it is remarkable, resembles in his person and lineaments more than one of the Apostles in the *Cartoons* of Raphael. He deserves to be added to the Twelve! [A]

[Footnote A: After all, the best as well as most amusing comment on the character just described was that made by Sheridan, who being picked up in no very creditable plight by the watch, and asked rather roughly who he was, made answer—"I am Mr. Wilberforce! " The guardians of the night conducted him home with all the honours due to Grace and Nature.]

* * * * *

MR. SOUTHEY.

Mr. Southey, as we formerly remember to have seen him, had a hectic flush upon his cheek, a roving fire in his eye, a falcon glance, a look at once aspiring and dejected—it was the look that had been impressed upon his face by the events that marked the outset of his life, it was the dawn of Liberty that still tinged his cheek, a smile betwixt hope and sadness that still played upon his quivering lip. Mr. Southey's mind is essentially sanguine, even to over-weeningness. It is prophetic of good; it cordially embraces it; it casts a longing, lingering look after it, even when it is gone for ever. He cannot bear to give up the thought of happiness, his confidence in his fellow-man, when all else despair. It is the very element, "where he must live or have no life at all. " While he supposed it possible that a better form of society could be introduced than any that had hitherto existed, while the light of the French Revolution beamed into his soul (and long after, it was seen reflected on his brow, like the light of setting suns on the peak of some high mountain, or lonely range of clouds, floating in purer ether!) while he had this hope, this faith in man left, he cherished it with child-like simplicity, he clung to it with the fondness of a lover, he was an enthusiast, a fanatic, a leveller; he stuck at nothing that he thought would banish all pain and misery from the world—in his impatience of the smallest error or injustice, he would have sacrificed himself and the existing generation (a holocaust) to his devotion to the right cause. But when he once believed after many staggering doubts and painful struggles, that this was no longer possible, when his chimeras and golden dreams of human perfectibility vanished from him, he turned suddenly round, and maintained that "whatever *is*, is right. " Mr. Southey has not fortitude of mind, has not patience to think that evil is inseparable from the nature of things. His irritable sense rejects the alternative altogether, as a weak stomach rejects the food that is distasteful to it. He hopes on against hope, he believes in all unbelief. He must either repose on actual or on imaginary good. He missed his way in *Utopia*, he has found it at Old Sarum—

"His generous *ardour* no cold medium knows: "

his eagerness admits of no doubt or delay. He is ever in extremes, and ever in the wrong!

The reason is, that not truth, but self-opinion is the ruling principle of Mr. Southey's mind. The charm of novelty, the applause of the multitude, the sanction of power, the venerableness of antiquity, pique, resentment, the spirit of contradiction have a good deal to do with his preferences. His inquiries are partial and hasty: his conclusions raw and unconcocted, and with a considerable infusion of whim and humour and a monkish spleen. His opinions are like certain wines, warm and generous when new; but they will not keep, and soon turn flat or sour, for want of a stronger spirit of the understanding to give a body to them. He wooed Liberty as a youthful lover, but it was perhaps more as a mistress than a bride; and he has since wedded with an elderly and not very reputable lady, called Legitimacy. *A wilful man*, according to the Scotch proverb, *must have his way*. If it were the cause to which he was sincerely attached, he would adhere to it through good report and evil report; but it is himself to whom he does homage, and would have others do so; and he therefore changes sides, rather than submit to apparent defeat or temporary mortification. Abstract principle has no rule but the understood distinction between right and wrong; the indulgence of vanity, of caprice, or prejudice is regulated by the convenience or bias of the moment. The temperament of our politician's mind is poetical, not philosophical. He is more the creature of impulse, than he is of reflection. He invents the unreal, he embellishes the false with the glosses of fancy, but pays little attention to "the words of truth and soberness. " His impressions are accidental, immediate, personal, instead of being permanent and universal. Of all mortals he is surely the most impatient of contradiction, even when he has completely turned the tables on himself. Is not this very inconsistency the reason? Is he not tenacious of his opinions, in proportion as they are brittle and hastily formed? Is he not jealous of the grounds of his belief, because he fears they will not bear inspection, or is conscious he has shifted them? Does he not confine others to the strict line of orthodoxy, because he has himself taken every liberty? Is he not afraid to look to the right or the left, lest he should see the ghosts of his former extravagances staring him in the face? Does he not refuse to tolerate the smallest shade of difference in others, because he feels that he wants the utmost latitude of construction for differing so widely from himself? Is he not captious, dogmatical, petulant in delivering his sentiments, according as he has been inconsistent, rash, and fanciful in adopting them? He maintains that there can be no possible ground for differing from him, because he looks only at his own side of the question! He sets up his own favourite notions as the standard of reason and honesty, because he has changed from one extreme to another! He treats his opponents with contempt, because he is himself afraid of meeting with disrespect! He says that "a Reformer is a worse character than a house-breaker, " in order to stifle the recollection that he himself once was one!

We must say that "we relish Mr. Southey more in the Reformer" than in his lately acquired, but by no means natural or becoming character of poet-laureat and courtier. He may rest assured that a garland of wild flowers suits him better than the laureat-wreath: that his pastoral odes and popular inscriptions were far more adapted to his genius than his presentation-poems. He is nothing akin to birth-day suits and drawing-room fopperies. "He is nothing, if not fantastical. " In his figure, in his movements, in his sentiments, he is sharp and angular, quaint and eccentric. Mr. Southey is not of the court, courtly. Every thing of him and about him is from the people. He is not classical, he is not legitimate. He is not a man cast in the mould of other men's opinions: he is not shaped on any model: he bows to no authority: he yields only to his own wayward peculiarities. He is wild, irregular, singular, extreme. He is no formalist, not he! All is crude and chaotic, self-opinionated, vain. He wants proportion, keeping, system, standard rules. He is not *teres et rotundus*. Mr. Southey walks with his chin erect through the streets of London, and with an umbrella sticking out under his arm, in the finest weather. He has not sacrificed to the Graces, nor studied decorum. With him every thing is projecting, starting from its place, an episode, a digression, a poetic license. He does not move in any given orbit, but like a falling star, shoots from his sphere. He is pragmatical, restless, unfixed, full of experiments, beginning every thing a-new, wiser than his betters, judging for himself, dictating to others. He is decidedly *revolutionary*. He may have given up the reform of the State: but depend upon it, he has some other *hobby* of the same kind. Does he not dedicate to his present Majesty that extraordinary poem on the death of his father, called *The Vision of Judgment*, as a specimen of what might be done in English hexameters? In a court-poem all should be trite and on an approved model. He might as well have presented himself at the levee in a fancy or masquerade dress. Mr. Southey was not *to try conclusions* with Majesty—still less on such an occasion. The extreme freedoms with departed greatness, the party-petulance carried to the Throne of Grace, the unchecked indulgence of private humour, the assumption of infallibility and even of the voice of Heaven in this poem, are pointed instances of what we have said. They shew the singular state of over-excitement of Mr. Southey's mind, and the force of old habits of independent and unbridled thinking, which cannot be kept down even in addressing his Sovereign! Look at Mr. Southey's larger poems, his *Kehama*, his *Thalaba*, his *Madoc*, his *Roderic*. Who will deny the spirit, the scope, the splendid imagery, the hurried and startling interest that pervades them? Who will say that they are not sustained on fictions wilder than his own Glendoveer, that they are not the daring creations of a mind curbed by no law, tamed by no fear, that they are not rather like the trances than the waking dreams of genius, that they are not the very paradoxes of poetry? All this is very well, very intelligible, and very harmless, if we regard the rank excrescences of Mr. Southey's poetry, like the red and blue flowers in corn, as the unweeded growth of a luxuriant and wandering fancy; or if we allow the yeasty workings of an ardent spirit to ferment and boil over—the variety, the boldness, the lively stimulus given to the mind may then atone for the violation of rules and the offences to bed-rid authority; but not if our poetic libertine sets up for a law-giver and judge, or an apprehender of vagrants in the regions either of taste or opinion. Our motley gentleman deserves the strait-waistcoat, if he is for setting others in the stocks of servility, or condemning them to the pillory for a new mode of rhyme or reason. Or if a composer of sacred Dramas on classic models, or a translator of an old Latin author (that will hardly bear translation) or a vamper-up of vapid cantos and Odes set to music, were to turn pander to prescription and palliater of every dull, incorrigible abuse, it would not be much to be wondered at or even regretted. But in Mr. Southey it was a lamentable falling-off. It is indeed to be deplored, it is a stain on genius, a blow to humanity, that the author of *Joan of Arc*—that work in which the love of Liberty is exhaled like the breath of spring, mild, balmy, heaven-born, that is full of tears and virgin-sighs, and yearnings of affection after truth and good, gushing warm and crimsoned from the heart—should ever after turn to folly, or become the advocate of a rotten cause. After giving up his heart to that subject, he ought not (whatever others might do) ever to have set his foot within the threshold of a court. He might be sure that he would not gain forgiveness or favour by it, nor obtain a single cordial smile from greatness. All that Mr. Southey is or that he does best, is independent, spontaneous, free as the vital air he draws—when he affects the courtier or the sophist, he is obliged to put a constraint upon himself, to hold in his breath, he loses his genius, and offers a violence to his nature. His characteristic faults are the excess of a lively, unguarded temperament: —oh! let them not degenerate into cold-blooded, heartless vices! If we speak or have ever spoken of Mr.

Southey with severity, it is with "the malice of old friends, " for we count ourselves among his sincerest and heartiest well-wishers. But while he himself is anomalous, incalculable, eccentric, from youth to age (the *Wat Tyler* and the *Vision of Judgment* are the Alpha and Omega of his disjointed career) full of sallies of humour, of ebullitions of spleen, making *jets-d'eaux,* cascades, fountains, and water-works of his idle opinions, he would shut up the wits of others in leaden cisterns, to stagnate and corrupt, or bury them under ground —

"Far from the sun and summer gale! "

He would suppress the freedom of wit and humour, of which he has set the example, and claim a privilege for playing antics. He would introduce an uniformity of intellectual weights and measures, of irregular metres and settled opinions, and enforce it with a high hand. This has been judged hard by some, and has brought down a severity of recrimination, perhaps disproportioned to the injury done. "Because he is virtuous, " (it has been asked,) "are there to be no more cakes and ale? " Because he is loyal, are we to take all our notions from the *Quarterly Review*? Because he is orthodox, are we to do nothing but read the *Book of the Church*? We declare we think his former poetical scepticism was not only more amiable, but had more of the spirit of religion in it, implied a more heartfelt trust in nature and providence than his present bigotry. We are at the same time free to declare that we think his articles in the *Quarterly Review,* notwithstanding their virulence and the talent they display, have a tendency to qualify its most pernicious effects. They have redeeming traits in them. "A little leaven leaveneth the whole lump: " and the spirit of humanity (thanks to Mr. Southey) is not quite expelled from the *Quarterly Review*. At the corner of his pen, "there hangs a vapourous drop profound" of independence and liberality, which falls upon its pages, and oozes out through the pores of the public mind. There is a fortunate difference between writers whose hearts are naturally callous to truth, and whose understandings are hermetically sealed against all impressions but those of self-interest, and a man like Mr. Southey. *Once a philanthropist and always a philanthropist.* No man can entirely baulk his nature: it breaks out in spite of him. In all those questions, where the spirit of contradiction does not interfere, on which he is not sore from old bruises, or sick from the extravagance of youthful intoxication, as from a last night's debauch, our "laureate" is still bold, free, candid, open to conviction, a reformist without knowing it. He does not advocate the slave-trade, he does not arm Mr. Malthus's revolting ratios with his authority, he does not strain hard to deluge Ireland with blood. On such points, where humanity has not become obnoxious, where liberty has not passed into a by-word, Mr. Southey is still liberal and humane. The elasticity of his spirit is unbroken: the bow recoils to its old position. He still stands convicted of his early passion for inquiry and improvement. He was not regularly articled as a Government-tool! —Perhaps the most pleasing and striking of all Mr. Southey's poems are not his triumphant taunts hurled against oppression, are not his glowing effusions to Liberty, but those in which, with a mild melancholy, he seems conscious of his own infirmities of temper, and to feel a wish to correct by thought and time the precocity and sharpness of his disposition. May the quaint but affecting aspiration expressed in one of these be fulfilled, that as he mellows into maturer age, all such asperities may wear off, and he himself become

"Like the high leaves upon the holly-tree! "

Mr. Southey's prose-style can scarcely be too much praised. It is plain, clear, pointed, familiar, perfectly modern in its texture, but with a grave and sparkling admixture of *archaisms* in its ornaments and occasional phraseology. He is the best and most natural prose-writer of any poet of the day; we mean that he is far better than Lord Byron, Mr. Wordsworth, or Mr. Coleridge, for instance. The manner is perhaps superior to the matter, that is, in his Essays and Reviews. There is rather a want of originality and even of *impetus*: but there is no want of playful or biting satire, of ingenuity, of casuistry, of

learning and of information. He is "full of wise saws and modern" (as well as ancient) "instances. " Mr. Southey may not always convince his opponents; but he seldom fails to stagger, never to gall them. In a word, we may describe his style by saying that it has not the body or thickness of port wine, but is like clear sherry with kernels of old authors thrown into it! —He also excels as an historian and prose-translator. His histories abound in information, and exhibit proofs of the most indefatigable patience and industry. By no uncommon process of the mind, Mr. Southey seems willing to steady the extreme levity of his opinions and feelings by an appeal to facts. His translations of the Spanish and French romances are also executed *con amore*, and with the literal fidelity and care of a mere linguist. That of the *Cid*, in particular, is a masterpiece. Not a word could be altered for the better, in the old scriptural style which it adopts in conformity to the original. It is no less interesting in itself, or as a record of high and chivalrous feelings and manners, than it is worthy of perusal as a literary curiosity.

Mr. Southey's conversation has a little resemblance to a common-place book; his habitual deportment to a piece of clock-work. He is not remarkable either as a reasoner or an observer: but he is quick, unaffected, replete with anecdote, various and retentive in his reading, and exceedingly happy in his play upon words, as most scholars are who give their minds this sportive turn. We have chiefly seen Mr. Southey in company where few people appear to advantage, we mean in that of Mr. Coleridge. He has not certainly the same range of speculation, nor the same flow of sounding words, but he makes up by the details of knowledge, and by a scrupulous correctness of statement for what he wants in originality of thought, or impetuous declamation. The tones of Mr. Coleridge's voice are eloquence: those of Mr. Southey are meagre, shrill, and dry. Mr. Coleridge's *forte* is conversation, and he is conscious of this: Mr. Southey evidently considers writing as his strong-hold, and if gravelled in an argument, or at a loss for an explanation, refers to something he has written on the subject, or brings out his port-folio, doubled down in dog-ears, in confirmation of some fact. He is scholastic and professional in his ideas. He sets more value on what he writes than on what he says: he is perhaps prouder of his library than of his own productions—themselves a library! He is more simple in his manners than his friend Mr. Coleridge; but at the same time less cordial or conciliating. He is less vain, or has less hope of pleasing, and therefore lays himself less out to please. There is an air of condescension in his civility. With a tall, loose figure, a peaked austerity of countenance, and no inclination to *embonpoint*, you would say he has something puritanical, something ascetic in his appearance. He answers to Mandeville's description of Addison, "a parson in a tye-wig. " He is not a boon companion, nor does he indulge in the pleasures of the table, nor in any other vice; nor are we aware that Mr. Southey is chargeable with any human frailty but—*want of charity*! Having fewer errors to plead guilty to, he is less lenient to those of others. He was born an age too late. Had he lived a century or two ago, he would have been a happy as well as blameless character. But the distraction of the time has unsettled him, and the multiplicity of his pretensions have jostled with each other. No man in our day (at least no man of genius) has led so uniformly and entirely the life of a scholar from boyhood to the present hour, devoting himself to learning with the enthusiasm of an early love, with the severity and constancy of a religious vow—and well would it have been for him if he had confined himself to this, and not undertaken to pull down or to patch up the State! However irregular in his opinions, Mr. Southey is constant, unremitting, mechanical in his studies, and the performance of his duties. There is nothing Pindaric or Shandean here. In all the relations and charities of private life, he is correct, exemplary, generous, just. We never heard a single impropriety laid to his charge; and if he has many enemies, few men can boast more numerous or stauncher friends. — The variety and piquancy of his writings form a striking contrast to the mode in which they are produced. He rises early, and writes or reads till breakfast-time. He writes or reads after breakfast till dinner, after dinner till tea, and from tea till bed-time—

> "And follows so the ever-running year
> With profitable labour to his grave—"

on Derwent's banks, beneath the foot of Skiddaw. Study serves him for business, exercise, recreation. He passes from verse to prose, from history to poetry, from reading to writing, by a stop-watch. He writes a fair hand, without blots, sitting upright in his chair, leaves off when he comes to the bottom of the page, and changes the subject for another, as opposite as the Antipodes. His mind is after all rather the recipient and transmitter of knowledge, than the originator of it. He has hardly grasp of thought enough to arrive at any great leading truth. His passions do not amount to more than irritability. With some gall in his pen, and coldness in his manner, he has a great deal of kindness in his heart. Rash in his opinions, he is steady in his attachments—and is a man, in many particulars admirable, in all respectable—his political inconsistency alone excepted!

* * * * *

MR. T. MOORE. —MR. LEIGH HUNT.

"Or winglet of the fairy humming-bird,
Like atoms of the rainbow fluttering round. "

CAMPBELL.

The lines placed at the head of this sketch, from a contemporary writer, appear to us very descriptive of Mr. Moore's poetry. His verse is like a shower of beauty; a dance of images; a stream of music; or like the spray of the water-fall, tinged by the morning-beam with rosy light. The characteristic distinction of our author's style is this continuous and incessant flow of voluptuous thoughts and shining allusions. He ought to write with a crystal pen on silver paper. His subject is set off by a dazzling veil of poetic diction, like a wreath of flowers gemmed with innumerable dewdrops, that weep, tremble, and glitter in liquid softness and pearly light, while the song of birds ravishes the ear, and languid odours breathe around, and Aurora opens Heaven's smiling portals, Peris and nymphs peep through the golden glades, and an Angel's wing glances over the glossy scene.

"No dainty flower or herb that grows on ground,
No arboret with painted blossoms drest,
And smelling sweet, but there it might be found
To bud out fair, and its sweet smells throw all around.

No tree, whose branches did not bravely spring;
No branch, whereon a fine bird did not sit;
No bird, but did her shrill notes sweetly sing;
No song, but did contain a lovely dit:
Trees, branches, birds, and songs were framed fit
For to allure frail minds to careless ease. "....

Mr. Campbell's imagination is fastidious and select; and hence, though we meet with more exquisite beauties in his writings, we meet with them more rarely: there is comparatively a dearth of ornament. But Mr. Moore's strictest economy is "wasteful and superfluous excess: " he is always liberal, and never at a loss; for sooner than not stimulate and delight the reader, he is willing to be tawdry, or superficial, or common-place. His Muse must be fine at any rate, though she should paint, and wear cast-off decorations.

Rather than have any lack of excitement, he repeats himself; and "Eden, and Eblis, and cherub-smiles" fill up the pauses of the sentiment with a sickly monotony. —It has been too much our author's object to pander to the artificial taste of the age; and his productions, however brilliant and agreeable, are in consequence somewhat meretricious and effeminate. It was thought formerly enough to have an occasionally fine passage in the progress of a story or a poem, and an occasionally striking image or expression in a fine passage or description. But this style, it seems, was to be exploded as rude, Gothic, meagre, and dry. Now all must be raised to the same tantalising and preposterous level. There must be no pause, no interval, no repose, no gradation. Simplicity and truth yield up the palm to affectation and grimace. The craving of the public mind after novelty and effect is a false and uneasy appetite that must be pampered with fine words at every step—we must be tickled with sound, startled with shew, and relieved by the importunate, uninterrupted display of fancy and verbal tinsel as much as possible from the fatigue of thought or shock of feeling. A poem is to resemble an exhibition of fireworks, with a continual explosion of quaint figures and devices, flash after flash, that surprise for the moment, and leave no trace of light or warmth behind them. Or modern poetry in its retrograde progress comes at last to be constructed on the principles of the modern OPERA, where an attempt is made to gratify every sense at every instant, and where the understanding alone is insulted and the heart mocked. It is in this view only that we can discover that Mr. Moore's poetry is vitiated or immoral, —it seduces the taste and enervates the imagination. It creates a false standard of reference, and inverts or decompounds the natural order of association, in which objects strike the thoughts and feelings. His is the poetry of the bath, of the toilette, of the saloon, of the fashionable world; not the poetry of nature, of the heart, or of human life. He stunts and enfeebles equally the growth of the imagination and the affections, by not taking the seed of poetry and sowing it in the ground of truth, and letting it expand in the dew and rain, and shoot up to heaven,

"And spread its sweet leaves to the air,
Or dedicate its beauty to the sun, "—

instead of which he anticipates and defeats his own object, by plucking flowers and blossoms from the stem, and setting them in the ground of idleness and folly—or in the cap of his own vanity, where they soon wither and disappear, "dying or ere they sicken! "

This is but a sort of child's play, a short-sighted ambition. In Milton we meet with many prosaic lines, either because the subject does not require raising or because they are necessary to connect the story, or serve as a relief to other passages—there is not such a thing to be found in all Mr. Moore's writings. His volumes present us with "a perpetual feast of nectar'd sweets"—but we cannot add, —"where no crude surfeit reigns. " He indeed cloys with sweetness; he obscures with splendour; he fatigues with gaiety. We are stifled on beds of roses—we literally lie "on the rack of restless ecstacy. " His flowery fancy "looks so fair and smells so sweet, that the sense aches at it. " His verse droops and languishes under a load of beauty, like a bough laden with fruit. His gorgeous style is like "another morn risen on mid-noon. " There is no passage that is not made up of blushing lines, no line that is not enriched with a sparkling metaphor, no image that is left unadorned with a double epithet—all his verbs, nouns, adjectives, are equally glossy, smooth, and beautiful. Every stanza is transparent with light, perfumed with odours, floating in liquid harmony, melting in luxurious, evanescent delights. His Muse is never contented with an offering from one sense alone, but brings another rifled charm to match it, and revels in a fairy round of pleasure. The interest is not dramatic, but melo-dramatic—it is a mixture of painting, poetry, and music, of the natural and preternatural, of obvious sentiment and romantic costume. A rose is a *Gul*, a nightingale a *Bulbul*. We might fancy ourselves in an eastern harem, amidst Ottomans, and otto of roses, and veils and spangles, and marble pillars, and cool fountains, and Arab maids and Genii, and magicians, and Peris, and cherubs, and what not? Mr. Moore has a little mistaken the art of poetry for the *cosmetic art*. He does not compose an historic group, or work out a single figure; but throws a variety of elementary sensations, of vivid impressions together, and calls it a description. He makes out an inventory of beauty—the smile on the lips, the dimple on the cheeks, *item*, golden locks, *item*, a pair of blue wings, *item*, a silver sound, with breathing fragrance and radiant light, and thinks it a character or a story. He gets together a number of fine things and fine names, and thinks that, flung on heaps, they make up a fine poem. This dissipated, fulsome, painted, patch-work style may succeed in the levity and languor of the *boudoir*, or might have been adapted to the Pavilions of royalty, but it is not the style of Parnassus, nor a passport to Immortality. It is not the taste of the ancients, "'tis not classical lore"—nor the fashion of Tibullus, or Theocritus, or Anacreon, or Virgil, or Ariosto, or Pope, or Byron, or any great writer among the living or the dead, but it is the style of our English

Anacreon, and it is (or was) the fashion of the day! Let one example (and that an admired one) taken from *Lalla Rookh*, suffice to explain the mystery and soften the harshness of the foregoing criticism.

"Now upon Syria's land of roses
Softly the light of eve reposes,
And like a glory, the broad sun
Hangs over sainted Lebanon:
Whose head in wintry grandeur towers,
And whitens with eternal sleet,
While summer, in a vale of flowers,
Is sleeping rosy at his feet.
To one who look'd from upper air,
O'er all th' enchanted regions there,
How beauteous must have been the glow,
The life, the sparkling from below!
Fair gardens, shining streams, with ranks
Of golden melons on their banks,
More golden where the sun-light falls, —
Gay lizards, glittering on the walls
Of ruin'd shrines, busy and bright
As they were all alive with light; —
And yet more splendid, numerous flocks
Of pigeons, settling on the rocks,
With their rich, restless wings, that gleam
Variously in the crimson beam
Of the warm west, as if inlaid
With brilliants from the mine, or made
Of tearless rainbows, such as span
The unclouded skies of Peristan!
And then, the mingling sounds that come
Of shepherd's ancient reed, with hum
Of the wild bees of Palestine,
Banquetting through the flowery vales—
And, Jordan, those sweet banks of thine,
And woods, so full of nightingales. " —

The following lines are the very perfection of Della Cruscan sentiment, and affected orientalism of style. The Peri exclaims on finding that old talisman and hackneyed poetical machine, "a penitent tear" —

"Joy, joy forever! my task is done—

The gates are pass'd, and Heaven is won!
Oh! am I not happy? I am, I am —
To thee, sweet Eden! how dark and sad
Are the diamond turrets of Shadukiam,
And the fragrant bowers of Amberabad. "

There is in all this a play of fancy, a glitter of words, a shallowness of thought, and a want of truth and solidity that is wonderful, and that nothing but the heedless, rapid glide of the verse could render tolerable: — — it seems that the poet, as well as the lover,

"May bestride the Gossamer,
That wantons in the idle, summer air,
And yet not fall, so light is vanity! "

Mr. Moore ought not to contend with serious difficulties or with entire subjects. He can write verses, not a poem. There is no principle of massing or of continuity in his productions—neither height nor breadth nor depth of capacity. There is no truth of representation, no strong internal feeling—but a continual flutter and display of affected airs and graces, like a finished coquette, who hides the want of symmetry by extravagance of dress, and the want of passion by flippant forwardness and unmeaning sentimentality. All is flimsy, all is florid to excess. His imagination may dally with insect beauties, with Rosicrucian spells; may describe a butterfly's wing, a flower-pot, a fan: but it should not attempt to span the great outlines of nature, or keep pace with the sounding march of events, or grapple with the strong fibres of the human heart. The great becomes turgid in his hands, the pathetic insipid. If Mr. Moore were to describe the heights of Chimboraco, instead of the loneliness, the vastness and the shadowy might, he would only think of adorning it with roseate tints, like a strawberry-ice, and would transform a magician's fortress in the Himmalaya (stripped of its mysterious gloom and frowning horrors) into a jeweller's toy, to be set upon a lady's toilette. In proof of this, see above "the diamond turrets of Shadukiam, " &c. The description of Mokanna in the fight, though it has spirit and grandeur of effect, has still a great alloy of the mock-heroic in it. The route of blood and death, which is otherwise well marked, is infested with a swarm of "fire-fly" fancies.

"In vain Mokanna, 'midst the general flight,
Stands, like the red moon, in some stormy night.
Among the fugitive clouds, that hurrying by,

Leave only her unshaken in the sky. "

This simile is fine, and would have been perfect, but that the moon is not red, and that she seems to hurry by the clouds, not they by her. The description of the warrior's youthful adversary,

— —"Whose coming seems
A light, a glory, such as breaks in dreams. " —

is fantastic and enervated—a field of battle has nothing to do with dreams: —and again, the two lines immediately after,

"And every sword, true as o'er billows dim
The needle tracks the load-star, following him" —

are a mere piece of enigmatical ingenuity and scientific *mimminee-pimminee.*

We cannot except the *Irish Melodies* from the same censure. If these national airs do indeed express the soul of impassioned feeling in his countrymen, the case of Ireland is hopeless. If these prettinesses pass for patriotism, if a country can heave from its heart's core only these vapid, varnished sentiments, lip-deep, and let its tears of blood evaporate in an empty conceit, let it be governed as it has been. There are here no tones to waken Liberty, to console Humanity. Mr. Moore converts the wild harp of Erin into a musical snuff-box[A]! — We *do* except from this censure the author's political squibs, and the "Two- penny Post-bag. " These are essences, are "nests of spicery", bitter and sweet, honey and gall together. No one can so well describe the set speech of a dull formalist[B], or the flowing locks of a Dowager,

"In the manner of Ackermann's dresses for May. "

His light, agreeable, polished style pierces through the body of the court—hits off the faded graces of "an Adonis of fifty", weighs the vanity of fashion in tremulous scales, mimics the grimace of affectation and folly, shews up the littleness of the great, and spears a phalanx of statesmen with its glittering point as with a diamond broach.

"In choosing songs the Regent named
'Had I a heart for falsehood fram'd: '

> While gentle Hertford begg'd and pray'd
> For 'Young I am, and sore afraid. '"

Nothing in Pope or Prior ever surpassed the delicate insinuation and adroit satire of these lines, and hundreds more of our author's composition. We wish he would not take pains to make us think of them with less pleasure than formerly. —The "Fudge Family" is in the same spirit, but with a little falling-off. There is too great a mixture of undisguised Jacobinism and fashionable *slang*. The "divine Fanny Bias" and "the mountains *à la Russe*" figure in somewhat quaintly with Buonaparte and the Bourbons. The poet also launches the lightning of political indignation; but it rather plays round and illumines his own pen than reaches the devoted heads at which it is aimed!

Mr. Moore is in private life an amiable and estimable man. The embellished and voluptuous style of his poetry, his unpretending origin, and his *mignon* figure soon introduced him to the notice of the great, and his gaiety, his wit, his good-humour, and many agreeable accomplishments fixed him there, the darling of his friends and the idol of fashion. If he is no longer familiar with Royalty as with his garter, the fault is not his—his adherence to his principles caused the separation—his love of his country was the cloud that intercepted the sunshine of court-favour. This is so far well. Mr. Moore vindicates his own dignity; but the sense of intrinsic worth, of wide-spread fame, and of the intimacy of the great makes him perhaps a little too fastidious and *exigeant* as to the pretensions of others. He has been so long accustomed to the society of Whig Lords, and so enchanted by the smile of beauty and fashion, that he really fancies himself one of the *set*, to which he is admitted on sufferance, and tries very unnecessarily to keep others out of it. He talks familiarly of works that are or are not read "in *our* circle; " and seated smiling and at his ease in a coronet-coach, enlivening the owner by his brisk sallies and Attic conceits, is shocked, as he passes, to see a Peer of the realm shake hands with a poet. There is a little indulgence of spleen and envy, a little servility and pandering to aristocratic pride in this proceeding. Is Mr. Moore bound to advise a Noble Poet to get as fast as possible out of a certain publication, lest he should not be able to give an account at Holland or at Lansdown House, how his friend Lord B——had associated himself with his friend L. H——? Is he afraid that the "Spirit of Monarchy" will eclipse the "Fables for the Holy Alliance" in virulence and plain speaking? Or are the members of the "Fudge Family" to secure a monopoly for the abuse of the

Bourbons and the doctrine of Divine Right? Because he is genteel and sarcastic, may not others be paradoxical and argumentative? Or must no one bark at a Minister or General, unless they have been first dandled, like a little French pug-dog, in the lap of a lady of quality? Does Mr. Moore insist on the double claim of birth and genius as a title to respectability in all advocates of the popular side—but himself? Or is he anxious to keep the pretensions of his patrician and plebeian friends quite separate, so as to be himself the only point of union, a sort of *double meaning*, between the two? It is idle to think of setting bounds to the weakness and illusions of self-love as long as it is confined to a man's own breast; but it ought not to be made a plea for holding back the powerful hand that is stretched out to save another struggling with the tide of popular prejudice, who has suffered shipwreck of health, fame and fortune in a common cause, and who has deserved the aid and the good wishes of all who are (on principle) embarked in the same cause by equal zeal and honesty, if not by equal talents to support and to adorn it!

We shall conclude the present article with a short notice of an individual who, in the cast of his mind and in political principle, bears no very remote resemblance to the patriot and wit just spoken of, and on whose merits we should descant at greater length, but that personal intimacy might be supposed to render us partial. It is well when personal intimacy produces this effect; and when the light, that dazzled us at a distance, does not on a closer inspection turn out an opaque substance. This is a charge that none of his friends will bring against Mr. Leigh Hunt. He improves upon acquaintance. The author translates admirably into the man. Indeed the very faults of his style are virtues in the individual. His natural gaiety and sprightliness of manner, his high animal spirits, and the *vinous* quality of his mind, produce an immediate fascination and intoxication in those who come in contact with him, and carry off in society whatever in his writings may to some seem flat and impertinent. From great sanguineness of temper, from great quickness and unsuspecting simplicity, he runs on to the public as he does at his own fire-side, and talks about himself, forgetting that he is not always among friends. His look, his tone are required to point many things that he says: his frank, cordial manner reconciles you instantly to a little over-bearing, over-weening self- complacency. "To be admired, he needs but to be seen: " but perhaps he ought to be seen to be fully appreciated. No one ever sought his society who did not come away with a more favourable opinion of him: no one was ever disappointed, except those who had entertained idle prejudices against him. He sometimes trifles with his readers, or tires of a subject (from not being urged on by the stimulus of immediate sympathy)—but in conversation he is all life and animation, combining the vivacity of the school-boy with the resources of the wit and the taste of the scholar. The personal character, the spontaneous impulses, do not appear to excuse the author, unless you are acquainted with his situation and habits—like some proud beauty who gives herself what we think strange airs and graces under a mask, but who is instantly forgiven when she shews her face. We have said that Lord Byron is a sublime coxcomb: why should we not say that Mr. Hunt is a delightful one? There is certainly an exuberance of satisfaction in his manner which is more than the strict logical premises warrant, and which dull and phlegmatic constitutions know nothing of, and cannot understand till they see it. He is the only poet or literary man we ever knew who puts us in mind of Sir John Suckling or Killigrew or Carew; or who united rare intellectual acquirements with outward grace and natural gentility. Mr. Hunt ought to have been a gentleman born, and to have patronised men of letters. He might then have played, and sung, and laughed, and talked his life away; have written manly prose, elegant verse; and his *Story of Rimini* would have been praised by Mr. Blackwood. As it is, there is no man now living who at the same time writes prose and verse so well, with the exception of Mr. Southey (an exception, we fear, that will be little palatable to either of these gentlemen). His prose writings, however, display more consistency of principle than the laureate's: his verses more taste. We will venture to oppose his Third Canto of the *Story of Rimini* for classic elegance and natural feeling to any equal number of lines from Mr. Southey's Epics or from Mr. Moore's Lalla Rookh. In a more gay and conversational style of writing, we think his *Epistle to Lord Byron* on his going abroad, is a masterpiece; —and the *Feast of the Poets* has run through several editions. A light, familiar grace, and mild unpretending pathos are the characteristics of his more sportive or serious writings, whether in poetry or prose. A smile plays round the features of the one; a tear is ready to start from the thoughtful gaze of the other. He perhaps takes too little pains, and indulges in too much wayward caprice in both. A wit and a poet, Mr. Hunt is also distinguished by fineness of tact and sterling sense: he has only been a visionary in humanity, the fool of virtue. What then is the drawback to so many shining qualities, that has made them useless, or even hurtful to their owner? His crime is, to have been Editor of the *Examiner* ten years ago, when some allusion was made in it to the age of the present king, and that, though his Majesty has grown older, our luckless politician is no wiser than he was then!

[Footnote A: Compare his songs with Burns's.]

[Footnote B:

> "There was a little man, and he had a little soul,
> And he said, Little soul, let us try, " &c. —

Parody on

> "There was a little man, and he had a little gun. " —

One should think this exquisite ridicule of a pedantic effusion might have silenced for ever the automaton that delivered it: but the official personage in question at the close of the Session addressed an extra-official congratulation to the Prince Regent on a bill that had *not* passed—as if to repeat and insist upon our errors were to justify them.]

* * * * *

ELIA, AND GEOFFREY CRAYON.

So Mr. Charles Lamb and Mr. Washington Irvine choose to designate themselves; and as their lucubrations under one or other of these *noms de guerre* have gained considerable notice from the public, we shall here attempt to discriminate their several styles and manner, and to point out the beauties and defects of each in treating of somewhat similar subjects.

Mr. Irvine is, we take it, the more popular writer of the two, or a more general favourite: Mr. Lamb has more devoted, and perhaps more judicious partisans. Mr. Irvine is by birth an American, and has, as it were, *skimmed the cream*, and taken off patterns with great skill and cleverness, from our best known and happiest writers, so that their thoughts and almost their reputation are indirectly transferred to his page, and smile upon us from another hemisphere, like "the pale reflex of Cynthia's brow: " he succeeds to our admiration and our sympathy by a sort of prescriptive title and traditional privilege. Mr. Lamb, on the contrary, being "native to the manner here, " though he too has borrowed from previous sources, instead of availing himself of the most popular and admired, has groped out his way, and made his most successful researches among the more obscure and intricate, though certainly not the least pithy or pleasant of our writers. Mr. Washington Irvine has culled and transplanted the flowers of modern literature, for the amusement of the general reader: Mr. Lamb has raked among the dust and cobwebs of a more remote period, has exhibited specimens of curious relics, and pored over moth-eaten, decayed manuscripts, for the benefit of the more inquisitive and discerning part of the public. Antiquity after a time has the grace of novelty, as old fashions revived are mistaken for new ones; and a certain quaintness and singularity of style is an agreeable relief to the smooth and insipid monotony of modern composition. Mr. Lamb has succeeded not by conforming to the *Spirit of the Age*, but in opposition to it. He does not march boldly along with the crowd, but steals off the pavement to pick his way in the contrary direction. He prefers *bye-ways* to *highways*. When the full tide of human life pours along to some festive shew, to some pageant of a day, Elia would stand on one side to look over an old book-stall, or stroll down some deserted pathway in search of a pensive inscription over a tottering door-way, or some quaint device in architecture, illustrative of embryo art and ancient manners. Mr. Lamb has the very soul of an antiquarian, as this implies a reflecting humanity; the film of the past hovers for ever before him. He is shy, sensitive, the reverse of every thing coarse, vulgar, obtrusive, and *common-place*. He would fain "shuffle off this mortal coil", and his spirit clothes itself in the garb of elder time, homelier, but more durable. He is borne along with no pompous paradoxes, shines in no glittering tinsel of a fashionable phraseology; is neither fop nor sophist. He has none of the turbulence or froth of new-fangled opinions. His style runs pure and clear, though it may often take an underground course, or be conveyed through old-fashioned conduit-pipes. Mr. Lamb does not court popularity, nor strut in gaudy plumes, but shrinks from every kind of ostentatious and obvious pretension into the retirement of his own mind.

> "The self-applauding bird, the peacock see: —
> Mark what a sumptuous pharisee is he!
> Meridian sun-beams tempt him to unfold
> His radiant glories, azure, green, and gold:
> He treads as if, some solemn music near,
> His measured step were governed by his ear:
> And seems to say — Ye meaner fowl, give place,
> I am all splendour, dignity, and grace!
> Not so the pheasant on his charms presumes,
> Though he too has a glory in his plumes.
> He, christian-like, retreats with modest mien
> To the close copse or far sequestered green,
> And shines without desiring to be seen. "

These lines well describe the modest and delicate beauties of Mr. Lamb's writings, contrasted with the lofty and vain-glorious pretensions of some of his contemporaries. This gentleman is not one of those who pay all their homage to the prevailing idol: he thinks that

> "New-born gauds are made and moulded of things past. "

nor does he

> "Give to dust that is a little gilt
> More laud than gilt o'er-dusted. "

His convictions "do not in broad rumour lie, " nor are they "set off to the world in the glistering foil" of fashion; but "live and breathe aloft in those pure eyes, and perfect judgment of all-seeing *time*. " Mr.

Lamb rather affects and is tenacious of the obscure and remote: of that which rests on its own intrinsic and silent merit; which scorns all alliance, or even the suspicion of owing any thing to noisy clamour, to the glare of circumstances. There is a fine tone of *chiaro-scuro*, a moral perspective in his writings. He delights to dwell on that which is fresh to the eye of memory; he yearns after and covets what soothes the frailty of human nature. That touches him most nearly which is withdrawn to a certain distance, which verges on the borders of oblivion: —that piques and provokes his fancy most, which is hid from a superficial glance. That which, though gone by, is still remembered, is in his view more genuine, and has given more "vital signs that it will live, " than a thing of yesterday, that may be forgotten to-morrow. Death has in this sense the spirit of life in it; and the shadowy has to our author something substantial in it. Ideas savour most of reality in his mind; or rather his imagination loiters on the edge of each, and a page of his writings recals to our fancy the *stranger* on the grate, fluttering in its dusky tensity, with its idle superstition and hospitable welcome!

Mr. Lamb has a distaste to new faces, to new books, to new buildings, to new customs. He is shy of all imposing appearances, of all assumptions of self-importance, of all adventitious ornaments, of all mechanical advantages, even to a nervous excess. It is not merely that he does not rely upon, or ordinarily avail himself of them; he holds them in abhorrence, he utterly abjures and discards them, and places a great gulph between him and them. He disdains all the vulgar artifices of authorship, all the cant of criticism, and helps to notoriety. He has no grand swelling theories to attract the visionary and the enthusiast, no passing topics to allure the thoughtless and the vain. He evades the present, he mocks the future. His affections revert to, and settle on the past, but then, even this must have something personal and local in it to interest him deeply and thoroughly; he pitches his tent in the suburbs of existing manners; brings down the account of character to the few straggling remains of the last generation; seldom ventures beyond the bills of mortality, and occupies that nice point between egotism and disinterested humanity. No one makes the tour of our southern metropolis, or describes the manners of the last age, so well as Mr. Lamb—with so fine, and yet so formal an air—with such vivid obscurity, with such arch piquancy, such picturesque quaintness, such smiling pathos. How admirably he has sketched the former inmates of the South- Sea House; what "fine fretwork he makes of their double and single entries! " With what a firm, yet subtle pencil he has embodied *Mrs.*

Battle's Opinions on Whist! How notably he embalms a battered *beau*; how delightfully an amour, that was cold forty years ago, revives in his pages! With what well-disguised humour he introduces us to his relations, and how freely he serves up his friends! Certainly, some of his portraits are *fixtures*, and will do to hang up as lasting and lively emblems of human infirmity. Then there is no one who has so sure an ear for "the chimes at midnight", not even excepting Mr. Justice Shallow; nor could Master Silence himself take his "cheese and pippins" with a more significant and satisfactory air. With what a gusto Mr. Lamb describes the inns and courts of law, the Temple and Gray's-Inn, as if he had been a student there for the last two hundred years, and had been as well acquainted with the person of Sir Francis Bacon as he is with his portrait or writings! It is hard to say whether St. John's Gate is connected with more intense and authentic associations in his mind, as a part of old London Wall, or as the frontispiece (time out of mind) of the Gentleman's Magazine. He haunts Watling-street like a gentle spirit; the avenues to the play-houses are thick with panting recollections, and Christ's-Hospital still breathes the balmy breath of infancy in his description of it! Whittington and his Cat are a fine hallucination for Mr. Lamb's historic Muse, and we believe he never heartily forgave a certain writer who took the subject of Guy Faux out of his hands. The streets of London are his fairy-land, teeming with wonder, with life and interest to his retrospective glance, as it did to the eager eye of childhood; he has contrived to weave its tritest traditions into a bright and endless romance!

Mr. Lamb's taste in books is also fine, and it is peculiar. It is not the worse for a little *idiosyncrasy*. He does not go deep into the Scotch novels, but he is at home in Smollett and Fielding. He is little read in Junius or Gibbon, but no man can give a better account of Burton's Anatomy of Melancholy, or Sir Thomas Brown's Urn-Burial, or Fuller's Worthies, or John Bunyan's Holy War. No one is more unimpressible to a specious declamation; no one relishes a recondite beauty more. His admiration of Shakespear and Milton does not make him despise Pope; and he can read Parnell with patience, and Gay with delight. His taste in French and German literature is somewhat defective: nor has he made much progress in the science of Political Economy or other abstruse studies, though he has read vast folios of controversial divinity, merely for the sake of the intricacy of style, and to save himself the pain of thinking. Mr. Lamb is a good judge of prints and pictures. His admiration of Hogarth does credit to both, particularly when it is considered that Leonardo da Vinci is his next greatest favourite, and that his love of the *actual* does not proceed from a want of taste for the *ideal*. His worst fault is an over-eagerness of enthusiasm, which occasionally makes him take a surfeit of his highest favourites. —Mr. Lamb excels in familiar conversation almost as much as in writing, when his modesty does not overpower his self-possession. He is as little of a proser as possible; but he *blurts* out the finest wit and sense in the world. He keeps a good deal in the back-ground at first, till some excellent conceit pushes him forward, and then he abounds in whim and pleasantry. There is a primitive simplicity and self-denial about his manners; and a Quakerism in his personal appearance, which is, however, relieved by a fine Titian head, full of dumb eloquence! Mr. Lamb is a general favourite with those who know him. His character is equally singular and amiable. He is endeared to his friends not less by his foibles than his virtues; he insures their esteem by the one, and does not wound their self-love by the other. He gains ground in the opinion of others, by making no advances in his own. We easily admire genius where the diffidence of the possessor makes our acknowledgment of merit seem like a sort of patronage, or act of condescension, as we willingly extend our good offices where they are not exacted as obligations, or repaid with sullen indifference. — The style of the Essays of Elia is liable to the charge of a certain *mannerism*. His sentences are cast in the mould of old authors; his expressions are borrowed from them; but his feelings and observations are genuine and original, taken from actual life, or from his own breast; and he may be said (if any one can) "to have coined his heart for *jests*, " and to have split his brain for fine distinctions! Mr. Lamb, from the peculiarity of his exterior and address as an author, would probably never have made his way by detached and independent efforts; but, fortunately for himself and others, he has taken advantage of the Periodical Press, where he has been stuck into notice, and the texture of his compositions is assuredly fine enough to bear the broadest glare of popularity that has hitherto shone upon them. Mr. Lamb's literary efforts have procured him civic honours (a thing unheard of in our times), and he has been invited, in his character of ELIA, to dine at a select party with the Lord Mayor. We should prefer this distinction to that of being poet-laureat. We would recommend to Mr. Waithman's perusal (if Mr. Lamb has not anticipated us) the *Rosamond Gray* and the *John Woodvil* of the same author, as an agreeable relief to the noise of a city feast, and the heat of city elections. A friend, a short time ago, quoted some lines[A] from the last-mentioned of these works, which meeting Mr. Godwin's eye, he was so struck with the beauty of the passage, and with a consciousness of having seen it before, that he was uneasy till he could recollect where, and after hunting in vain for it in Ben Jonson, Beaumont and Fletcher, and other not unlikely places, sent to Mr. Lamb to know if he could help him to the author!

Mr. Washington Irvine's acquaintance with English literature begins almost where Mr. Lamb's ends, —with the Spectator, Tom Brown's works, and the wits of Queen Anne. He is not bottomed in our elder writers, nor do we think he has tasked his own faculties much, at least on English ground. Of the merit of his *Knicker-bocker,* and New York stories, we cannot pretend to judge. But in his *Sketch-book* and *Bracebridge-Hall* he gives us very good American copies of our British Essayists and Novelists, which may be very well on the other side of the water, and as proofs of the capabilities of the national genius, but which might be dispensed with here, where we have to boast of the originals. Not only Mr. Irvine's language is with great taste and felicity modelled on that of Addison, Sterne, Goldsmith, or Mackenzie; but the thoughts and sentiments are taken at the rebound, and as they are brought forward at the present period, want both freshness and probability. Mr. Irvine's writings are literary *anachronisms.* He comes to England for the first time; and being on the spot, fancies himself in the midst of those characters and manners which he had read of in the Spectator and other approved authors, and which were the only idea he had hitherto formed of the parent country. Instead of looking round to see what *we are*, he sets to work to describe us as *we were*—at second hand. He has Parson Adams, or Sir Roger de Coverley in his *"mind's eye"*; and he makes a village curate, or a country 'squire in Yorkshire or Hampshire sit to these admired models for their portraits in the beginning of the nineteenth century. Whatever the ingenious author has been most delighted with in the representations of books, he transfers to his port-folio, and swears that he has found it actually existing in the course of his observation and travels through Great Britain. Instead of tracing the changes that have taken place in society since Addison or Fielding wrote, he transcribes their account in a different hand-writing, and thus keeps us stationary, at least in our most attractive and praise-worthy qualities of simplicity, honesty, hospitality, modesty, and good-nature. This is a very flattering mode of turning fiction into history, or history into fiction; and we should scarcely know ourselves again in the softened and altered likeness, but that it bears the date of 1820, and issues from the press in Albemarle-street. This is one way of complimenting our national and Tory prejudices; and coupled with literal or exaggerated portraits of *Yankee* peculiarities, could hardly fail to please. The first Essay in the *Sketch-book*, that on National Antipathies, is the best; but after that, the sterling ore of wit or feeling is gradually spun thinner and thinner, till it fades to the shadow of a shade. Mr. Irvine is himself, we believe, a most agreeable and deserving man, and has been led into the natural and pardonable error we speak of, by the tempting bait of European popularity, in which he thought there was no more likely method of succeeding than by imitating the style of our standard authors, and giving us credit for the virtues of our forefathers.

[Footnote A: The description of sports in the forest:

"To see the sun to bed and to arise,
Like some hot amourist with glowing eyes, " &c.]

* * * * *

We should not feel that we had discharged our obligations to truth or friendship, if we were to let this volume go without introducing into it the name of the author of *Virginius*. This is the more proper, inasmuch as he is a character by himself, and the only poet now living that is a mere poet. If we were asked what sort of a man Mr. Knowles is, we could only say, "he is the writer of Virginius. " His most intimate friends see nothing in him, by which they could trace the work to the author. The seeds of dramatic genius are contained and fostered in the warmth of the blood that flows in his veins; his heart dictates to his head. The most unconscious, the most unpretending, the most artless of mortals, he instinctively obeys the impulses of natural feeling, and produces a perfect work of art. He has hardly read a poem or a play or seen any thing of the world, but he hears the anxious beatings of his own heart, and makes others feel them by the force of sympathy. Ignorant alike of rules, regardless of models, he follows the steps of truth and simplicity; and strength, proportion, and delicacy are the infallible results. By thinking of nothing but his subject, he rivets the attention of the audience to it. All his dialogue tends to action, all his situations form classic groups. There is no doubt that Virginius is the best acting tragedy that has been produced on the modern stage. Mr. Knowles himself was a player at one time, and this circumstance has probably enabled him to judge of the picturesque and dramatic effect of his lines, as we think it might have assisted Shakespear. There is no impertinent display, no flaunting poetry; the writer immediately conceives how a thought would tell if he had to speak it himself. Mr. Knowles is the first tragic writer of the age; in other respects he is a common man; and divides his time and his affections between his plots and his fishing-tackle, between the Muses' spring, and those mountain-streams which sparkle like his own eye, that gush out like his own voice at the sight of an old friend. We have known him almost from a child, and we must say he appears to us the same boy-poet that he ever was. He has been cradled in song, and rocked in it as in a dream, forgetful of himself and of the world!

THE END.

Printed in the United Kingdom
by Lightning Source UK Ltd.
128684UK00001B/171/A